JESUS

HIS LIFE AND MINISTRY

DEREK PRIME

OLIVER
NELSON

THOMAS NELSON PUBLISHERS
Nashville • Atlanta • London • Vancouver

Published in Nashville, Tennessee, by Thomas Nelson, Inc., Publishers, and distributed in Canada by Word Communications, Ltd., Richmond, British Columbia.

Library of Congress Cataloging-in-Publication Data

Prime, Derek.
    Jesus : His life and ministry / Derek Prime.
      p. cm.
    ISBN 0-7852-8133-9 (pbk.)
    1. Jesus Christ—Biography—Study and teaching. 2. Jesus Christ—Person and offices—Study and teaching. I. Title.
BT307.P715 1995
232—dc20
[B]
                              95-17914
                                  CIP

Printed in the United States of America.

1 2 3 4 5 6 — 00 99 98 97 96 95

JESUS
HIS LIFE AND MINISTRY

CONTENTS

PREFACE

This book has several purposes in view. First and foremost, it is an introduction to the life and ministry of our Lord Jesus Christ as recorded in the four Gospels. It follows the basic pattern the apostles used as they preached the gospel to those who had never heard it before (see, for example, the detailed outline of Peter's preaching of the good news to Cornelius in Acts 10:34–43).

This outline is followed deliberately in this book because it reminds us that to proclaim Jesus Christ is to proclaim the gospel, and that the gospel narratives show how the early Christians declared the truth about Jesus to the world.

We dare not take for granted people's knowledge of Jesus' life and ministry. We need to take the same care as the apostles did in providing seekers and new hearers of the gospel with the basic truths concerning His earthly life.

Part 1: Three Suggestions

First, the book can be read as an introduction to Jesus' life and ministry without using either the recommended Bible passages at the beginning of every chapter or the suggestions for meditation and the questions at each chapter's close.

There is value in considering Jesus' life and ministry in one sweep, as it were, in brief compass, for if we begin by concentrating only on small details, we may lose sight of the main impressions we should have.

The second use is for personal study and reading of the Gospels as a stimulus to meditation on Jesus' life—perhaps considering a chapter each week.

There is no substitute for meditation on the person and work of Jesus Christ as a strength and stimulus to faith (Heb. 3:1; 12:2). Contemporary life tends to be marked by haste, and deliberate meditation places a necessary brake on superficial reading of biblical truth. Each chapter has seven Bible passages listed at its beginning, and seven subjects for meditation at its conclusion, so that they may be read during the course of a week. Each subject for meditation arises from the Bible passage for the day.

The third use is for group Bible study, and seven questions are to be found at the conclusion of each chapter. Ideally, each member of the group should be encouraged to read the seven Bible passages and the relevant chapter in the preceding week in preparation for discussing the answers to the questions. By this means, group Bible study is anchored in Bible reading and preparation.

Part 2

Part 2 of the book is "An A Through Z of Bible Words, Names, and Places." Its purpose is to provide quick and convenient information where these words, names, and places arise—often in passing—in the preceding chapters.

We sometimes—and perhaps often—refer to places without being sure where they were or are, or to subjects without being clear about exactly what the Bible teaches concerning them. I hope this section will help to remedy this. It is not intended to be comprehensive, and the ground for inclusion of any subject is its mention in the preceding chapters concerning Jesus' life and ministry.

PART 1

INTRODUCTION

Jesus Our Contemporary

Why study the life and teaching of Jesus? The first reason is the most important. Although we may learn about famous men and women of the past—such as Napoleon and Florence Nightingale—we cannot know them personally. Jesus Christ, who lived in first-century Palestine, however, is our contemporary, for He is the risen and living Lord (Rev. 1:9–18), "the same yesterday, today, and forever" (Heb. 13:8). Learning about Him, we may come to know Him better. To know Him is to know God and to possess eternal life (John 17:3). But there are other reasons for such a study.

The Good News

Jesus is the center of God's good news. But He is more than that—He is Himself the good news. Philip, an evangelist of the early church, met on a desert road an Ethiopian reading Isaiah 53. The Ethiopian said, "I ask of you, of whom does the prophet say this, of himself or of some other man?" Philip began with that passage and "preached Jesus to him" (Acts 8:34–35). To appreciate who Jesus is, and why He came into the world, is to possess the key to God's plan of salvation. It is rather like focusing a camera's lenses. As we fix our attention on the central figure or feature, then all around it falls into proper focus. With Jesus Christ in rightful focus, everything else God wants us to know and understand falls into place.

The Word

Jesus is the Word of God (John 1:1; Heb. 1:1–2): God speaks to us through Him as through no one else. If we would hear God speak to us, we must listen to His Son. "Hear Him!" was God's instruction to Peter, James, and John at the Transfiguration (Luke 9:35); and God says the same to us.

The Visible Image

Jesus is the visible image of the invisible God (Col. 1:15). What had never been seen before was witnessed when Jesus, the Eternal Word, became flesh and revealed God's glory. "He who has seen Me has seen the Father," He explained to Philip, one of His first disciples (John 14:9). To understand what God is like, we must deliberately fix our attention on the person and work of Jesus Christ.

The Centrality of the Cross

The Cross is both the great mystery and the triumph of Jesus' life (Matt. 16:21–23). Examining Jesus' life carefully, we soon appreciate His perfection and sinlessness, and the all-sufficient sacrifice He alone was able to make, therefore, for our sins and the sins of the whole world.

The Object of Faith

Jesus is the supreme object of Christian faith. Through Him alone, we come to believe in God and discover His salvation (1 Pet. 1:21). Faith comes to birth as we understand who Jesus is and what He has done for us (Acts 8:35, 37; 1 Cor. 15:1–5).

God the Holy Spirit's activity in our lives is the secret of this birth of faith, a work as powerful and wonderful as God's initial act of creation: "For it is the God who commanded light to shine out of darkness, who has shone in our hearts to give the light of the knowledge of the glory of God in the face of Jesus Christ" (2 Cor. 4:6). But that is only the beginning of faith. It continues to grow by the same principle. As it came into being through our first looking to Jesus Christ, so it increases as we continue to look to Him. Most defects in faith stem from failure to consider Jesus—what the writer of Hebrews describes as "looking unto Jesus" (12:2; cf. 3:1). It is a simple secret, overlooked often because of its simplicity.

The Example

Jesus is the example for all disciples to follow (1 Pet. 2:21). Once He has become our Savior, we are to walk in His footsteps. But to follow His example, we must know it well. An apprentice watches his teacher carefully, considers all he does and how he does it. A disciple is no less committed to watch, learn, and copy. Our failures to be Christlike have much to do with our neglect of our Master's life and example.

Four Gospels

It is no accident that God the Holy Spirit—the Author and Inspirer of Scripture—has seen fit to provide four records of Jesus' life and ministry. When we choose to say something several times, we underline its fundamental importance. The same significance must be seen in the provision of not just one, but four Gospels.

The Danger of Neglect

Nevertheless, the life of Jesus tends to be neglected. We are inclined to think we know the events of His life and ministry. Our preoccupation instead may be more with the New Testament letters or our particular biblical interests. But as soon as this happens, we quickly cease to be obedient disciples, and we end up living the Christian life without the vitality and power that come from Jesus' mind and attitudes in us.

We must not lose the basic simplicity of the Christian life—it is following Jesus Christ.

M E D I T A T I O N

1. Jesus Christ is the Word of God: "God, who at various times and in various ways spoke in time past to the fathers by the prophets, has in these last days spoken to us by His Son" (Heb. 1:1–2).

2. Jesus is the visible image of the invisible God. Jesus said, "He who has seen Me has seen the Father" (John 14:9; cf. Col. 1:15).

3. Jesus is the object of our faith: "We beheld His glory, the glory as of the only begotten of the Father, full of grace and truth" (John 1:14); "[Look] unto Jesus, the author and finisher of our faith" (Heb. 12:2).

4. Jesus' death on the cross was central to all He had come to do. He said, "The Son of Man did not come to be served, but to serve, and to give His life a ransom for many" (Mark 10:45).

5. Jesus Christ is Himself the good news: "Philip . . . preached Jesus to him" (Acts 8:35); "We preach Christ crucified" (1 Cor. 1:23).

6. Jesus is the example for disciples to follow: "Christ also suffered for us, leaving us an example, that you should follow His steps" (1 Pet. 2:21).

7. Jesus Christ is our contemporary: "I am He who lives, and was dead, and behold, I am alive forevermore" (Rev. 1:18); "Jesus Christ is the same yesterday, today, and forever" (Heb. 13:8).

Q U E S T I O N S

1. How does God speak to us through Jesus, and how does Jesus show us the Father?

2. What are the foremost truths that Jesus' character and teaching revealed of the Father?

3. What does it mean in practice to look unto Jesus?

4. What understanding does Isaiah 53 give of God's purposes in the Cross?

5. Putting ourselves in Philip's place in Acts 8:35, how do we imagine him explaining the good news to the Ethiopian?

6. To which aspects of Jesus' example does the New Testament particularly draw our attention (e.g., John 13:15; Rom. 15:3, 7; Phil. 2:5–11; 1 Pet. 2:21)?

7. How may we know Jesus Christ? What are the expected evidences of such knowledge in our lives?

Chapter One

THE PROPER STARTING POINT

Where should we start in our study of Jesus' life and ministry? Should we begin with His virgin conception? Or perhaps with His baptism? If we let the Bible direct us, we have to go back farther than that!

Key Passages

Three New Testament passages guide us: John 1:1–3, 14; Philippians 2:5–7; and Hebrews 1:1–3.

The first is John's introduction to his gospel:

In the beginning was the Word, and the Word was
with God, and the Word was God. He was in the beginning with God. All things were made through Him,
and without Him nothing was made that was made. . . .
And the Word became flesh and dwelt among us, and
we beheld His glory, the glory as of the only begotten
of the Father, full of grace and truth (John 1:1–3, 14).

John's prologue identifies Jesus as the Word. Words are
our principal means of communication. It is by our words
that we speak to one another. The description of Jesus as
the Word emphasizes that He is the One through whom
God uniquely speaks to us. He is not "*a* Word" but "*the*
Word."

The most important truth John tells us about Jesus as the
Word is that He is God, and God the Creator (cf. Col. 1:16;
1 Cor. 8:6). The birth of Jesus at Bethlehem in a stable was
not the beginning of His existence.

The second key passage is Philippians 2:5–7, where Paul
probably quotes an early Christian hymn, perhaps of his
own composing: "Christ Jesus . . . being in the form of
God, did not consider it robbery to be equal with God, but
made Himself of no reputation, taking the form of a bond-
servant, and coming in the likeness of men." Jesus did not
need to grasp after deity because it was His already. Like
John's prologue, Paul's words emphasize Jesus' preexistence.

The third key passage is Hebrews 1:1–3, where the writer
declares Jesus to be the eternal Son of God:

God, who at various times and in various ways spoke in
time past to the fathers by the prophets, has in these
last days spoken to us by His Son, whom He has ap-

pointed heir of all things, through whom also He made the worlds; who being the brightness of His glory and the express image of His person, and upholding all things by the word of His power.

Jesus' *human* life began at Bethlehem, but it was not the beginning of His existence. He enjoyed fellowship and glory with the Father before the world began (John 17:5). The One born in Bethlehem, who walked the hills and streets of Galilee, was the Creator of the universe, the mighty God. He preceded time, and He is above time.

John's statement, that "no one has ever seen God, but God the One and Only, who is at the Father's side, has made him known" (John 1:18 NIV), implies that whenever God chose to show Himself in visible form—in the Old Testament period as well as the New—it was through His Son Jesus Christ (cf. Isa. 6:1–3 with John 12:41). On that account we may conclude that Jesus the Son of God was the One who appeared to Moses (Exod. 3:1–6), Joshua (Josh. 5:13–15), Manoah (Judg. 13:1–25), and Isaiah (Isa. 6:1–13).

The Preexistence of Christ

The proper starting point of our study, therefore, is the preexistence of Jesus Christ. He declared, "Before Abraham was, I AM" (John 8:58). The Son of God *was* before His historical manifestation (1 John 1:1–2). Pilate asked Jesus, "Where are You from?" Jesus gave him no answer (John 19:9). Pilate would not have understood.

The Hope of All the Ages

Linked with Jesus' preexistence as our proper starting point is the truth that in His coming into the world, He was the hope of all the ages. As the writer to the Hebrews explains, "In the past God spoke to our forefathers through the prophets at many times and in various ways" (Heb. 1:1 NIV). All the Old Testament prophets looked forward to Jesus' coming. The prophets "searched carefully . . . searching what, or what manner of time, the Spirit of Christ who was in them was indicating when He testified beforehand the sufferings of Christ and the glories that would follow" (1 Pet. 1:10–11).

The Old Testament prophets were on the tiptoes of expectation as the Holy Spirit gave hints and intimations of God's breathtaking plan of salvation. As they looked into the future, their focus was directed to one particular person, unique in His relationship with God, and in His ability to achieve God's saving purposes.

The details they gave bore the character of an Identikit. The more clues given as to His person and work, the clearer it became that His coming into the world demanded a death that would be the amazing secret of the good news He came to proclaim. The prophets all said, in effect, "The Lamb of God is coming," until that vital moment when the last of the prophets before Jesus' ministry, John the Baptist, saw Him and said, "Behold! The Lamb of God who takes away the sin of the world!" (John 1:29).

The Key

The Incarnation was the key to God's amazing plan of salvation. It was necessary that the Lord Jesus Christ, the Son of God, should be truly and fully man so that He might be able to stand in our place as our substitute and by this means accept on our behalf God's righteous wrath against our sins.

Only by becoming man could He mediate between God and humankind (1 Tim. 2:5). His death was to have sufficient value to God that it would be an atoning sacrifice—a propitiation—for the sins of "the whole world" (1 John 2:2).

Let us turn our attention now to that period between our Savior's birth at Bethlehem and His appearance on the scene as John the Baptist baptized repentant Jews in the river Jordan and gave his testimony to Jesus.

The Nazarene

We begin at Nazareth. Jesus was commonly called "Jesus of Nazareth" in the Gospels (Matt. 26:71; Mark 1:24; Luke 4:34; 18:37; 24:19; John 1:45; 18:5, 7; 19:19) and in the Acts of the Apostles (Acts 2:22; 3:6; 4:10; 6:14; 10:38; 22:8–9) since that was the home of Mary and Joseph. No doubt He spoke with a Nazarene accent. He was known as "the Nazarene" (Mark 14:67; 16:6 NIV), so the early Christians were identified as belonging to the "Nazarene sect" (Acts 24:5 NIV).

Nazareth in Lower Galilee remained outside the mainstream of Jewish life in New Testament times. Somewhat aloof from much of Israel, it lay close to main trade routes so as to have easy contact with the outside world. Its position as a frontier town contributed to its aloofness. Its independence of outlook probably caused it to be held in a degree of scorn by strict Jews.

Jesus' Birth Was Foretold to Mary

God sent the angel Gabriel to Mary, "a virgin betrothed to a man whose name was Joseph, of the house of David" (Luke 1:27). The angel explained that "the power of the Highest" was to "overshadow" her (Luke 1:35), in that Jesus' conception in her womb was to be a work of God hidden from human eyes.

Fears and questions understandably came to Mary's mind (Luke 1:29–30, 34), but in describing herself as "the maidservant of the Lord" (Luke 1:38), she expressed her willingness to give complete obedience to God. She was told wonderful things about the son who was to be born to her (Luke 1:31–35), including His unique sinlessness.

Mary Visited Her Cousin Elizabeth

As soon as the angel left her, Mary visited her cousin Elizabeth since the angel had told her that Elizabeth was expecting a child in her old age (Luke 1:36)—a child who grew up to be John the Baptist.

The remarkable response of the yet unborn child in Elizabeth's womb, as he leaped for joy at Mary's visit (Luke 1:44), and Elizabeth's immediate spiritual insight into the significance of Mary's pregnancy (Luke 1:43–45), confirmed God's amazing promise to Mary through the angel.

Mary—a virgin—was to give birth to the Son of God. The words themselves are simple, but the truth they convey is impossible to fathom.

The Virgin Conception

We speak often of "the virgin birth," but more accurately, we should speak of "the virgin conception." So far as we know there was nothing different or unusual about Jesus' actual birth; the conception itself in the virgin's womb was unique. Jesus was born of a human mother, without any human father (Matt. 1:20; Luke 1:34–35; Gal. 4:4). He became flesh through being conceived by the power of the Holy Spirit in Mary's womb.

A Fundamental Truth

How important is the virgin conception? The answer must be that it is of fundamental importance. Because it is so amazing a happening, and something beyond human understanding or the possibility of scientific proof, the tendency of unbelieving men and women has been to put it in the category of fairy tale or myth. But we are thinking and speaking of God when we consider the Incarnation.

God became flesh. That itself is as remarkable as the virgin conception and equally beyond human understanding unless God enlightens our minds. Jesus Christ's later resurrection was an act of the same almighty God. Assured of the Resurrection, I find no difficulty in accepting the reality of the virgin conception.

It is always reassuring when we find truths fitting together, even though we may not fully understand them. This is the case as we ponder the mystery of Jesus being truly God and truly man. In ways the Bible does not choose to explain, Jesus laid aside some aspects of His visible divine glory, although not His divine attributes, in becoming man (Phil. 2:6–7). At the same time, in His becoming perfectly like us, there was one great difference—although open to temptation, there was no sin in Him, and He never sinned.

If we ask, "How was this possible?" the answer is found partly in His virgin conception. Not being born of a human mother and father, as we were, He did not inherit a sinful nature as we did. But what then of Mary's sinful nature? The angel explained to Mary that "the power of the Highest" would "overshadow" her so that the "Holy One who is to be born" would be called the Son of God (Luke 1:35). The Holy Spirit's overshadowing safeguarded Jesus Christ's perfect holiness as He was conceived in Mary's womb.

We might be inclined to think that it follows that Jesus was not tempted as we are. But we would be wrong. Adam, our first forefather, was tempted before he ever sinned—in other words, while he was sinless. Temptation was more intense and unrelieved for Jesus than it is for us. Because He never gave in, the pressure was always on Him. The person who has never given in to temptation alone knows its full power.

Joseph

Joseph, to whom Mary was pledged to be married, stands out as a most honorable man. Mary's pregnancy must have distressed him considerably and caused great alarm. Before an angel of the Lord appeared to him in a dream confirming the truth of what had been promised Mary, he had determined to divorce her quietly (Matt. 1:19).

Obedient, however, to the angel's instruction, Joseph took Mary home as his wife, and he had no union with her until she gave birth to her son (Matt. 1:25).

"The Mystery" Taking Place

As we reflect on the circumstances of Jesus' coming into the world, we are able to discern important factors fitting together, providing evidence of the divine plan—the mystery (Col. 1:27)—taking place.

Joseph and Mary belonged to Nazareth, and that was where Joseph worked as a carpenter, and where both he and Mary received their special revelation from God.

The prophet declared centuries before that the Messiah would be born in Bethlehem:

> But you, Bethlehem Ephrathah,
> Though you are little among the thousands of Judah,
> Yet out of you shall come forth to Me
> The One to be Ruler in Israel,
> Whose goings forth are from of old,
> From everlasting (Mic. 5:2).

It was no accident, therefore, that "when the fullness of the time had come" (Gal. 4:4), "in those days that a decree went out from Caesar Augustus that all the world should be registered. . . . So all went to be registered, everyone to his own city" (Luke 2:1, 3).

Belonging to the house and line of David, Joseph went up to Bethlehem, the town of David, to register with Mary. While they were there, Jesus was born (Luke 2:6).

Mothers possess a unique capacity of almost total recall of the events surrounding their children's childhoods, and Mary in particular treasured all the things that happened at her son's birth and "pondered them in her heart" (Luke 2:19). She is an example because we often lose the power and significance of truth by not turning it over in our minds until we fully grasp it.

Mary's total recall of those early events—no doubt assisted by God the Holy Spirit—explains the detailed narrative we have in Luke's gospel. (Luke plainly had recourse to material relating to Mary's recollections, and perhaps he met and knew Mary.)

The shepherds' visit, with their surprising news of the heavenly messengers, was one of the first memories (Luke 2:8–16), and the way they then spread the news of the Savior, the Messiah, who had come (Luke 2:17–18).

Jesus' Circumcision

On the eighth day, according to Jewish practice, Jesus was circumcised, and obedient to divine instructions, Mary and Joseph called the baby "JESUS" (Luke 2:21). The linking of the child's name with circumcision is not without significance.

Circumcision was, first, the symbol of God's special promises to the Jewish people. But, second, it symbolized the abandoning of heathen ways and human stubbornness (Josh. 5:9; Deut. 10:16). From the latter point of view, it was completely out of place for the Son of God. But His name is Jesus, meaning Savior, and from that point of view, circumcision was entirely appropriate because He had come to identify Himself with those for whose salvation He was to die.

The Magi

Mary recalled, too, the somewhat mysterious visitors who came after Jesus' birth when she, Joseph, and the child had moved out of the stable into a house (Matt. 2:1–12).

With amazement she heard their testimony about the star that had directed them. Her astonishment must have increased when they "fell down and worshiped" her infant son (Matt. 2:11). The gifts they brought plainly had significance, although their meaning was probably not immediately recognizable to Mary and Joseph. Christians have regarded the gifts as symbols: gold representing Jesus' deity, frankincense His priestly ministry, and myrrh (used in preparing bodies for burial) His humanity since He was to experience death.

Jesus Presented in the Temple

Mary must have often pondered the visit she and Joseph made to the temple with the young child Jesus thirty-three days after His circumcision, according to Jewish practice. They had two purposes in view: (1) Mary's ceremonial purification after the birth of her son and (2) the dedication of a firstborn child.

For forty days after the birth of a son, a woman was regarded as ceremonially impure. Then on the fortieth day, she offered a sacrifice of a lamb with a young pigeon or turtledove. If she was poor, however, two doves or pigeons, "one as a burnt offering and the other as a sin offering" (Lev. 12:8), were acceptable. Luke's reference to the latter option (2:24) indicates that Joseph and Mary were considered poor.

Then like Samuel, Jesus was offered to God. Up until that point, there was nothing unusual about Mary and Joseph's visit to the temple. What made it memorable were the surprising responses of Simeon and Anna; their enthusiastic and perceptive welcome of Jesus confirmed that He is the hope of all the ages, the One for whom the prophets looked (Luke 2:25–38).

The Flight to Egypt

Mary vividly remembered their escape to Egypt once Joseph had been warned by an angel in a dream that the child's life would be in danger if they remained in Palestine (Matt. 2:13–15). The gifts of gold, frankincense, and myrrh no doubt solved the initial financial demands of their time as refugees.

The Boy Jesus at the Temple

The final recorded recollection of those early years—again uniquely in Luke—was when at the age of twelve, Jesus went up with Joseph and Mary to Jerusalem for the Feast of the Passover (Luke 2:41–52).

The purpose of the visit so far as Jesus was concerned was probably to prepare Him for the ceremony of the following year when, as a thirteen-year-old boy, He would be permitted to join the religious community as a responsible member.

At that early age Jesus showed Himself aware of His relationship with God, His unique sonship, in His answer to His mother's request about His being in the temple: "Did you not know that I must be about My Father's business?" (Luke 2:49), although as Luke says, "They did not understand the statement which He spoke to them" (2:50).

Those who listened to what He asked the religious teachers, and the manner in which He answered their questions, saw evidences of the wisdom and authority that were later to confound and amaze the Jewish people: "All who heard Him were astonished at His understanding and answers" (Luke 2:47).

The Silent Years

Then followed what we may describe as the silent years. The Gospels record nothing at all between our Lord's visit to Jerusalem at the age of twelve and the beginning of His public ministry at the time of John the Baptist's arrest some eighteen or so years later, apart from the statement in Luke 2: "Then He went down with them and came to Nazareth, and was subject to them. . . . Jesus increased in wisdom and stature, and in favor with God and men" (vv. 51–52).

He certainly worked as a carpenter in Nazareth, for the crowds asked early on in His public ministry, "Is this not the carpenter?" (Mark 6:3). From the lack of mention of Joseph in the gospel narratives during Jesus' public ministry, it seems correct to assume that he had died (Mark 3:32; John 19:26), and Jesus, as the oldest child in the family, became the principal breadwinner. He would have acted as the head of the family, with early and heavy responsibilities for His younger brothers—of whom there were four—and His sisters (Mark 6:3).

Jesus' public ministry may not have begun until other members of the family could take responsibility for Mary and her children. The One who fulfilled all God's law perfectly obeyed the fifth commandment: "Honor your father and your mother" (Exod. 20:12).

We may apply an Old Testament prophecy to the early and silent years of Jesus' earthly life. In the book of Isaiah, the Messiah is heard to say,

> He has made My mouth like a sharp sword;
> In the shadow of His hand He has hidden Me,
> And made Me a polished shaft;
> In His quiver He has hidden Me.
> And He said to me, "You are My servant, O Israel,
> In whom I will be glorified" (49:2–3).

The Lord Jesus Christ was "a polished shaft." As an archer may polish the shaft of his arrow to make it perfectly effective for the moment of its use, so God prepared His Son during those silent years for the work He was to do in the few years of His public ministry. God is never in a hurry. The work of preparation and the discipline of waiting are as important as the moment of action.

The early, silent years, in which Jesus knew all the discipline, routine, and responsibilities of an ordinary, humble home in a small town, underline Jesus' sharing of our humanity. That is the kind of background from which most of us come.

Jesus shared our flesh and blood. He was like us in every way, except He was without sin (2 Cor. 5:21; Heb. 4:15). Besides the human responsibilities of being the eldest son, He knew human experiences like tiredness, thirst, tears, and suffering—and His future ministry was to confirm these realities.

We may wonder why the Gospels are silent concerning the early years. One reason at least is that the apostles were told to be witnesses of what they had both heard and seen of Jesus —His person, His teaching, His miracles, His death and resurrection. These are the fundamentals of the gospel, and the New Testament focuses on them. Mark, for example, plunges straight into his record of Jesus' ministry by beginning with John the Baptist—whom we must consider next.

M E D I T A T I O N

1. Jesus is God the Creator, the second person of the Trinity, made flesh, through whom God uniquely speaks to us:

   And without controversy great is the mystery of godliness:

God was manifested in the flesh,
Justified in the Spirit,
Seen by angels,
Preached among the Gentiles,
Believed on in the world,
Received up in glory (1 Tim. 3:16).

2. The virgin conception was the work of God's Spirit. Mary said to the angel, "How can this be, since I do not know a man?" The angel answered, "The Holy Spirit will come upon you, and the power of the Highest will overshadow you; therefore, also, that Holy One who is to be born will be called the Son of God" (Luke 1:34–35).

3. Even in Elizabeth's womb, John the Baptist leaped for joy in recognition of Jesus conceived in Mary's womb. Those who believe in Jesus "rejoice with joy inexpressible and full of glory" (1 Pet. 1:8).

4. Joseph heard this message: "You shall call His name JESUS, for He will save His people from their sins. . . . 'They shall call His name Immanuel,' which is translated, 'God with us'" (Matt. 1:21, 23).

5. What happened at Bethlehem was the unfolding of God's eternal purpose of salvation, long promised:

But you, Bethlehem Ephrathah,
Though you are little among the thousands of Judah,
Yet out of you shall come forth to Me
The One to be Ruler in Israel,
Whose goings forth are from of old,
From everlasting (Mic. 5:2).

6. The Magi's response on finding the King of kings is one to be emulated: "[They] fell down and worshiped Him.

And when they had opened their treasures, they presented gifts to Him" (Matt. 2:11).

7. "And Jesus increased in wisdom and stature, and in favor with God and men" (Luke 2:52). The Father was to give conspicuous testimony to the favor in which He held His Son as Jesus followed His path of obedience to the Father's will (Luke 2:22; 9:35). Through Jesus' perfect obedience and sacrifice, the Father now views Christian believers with equal favor.

Q U E S T I O N S

1. How did Jesus' humility show itself, in the manner of His coming and in His life and ministry? What should we, as disciples, learn from His example?

2. Why is Jesus' virgin conception so significant?

3. What does Mary's song tell us about her character and faith?

4. How far do the names *Immanuel* and *Jesus* sum up the coming and mission of God's Son?

5. What is the likely significance of the angels' involvement in the birth narrative in Luke 2:8–20?

6. What does the visit of the Magi from the East tell us about the intended recipients of the good news of Jesus (cf. Mal. 1:11; John 10:16; Acts 10:34–43)?

7. What does Luke's account of Jesus' visit as a boy to Jerusalem reveal of His character and purpose (Luke 2:41–52)?

Chapter Two

THE FORERUNNER AND THE SIGNAL

We might be inclined to go straight from Jesus' birth and early years to the beginning of His ministry, leaving out John the Baptist. But the Gospels do not allow us to do so.

Once Matthew and Luke have recorded the early years of Jesus' life, they continue their narrative with an account of John the Baptist's work (Matt. 3; Luke 3:1–20). No sooner has John, the writer of the fourth gospel, introduced Jesus as the Eternal Word than he, too, writes of John the Baptist. Mark begins his gospel record with John the Baptist's preparatory ministry for Jesus. All four gospel writers reflect the apostolic preaching of the gospel (Acts 10:37).

Forerunner and Witness

Picture a waiting and expectant people. They know their King is coming, but not exactly when. They realize, however, that His coming will be heralded by a forerunner. The latter will run ahead of the King with the glad message, "The King is coming! He will soon be here!" That was John the Baptist's privileged task in relation to Jesus.

John the Baptist's work made the people ready for Jesus' greater work. The more we examine John's ministry, the more impressive is the perfect preparation he provided for the Savior King's coming.

John was especially commissioned by God. As gospel writer John puts it, "There was a man sent from God, whose name was John" (1:6). The Greek can be translated, "There appeared on the stage of history a man sent from God." John's work was no accident; it was of divine origin and plan.

John's birth, too, had been a subject of special promise and surprising circumstance (Luke 1:5–25). His parents, Zacharias and Elizabeth, were outstanding for their godliness (v. 6). Their married life had been marred by a personal tragedy—Elizabeth was barren, and consequently, they were childless (v. 7). At the time the narrative describes, they were beyond the age to have any expectation of children. But at that point the unthinkable happened: "For with God nothing will be impossible" (Luke 1:37).

An angel of the Lord visited Zacharias in the course of his priestly duties and informed him that his prayer had been heard, and that his wife, Elizabeth, would bear him a son

(v. 13). Previously in Israel's history, children born to child-less parents were children of special promise, as in the case of Abraham and Sarah (Gen. 17:15–22), and Manoah and his wife (Judg. 13:2–7).

The child's name was chosen by God (v. 13): it was to be John, which means "the Lord is gracious." John's character and mission were also disclosed to Zacharias by the angel. He was to be a joy and delight to his parents (v. 14). Many were to "rejoice at his birth" (v. 14), and he was to be "great in the sight of the Lord" (v. 15).

He would never take wine or other fermented drink, an indication that he was not going to allow his life to be open to any false control or unhelpful influence. Rather, he would be filled with the Holy Spirit even from birth (v. 15). In Ephesians 5:18, we find the same contrast between the stimulation prompted by wine and the altogether different invigoration provided by the Holy Spirit.

The angel declared that John's work would be one of spiritual restoration: "And he will turn many of the children of Israel to the Lord their God" (v. 16). That had been characteristic of the ministry of many of the Old Testament prophets, especially Elijah, and John's future service was put on a par with his, since he was to do his work "in the spirit and power of Elijah" (v. 17).

Malachi's prophecy is quoted by Luke: John was "'to turn the hearts of the fathers to the children,' and the disobedient to the wisdom of the just" (Luke 1:17; see Mal. 4:5–6). Disunity among families was to be healed as they responded to the good news John proclaimed. It was all preparation for Jesus' coming; he was "to make ready a people prepared for the Lord" (Luke 1:17). The precise and detailed nature of the prophecy is impressive. John's ministry was not an end in itself. He was to prepare the way for another—for the Lord Himself.

Zacharias's unbelief at the promise of a son brought the severe discipline of losing his speech until the child's birth and naming. Godly and prayerful as he was, Zacharias found such good news difficult to take in.

John's Birth

When Elizabeth's son was born, the immediate assumption was that he would be named after his father—a common practice, and all the more so when an only and long-awaited son was born. But to everyone's surprise, Elizabeth spoke up and said, "No; he shall be called John" (Luke 1:60). As soon as Zacharias confirmed the name by writing it down, he opened his mouth to give voice to a most profound expression of praise to God and a prophecy concerning his son.

The praise Zacharias offered filled the people who heard it with awe (Luke 1:65). The baby's birth became a talking point. "What kind of child will this be?" they asked (Luke 1:66). The amazing circumstances of his birth and naming conveyed a marked sense of destiny.

Zacharias's Song

Zacharias's song has as its theme salvation or deliverance, in the light of the promises made through the centuries by the prophets (Luke 1:67–79). Zacharias identified his son as a "prophet of the Highest" (v. 76). A prophet in Bible language is not only someone who may predict what is going to happen in the future, but one who speaks by direct inspiration to declare God's truth to His people.

Zacharias saw John clearly in his role as forerunner to Jesus: "You will go before the face of the Lord to prepare His ways" (v. 76). He was to be the forerunner in the gist of the message. He was "to give knowledge of salvation to His people by the remission of their sins" (v. 77). That is a superb summary of the gospel. There can be no salvation—no deliverance from the just penalty our sins deserve of spiritual separation from God, death, judgment, and hell—without the experience of forgiveness.

John—a fallen human being like us—was to have no part in achieving this forgiveness, but he was to point to the One who was to accomplish it:

> Through the tender mercy of our God,
> With which the Dayspring from on high has visited us;
> To give light to those who sit in darkness and the
>   shadow of death,
> To guide our feet into the way of peace (vv. 78–79).

Once more we have cause to marvel at such a succinct and precise understanding of Jesus' ministry, of which John was to be the forerunner. Zacharias's ability to make this remarkable prophecy is explained by the statement that he was "filled with the Holy Spirit" (v. 67).

John's Childhood

We have two comments on John's childhood. The first is in Luke 1:66: "And the hand of the Lord was with him." "The hand of God" is an expression often used in the Bible as a synonym for the Holy Spirit's presence with an individual, and it fits in with the promise that John would be filled with the Holy Spirit from his birth (Luke 1:15). (The Greek, literally, is "from his mother's womb.") The second statement is in Luke 1:80: "The child grew and became strong in spirit."

The School of the Desert

All we are told about John's adulthood before the commencement of his ministry is that he "was in the deserts till the day of his manifestation to Israel" (Luke 1:80). The desert is the place of preparation in the Old Testament record of godly men God used. Moses tended "the flock of Jethro his father-in-law, the priest of Midian" in the desert, and there he received the revelation at the burning bush and the commission to begin his work (Exod. 3). David, another forerunner of the Messiah, looked after his sheep in the desert (1 Sam. 17:28) and was prepared there for his ministry as prophet and king.

The Word of the Lord Came to John

Luke, a most careful historian, records the exact period John began his ministry: "In the fifteenth year of the reign of Tiberius Caesar, Pontius Pilate being governor of Judea, Herod being tetrarch of Galilee, his brother Philip tetrarch of Iturea and the region of Trachonitis, and Lysanias tetrarch of Abilene, while Annas and Caiaphas were high priests, the word of God came to John the son of Zacharias in the wilderness" (3:1–2). The period that John commenced his ministry seems to be A.D. 27–29.

An element of drama marked John's sudden appearance on the stage of Israel's history, for it was something like four hundred years since there had been a prophet sent by God to His people: "The word of God came to John the son of Zacharias in the wilderness" (Luke 3:2). Those first words echo the Old Testament prophets' experience, and that must clearly be Luke's thought.

The regular formula in the Old Testament prophetic writings is "the word of the LORD came by the prophet" (1 Kings 16:7), or "the word of the LORD came expressly to Ezekiel" (Ezek. 1:3), or "the word of the LORD came to me" (Jer. 1:4). John did not decide for himself the time to begin his ministry—the coming of the Lord's word to him did. And he was in the desert when it happened.

An Unusual Figure

The forerunner's dress was distinctive: "John himself was clothed in camel's hair, with a leather belt around his waist" (Matt. 3:4; cf. Mark 1:6). So, too, was his food: "His food was locusts and wild honey" (Matt. 3:4). Numerous kinds of locusts exist. Although food only for the poorest, they may still be eaten, roasted or salted, by the Bedouin. John's lifestyle was the simplest possible.

The Sphere of John's Ministry

The Jordan was the immediate sphere of John's activity: "He went into all the region around the Jordan, preaching a baptism of repentance for the remission of sins" (Luke 3:3). *Jordan* means "descender" because the headwaters of the river, fed by springs, collect into Lake Huleh, 230 feet above sea level. Ten miles south at Lake Tiberias, it is nearly 700 feet below the Mediterranean, while at the north end of the Dead Sea the floor of the trench has dropped another 580 feet below sea level.

The distance from Lake Huleh to the Dead Sea is about seventy-five miles, but the course of the river is more than doubled by its meanders. The Jordan Valley, running for over sixty-five miles between Lake Tiberias and the Dead Sea, was the sphere of John's work, and in particular an area of about sixteen miles between the Jabbok and Beth Nimrah, where there were no streams entering the Jordan and little settlement. Despite oases, the valley was a desert.

John's Message

The period of John's ministry seems to have been short, but it was a strategic preparation for the work of the Son of God, especially in the message John proclaimed.

John's first emphasis was on repentance (Matt. 3:7–10; Luke 3:7–9). Repentance is basically a change of mind. In repentance we change our minds about sin; we recognize that to go our own way, contrary to God's will and commands, is wrong, and instead we choose to go God's way, confessing our sins to Him and turning from them.

John's message was clear and straightforward: he preached a baptism of repentance for the forgiveness of sins (Luke 3:3). It was good news that he preached (Luke 3:18).

Because of common depictions of John, we may be tempted to think of him as rather forbidding, somewhat awesome, aloof, and frightening. But John must have exhibited something of the joy of the good news he preached. With the repentance he taught went forgiveness, and there is no joy to be compared with the experience of God's gracious pardon and everlasting forgetfulness of our sins.

It is important not to pass too quickly over the word *preached* (Luke 3:18), in that the verb implies that John preached for a decision. He spoke not his own word but God's, and God's invitation to salvation required an immediate response.

The proper response was symbolized by baptism: he preached "a baptism of repentance" (Luke 3:3). Although there has been some debate about it, there seems little doubt that baptism was not new in the first century. The indications are that the Jews practiced it when they accepted gentile converts—"proselytes"—into the Jewish faith. Such would have been required to have been first circumcised and then baptized. Jews considered all of humankind except themselves to be in a state of total uncleanness and incapable of entering into covenant with God without a washing or baptism to symbolize purification from their spiritual defilement.

The difference with John's baptism was that it was not for converts to Judaism—for proselytes—but it was for the Jewish people themselves! It was not enough to be a Jew;

you had to be a converted Jew! So insistent was John on that as the required symbolic response that he was given the nickname "the Baptist."

Those with discernment saw in John the fulfillment of the prophet's promise:

> As it is written in the book of the words of Isaiah the prophet, saying:

> "The voice of one crying in the wilderness:
> 'Prepare the way of the LORD;
> Make His paths straight.
> Every valley shall be filled
> And every mountain and hill brought low;
> The crooked places shall be made straight
> And the rough ways smooth;
> And all flesh shall see the salvation of God'" (Luke 3:4–6; Isa. 40:3–5).

Crowds went out to be baptized by John (Luke 3:7). A danger in any crowd's mass response to preaching is that people may be prompted by emotion rather than reason, or moved by the actions of others rather than by conviction. John sought to sift out his hearers by forthrightly laying down the cost and the spiritual reality and moral honesty God requires.

John warned against baptism without genuine repentance. He "said to the multitudes that came out to be baptized by him, 'Brood of vipers! Who warned you to flee from the wrath to come? Therefore bear fruits worthy of repentance'" (Luke 3:7–8). He called for evidence of repentance. Profession on its own was not enough—changed lives were necessary.

By insisting that trueborn Jews needed to be baptized just as much as gentile converts to the Jewish faith, John showed that religious activity and background do not provide salvation: "And do not begin to say to yourselves, 'We have Abraham as our father.' For I say to you that God is able to raise up children to Abraham from these stones" (Luke 3:8). Behind this warning there is the clear implication of the truth of new birth—regeneration—being more important than religious privileges arising from the "accident" of natural birth (Luke 3:8; cf. John 1:11–13). John sought to arouse his Jewish hearers from any false sense of security.

To underline the urgency and seriousness of his message, John proclaimed God's judgment: "The ax is laid to the root of the trees. Therefore every tree which does not bear good fruit is cut down and thrown into the fire" (Luke 3:9). In the implicit idea of new birth and the use of the picture of a tree representing a person's life, we see the germs, the seeds of instruction, that Jesus was to amplify and bring to fullness. John's emphases perfectly prepared the way for Jesus' teaching (cf. Acts 13:24).

John gave specific instruction concerning the practical outworking of repentance to the different groups of people who presented themselves for baptism (Luke 3:10–14). Three examples are given. To rich or reasonably well-off people, his instruction was that "he who has two tunics, let him give to him who has none; and he who has food, let him do likewise" (v. 11). To the tax collectors, he said, "Collect no more than what is appointed for you" (v. 13). To soldiers, he said, "Do not intimidate anyone or accuse falsely, and be content with your wages" (v. 14).

John and the Messiah

In view of John the Baptist's dramatic ministry—especially as he was filled with the Spirit from birth and God's hand was with him—it is not surprising that some wondered if he were, in fact, the Christ, the promised Messiah.

John emphatically denied being the Messiah (John 1:19–28). It was not that the thought came to his mind, but it did occur to others. As Luke tells us, "The people were in expectation, and all reasoned in their hearts about John, whether he was the Christ or not" (3:15). This indicates how well John had done his work, of how effectively he prepared the way for his Master and Lord.

John's preaching focused on the coming Messiah (Matt. 3:11–12; Mark 1:7–8; Luke 3:15–18). He drew a contrast between his baptizing with water and Jesus' baptizing with the Holy Spirit (Luke 3:16). He spoke of his inferiority and worthlessness compared with the One of whom he testified: "One mightier than I is coming, whose sandal strap I am not worthy to loose" (Luke 3:16). He also spoke of Jesus as the Judge (Luke 3:17).

John's Witness to Jesus

John bore witness to Jesus as the true Light of the World. He "came for a witness, to bear witness of the Light, that all through him might believe. He was not that Light, but was sent to bear witness of that Light" (John 1:7–8). Nothing else that John did is as important as this (John 1:15, 20, 32, 34; 3:26; 5:33).

John witnessed to Jesus' preexistence: "This was He of whom I said, 'He who comes after me is preferred before me, for He was before me'" (John 1:15). John knew full well that Jesus was conceived and born *after* him, but he knew that Jesus was *before* him!

John witnessed to Jesus' deity, that Jesus is the Lord. In the words of the prophet Isaiah, he explained,

I am

"The voice of one crying in the wilderness:
'Make straight the way of the LORD'" (John 1:23).

He identified that Lord with the One whom he said stood among them, "whose sandal strap I am not worthy to loose" (John 1:27).

John witnessed to Jesus' atoning work. Seeing Jesus coming toward him, he said, "Behold! The Lamb of God who takes away the sin of the world!" (John 1:29). He made that statement more than once (John 1:36). The whole Jewish race was familiar with the sacrificial system. Jewish people knew that the holy God could be approached by sinful men and women only through sacrifice. And yet those sacrifices could never take away sin. Each animal sacrifice pointed to the one sacrifice of the promised Lamb of God who could effectively and once and for all deal with sin.

John witnessed to Jesus' identity as the Son of God, as he understood the events that accompanied Jesus' baptism. John explained, "I saw the Spirit descending from heaven like a dove, and He remained upon Him. I did not know Him, but He who sent me to baptize with water said to me, 'Upon whom you see the Spirit descending, and remaining on Him, this is He who baptizes with the Holy Spirit.' And I have seen and testified that this is the Son of God" (John 1:32–34).

The more we ponder this statement, the more remarkable it is. Jesus had not yet revealed His glory, yet John saw it. John received special insight from God to enable him to be a unique witness to Jesus as the Christ, the Son of God. After he gave that witness, John's work neared completion (cf. Acts 13:25).

John's Baptism of Jesus

John's baptism of Jesus was a momentous event for John and Jesus. It marked the beginning of Jesus' public life, although not of His public ministry (Matt. 3:13–17; Mark 1:9–11; Luke 3:21–23).

John was reluctant to baptize Jesus because of his appreciation of Jesus' identity (Matt. 3:14). Since John's baptism was for repentance, and Jesus, the sinless Son of God, had no sin of which to repent, John's baptism seemed—and seems—quite out of place.

Jesus' answer was that it is fitting to do all we know to be God's will (Matt. 3:15). By His baptism, He showed the reason for His coming into the world: He had come to stand alongside sinners and to be completely identified with them as their Savior. And so it was that He willingly submitted to being baptized by John. His baptism was a way of saying yes to the Father's will that He should go to the cross. Calvary's shadow fell on the flowing Jordan as He was baptized. Jesus knew from the beginning to what He was committing Himself.

The Father's approval of His Son and of His action was immediate (Matt. 3:16–17). Pleasing the Father perfectly in everything, Jesus was able to offer Himself—without spot or blemish—as the Lamb of God whom John rightly proclaimed Him to be.

John's Direction of Disciples to Jesus

Following Jesus' baptism, John pointed Jesus' first disciples to Him. John repeated his testimony to Him as the Lamb of God (John 1:36). As a consequence, two disciples followed Jesus and spent the day with Him (John 1:39). Andrew was one of the two, and "he first found his own brother Simon, and said to him, 'We have found the Messiah' (which is translated, the Christ)" (John 1:41). Although not stated, the implication is that Philip was also one of John the Baptist's disciples, perhaps Andrew's companion in the day visit to Jesus; and he, in turn, told Nathanael the good news (John 1:43–45).

The Importance of John's Witness

John's witness was of great importance. First, it was the fulfillment of prophecy (Mark 1:2–3; Mal. 3:1; Isa. 40:3).

Second, it showed the continuity of Jesus' ministry with the Old Testament. John the Baptist was the link between the Old Testament prophets and the coming of the Great Prophet they all anticipated.

Third, it prepared the way for Jesus' ministry. It was like the turning over of soil in preparation for seed. It set the pattern for Jesus' ministry even from the point of view of the treatment John received: the treatment meted out to John was a sample of what Jesus was going to experience (Matt. 17:12; Mark 9:12–13).

Fourth, wonderful as John's ministry was, it demonstrated the superiority of Jesus' ministry to all that had gone before, including John's. A typical difference between Jesus' teaching and John's was that concerning fasting (Matt. 9:14–17; Mark 2:18–22; Luke 5:33–39). John's ministry marked the end of the old chapter of God's dealings with His people; and Jesus' marked the beginning of the new.

Fifth, it is an example to us, for our task—under the Holy Spirit's influence and enabling—is to bear witness to Jesus. "You shall be witnesses to Me," was Jesus' last commission to His disciples immediately before His ascension (Acts 1:8). John was prepared to be a link in a chain, a signpost, pointing others to the Son of God.

"I Must Decrease"

The time quickly came when Jesus gained and baptized more disciples than John (John 4:1; cf. 3:26). Some of John's disciples were jealous and concerned for John's reputation. John used a very human illustration of his joy when he said,

A man can receive nothing unless it has been given to him from heaven. You yourselves bear me witness, that I said, "I am not the Christ," but, "I have been sent before Him." He who has the bride is the bridegroom; but the friend of the bridegroom, who stands and hears him, rejoices greatly because of the bridegroom's voice. Therefore this joy of mine is fulfilled. He must increase, but I must decrease (John 3:27–30).

John's Imprisonment

John's imprisonment came about through his honest rebuking of Herod the tetrarch because of Herodias, his brother's wife, and "for all the evils which Herod had done" (Luke 3:19); Herod "added this, above all, that he shut John up in prison" (Luke 3:20).

John's imprisonment was like a starter's pistol for the commencement of Jesus' work, and especially His preaching ministry (Matt. 4:12).

John's Disciples

Not all of John's disciples followed his instruction to focus on Jesus rather than on himself. Even at the time of the apostle John's writing of his gospel, disciples of John the Baptist continued to exist, and he goes to great pains to emphasize that John the Baptist was not the one promised but the one who gave witness to the Promised One (1:6–8; cf. 1:15, 19–20).

John sent two of his disciples to Jesus to ask, "Are You the Coming One, or do we look for another?" When the men arrived, they asked their question and also witnessed Jesus' healing of many who had diseases, sicknesses, and evil spirits and His giving of sight to people who were blind. Jesus replied to the messengers, "Go and tell John the things you have seen and heard: that the blind see, the lame walk, the lepers are cleansed, the deaf hear, the dead are raised, the poor have the gospel preached to them. And blessed is he who is not offended because of Me" (Luke 7:18–23; cf. Matt. 11:1–6).

Was John perhaps uncertain of Jesus' identity? That does not really make sense when we remember his testimony to Jesus and the promise that John would be filled with the Holy Spirit. What makes better sense is that he wanted his own disciples, who were uncertain of Jesus' identity, to see Him and His powerful works with their own eyes, and to hear from His lips the declaration of His messiahship, and for them to share it then with their fellow disciples. The purpose of John's disciples' mission was for their benefit rather than his.

Jesus used the visit of John's disciples to speak in the warmest possible manner of John (Matt. 11:7–19; Luke 7:24–28; cf. Matt. 21:32). He declared John to be a prophet, but more than a prophet (Luke 7:26): "I tell you, among those born of women there is no one greater than John" (Luke 7:28 NIV). Paradoxically, He went on to say, "But he who is least in the kingdom of God is greater than he" (Luke 7:28). Wonderful as it was to be a prophet, and to be the last of the great prophets, that is not as great a privilege as being a member of God's kingdom.

M E D I T A T I O N

1. Experiences of disappointment and suffering are not to be read as signs of God's discipline—godliness's genuineness may be demonstrated in them, and God's purposes worked out:

   There was in the days of Herod, the king of Judea, a certain priest named Zacharias, of the division of

Abijah. His wife was of the daughters of Aaron, and her name was Elizabeth. And they were both righteous before God, walking in all the commandments and ordinances of the Lord blameless. But they had no child, because Elizabeth was barren, and they were both well advanced in years (Luke 1:5–7).

2. Jesus is the Dayspring who gives "light to those who sit in darkness and the shadow of death, to guide our feet into the way of peace" (Luke 1:79). He says to us, "I am the light of the world. He who follows Me shall not walk in darkness, but have the light of life" (John 8:12).

3. God's answers to our prayers may come later than we expect since He is not limited by what we consider impossible: "But the angel said to him, 'Do not be afraid, Zacharias, for your prayer is heard; and your wife Elizabeth will bear you a son, and you shall call his name John" (Luke 1:13).

4. "Behold! The Lamb of God who takes away the sin of the world!" (John 1:29).

   All we like sheep have gone astray;
   We have turned, every one, to his own way;
   And the LORD has laid on Him the iniquity of us all
     (Isa. 53:6).

5. John "went into all the country around the Jordan, preaching a baptism of repentance for the forgiveness of sins" (Luke 3:3 NIV). In many ways John was Jesus' forerunner, but not least in the prominence he gave to the first benefit of salvation—forgiveness.

6. Jesus' words at His baptism—"It is fitting for us to fulfill all righteousness"—provide us with insight into Jesus' perfect obedience to His Father and the example He gives us.

7. "Assuredly, I say to you, among those born of women there has not risen one greater than John the Baptist; but he who is least in the kingdom of heaven is greater than he" (Matt. 11:11). Membership in the kingdom of heaven means birth into God's family, and that privilege is greater than any human position or status that a person may attain.

Q U E S T I O N S

1. Why is it unhelpful to consider Jesus' ministry without first considering that of John the Baptist?

2. In what particular ways was John the Baptist the forerunner of Jesus? How did he in practice prepare Jesus' way?

3. Why might the priests and Levites have thought that John the Baptist was the Messiah?

4. How would a discerning Jew have interpreted John's repeated testimony to Jesus as the Lamb of God?

5. How would you summarize John the Baptist's message?

6. What were the reasons for, and significance of, Jesus' baptism?

7. What insights into John the Baptist's works may we gain from Jesus' commendation of him (Matt. 11:1–19)?

Chapter Three

JESUS AT WORK

Teaching, preaching, doing good, and healing—these four activities sum up the three years of Jesus' public ministry.

A Clear Objective

Jesus always had one great end in view. His ministry was not simply to teach and preach, do good and heal: His objective, from the beginning, was His final journey to Jerusalem and His death there as the substitute for sinners (Luke 19:10; Matt. 20:28; Mark 10:45). This single-minded purpose brought Him into immediate and constant conflict with Satan, the god of this world, for Jesus' sacrificial death was the key to Satan's defeat (Heb. 2:14–15). For this reason Jesus' temptation in the wilderness, immediately after His baptism (Matt. 4:1–11), preceded His public ministry.

The Temptation

God the Holy Spirit, the Director of our Lord's earthly life, led Him into the desert to be tempted by the devil (Matt. 4:1; Mark 1:12). That period of testing, therefore, was no accident.

God's will was that Jesus should stand up successfully under temptation and so prove Himself the perfectly qualified Messiah to deliver His people from their sins. The desert's loneliness accentuated the acuteness of the temptations (Matt. 4:1).

The devil tried to undermine Jesus' assurance of His unique relationship with God as His Son. At His baptism, Jesus had been saluted as God's Son, the Messiah (Matt. 3:17). Significantly, two of the devil's temptations began with the words "If You are the Son of God" (Matt. 4:3, 6).

The Gospels record three specific temptations. The first was that Jesus should demonstrate His messiahship by meeting people's economic needs (Matt. 4:3), as the feeding of the five thousand, for example, showed He could have done if He had chosen (John 6:1–15). The second was that He should use startling and spectacular ways to win people's allegiance (Matt. 4:6). The third was that He should bypass the Cross altogether and instead obtain authority and glory from the devil (Matt. 4:8–9).

Jesus tested and answered the devil's tempting suggestions by the Scriptures—the Spirit's sword (Eph. 6:17). The timely encouragement of the angels at the end of Jesus' period of temptation (Matt. 4:11) gives a clue to the intensity of the testing through which He passed.

That was not the end of the conflict, for it continued throughout the next three years. Jesus was frequently tempted to shrink from full obedience to His Father's will. The people regularly asked Him for a spectacular sign as a ground for believing in His identity as the Messiah (Mark 8:11; John 2:18; 6:30). As the Cross drew nearer, the devil made temptation all the greater. But at the beginning, Jesus showed the way He was determined to go.

Early Events

John's gospel differs in a number of ways from the gospels of Matthew, Mark, and Luke. The latter three give prominence to Jesus' Galilean ministry. John concentrates much more on Jesus' ministry in Jerusalem and its immediate area. He records some of the early events in His ministry, which sum up its main features, but which the other gospel writers record later in greater detail.

John tells how Jesus began to call His first disciples after they had been pointed in His direction by John the Baptist (John 1:35–51). Soon after, Jesus gave them a glimpse of His glory at the wedding in Cana of Galilee when He turned water into wine (John 2:11). Such clues to His identity—that is to say, that the Creator was present with His creatures—were to increase as the months passed (Luke 5:1–11).

Then after a brief stay in Capernaum (John 2:12), Jesus went up to Jerusalem and dramatically cleansed the temple. Some have thought that is the same incident the other gospel writers describe toward the conclusion of our Lord's ministry. But there are no real grounds for making this assumption. Three years is a long time in terms of human activity and greed. If people do not listen to what is said or refuse to pay heed to a lesson, they quickly return to how they were.

The buying and selling to which our Lord objected took place in the outer courtyard, the court of the Gentiles.

Pilgrims from a distance had to buy sacrifical victims on their arrival. Visitors from other countries required facilities to change their money into coinage acceptable to the temple. Commercialism had taken over.

Those with discernment recognized the cleansing of the temple to be a messianic act (John 2:18). Miraculous signs that accompanied this visit to Jerusalem confirmed Jesus' authority to execute judgment. Powerful acts prompting searching questions marked His ministry.

Nicodemus came to Jesus at night following His action in the temple and His miracles (John 3:2). Jesus taught Nicodemus the revolutionary truth of new birth that underlies all the teaching He gave subsequently about the kingdom of God.

John uniquely provides details of Jesus' detour into Samaria on the way to Galilee (John 4:3–4) and His meeting with the Samaritan woman whom He pointed to repentance and faith in Himself. The incident indicates that from the beginning, Jesus knew that His mission and death were for the benefit of more than the Jews. Jesus' words to the Samaritan woman anticipated Acts 1:8 when Jesus commissioned His disciples to be His witnesses "in Jerusalem, and in all Judea and Samaria, and to the end of the earth." The harvest of His preaching during His brief visit to Samaria indicated that the salvation He had come to bring was for people of every race and nation (John 4:39–42).

The other gospel writers illustrate these themes through more detailed accounts of Jesus' ministry in Judea, and especially in Galilee.

The Signal

John the Baptist's imprisonment seems to have signaled the time for Jesus to begin His public work in Galilee, the area where He initially concentrated His ministry

(Luke 4:14–15). As Matthew records, "When Jesus heard that John had been put in prison, He departed to Galilee" (4:12).

Early on He went to Nazareth, His hometown (Luke 4:14–30). By means of a pointed reading of the prophet Isaiah in the synagogue, Jesus indicated His identity as the promised Messiah (v. 21). He was not merely rejected by the people in the synagogue; they sought to kill Him (v. 29).

He then made Capernaum, a city on the northwest shore of the Sea of Galilee, His headquarters (Mark 1:21; Luke 4:31). An important city, it served as a strategic base for the surrounding area, and much of Jesus' teaching and many of His miracles of healing occurred there (Matt. 8:5–13). It became known as Jesus' "own city" (Matt. 9:1). (The centurion's presence [Matt. 8:5] probably indicates that a Roman military post was close by or in the city itself.)

The Use of the Synagogues

Jesus regularly taught in the synagogues where possible (Matt. 4:23–25; Mark 1:39; Luke 4:44). Synagogues had arisen as places of instruction in the Scriptures and prayer during the period of the Exile, beginning in the sixth century B.C., when worship in Jerusalem was impossible. The word *synagogue* first described a gathering of individuals, and then later the building in which gatherings were held.

Synagogue buildings were probably modeled on the temple in Jerusalem. The scrolls of the Law and the Prophets were kept in a portable ark (i.e., chest), which faced the entrance of the building, and it was carried in procession on feast days. In front of the ark, and facing the worshipers, were "the best seats" (Matt. 23:6) for the religious and governing leaders of the synagogue. The Law was read from a central platform. The synagogues were the obvious starting point for Jesus to proclaim God's Word.

It was especially appropriate that Jesus should teach in the synagogues since He was the One whom the scrolls of the Law and the Prophets proclaimed, and whom the people claimed to expect (cf. Luke 4:17–27).

Healings

With Jesus' teaching there went healings. The early accounts in the Gospels indicate the great crowds wanting to be healed in every place (Mark 1:32–34). The variety of need was great: fever, leprosy, paralysis, perpetual hemorrhage, blindness, inability to speak, deafness, epilepsy, spinal deformity, and dropsy, as well as demon possession and death itself (Matt. 9:18–26; Luke 8:40–56). The Gospels record that Jesus healed all who were sick (Luke 4:40; cf. Matt. 8:16–17; 12:15–21; 14:34–36).

An Unseen Opposition

The most dramatic healings were those of demon possession (Mark 1:21–28, 34; Luke 4:31–37, 41). A sense of the opposition of the forces of evil to Jesus' power was always present. And yet they could never withstand His authority. Every time He cast out an evil spirit, the ultimate overthrow of Satan's kingdom was anticipated. Invariably, the evil spirits recognized Jesus' identity, and He regularly rebuked them and commanded their silence (Mark 1:34; 3:11–12).

Growing Crowds

The constant pressure of great numbers of people on Jesus must have been both physically and spiritually demanding, especially with His increasing popularity with the people (Luke 4:40–42; 5:15; 6:17–19). Virtue or power went out of Him (Mark 5:30; Luke 6:19; 8:46). His reputation spread far and wide (Matt. 4:24–25; Mark 3:7–8; Luke 6:17–19).

So vast were the crowds that on occasion Jesus used a boat at the lakeside to keep the crowd from overwhelming Him (Mark 3:7–12). The numbers grew even greater, with the crowds attracted more and more by His healing power, many of them simply trying to touch Him (Matt. 12:15–21; Luke 6:19).

The Primary Emphasis—Teaching

Jesus did not consider healing His priority: His main task was teaching and preaching the gospel. His healing ministry comes at the bottom of the list of His activities (Matt. 9:35). As a witness to His deity, the miracles underlined the authority of His teaching. But the crowds' preoccupation with the healings sometimes blunted their hearing of His message. He chose to withdraw from them often when that happened (Luke 5:16).

Seized Opportunities

Jesus gave much of His teaching in answer to questions. Some questions implied criticism of Him, but He turned them to good effect. When asked why His disciples did not fast like John's disciples, He explained the newness of His message (Matt. 9:14–17; Mark 2:18–22; Luke 5:33–39).

Questioned about His disciples picking heads of grain to eat on the Sabbath, He demonstrated that the Sabbath was made for people, and not the other way around, and that the Son of man is Lord of the Sabbath (Matt. 12:1–8; Mark 2:23–28; Luke 6:1–5).

Asked about His disciples eating food with unwashed hands, Jesus taught the perils of hypocrisy, especially in making the outside clean while neglecting the inside (Mark 7:1–16).

Some questions deliberately tested Jesus. A question about divorce was one such (Matt. 19:1–12; cf. Mark 10:1–12), and it provided Him with the opportunity to give teaching we do not find elsewhere. The lawyer's question to test Jesus, "What shall I do to inherit eternal life?" gave rise to Jesus' story of the good Samaritan (Luke 10:25–37).

The disciples, too, asked questions. They were privileged to have intimate access to Jesus. Often they followed up the answers He gave to other people's questions by further questions. They questioned Him on the divorce issue (Mark 10:10). Not understanding the parable of the sower—the most basic of Jesus' parables in establishing the principles of His ministry—they asked Him to explain it to them (Luke 8:9–15). When they failed to heal a boy with an evil spirit, they asked, "Why could we not cast it out?" (Mark 9:28; Luke 9:37–43), and they were taught the priority of prayer—something they had neglected (Mark 9:29).

In Training

Day in and day out, Jesus trained His disciples, and by different means, He revealed His glory so that at the end, they had no doubt at all of His identity and mission (1 John 1:1–3). They acquired much of their training through their observation of Him and the questions they put to Him. They had the unique opportunity of making requests, for example, "Lord, teach us to pray" (Luke 11:1).

At the same time Jesus devoted Himself to more formal instruction, such as the Sermon on the Mount (Matt. 5—7; Luke 6:20–49).

A Background of Prayer

Like the gentle lifting of a curtain, moments in the Gospels reveal the priority Jesus gave to prayer—a priority that prompted the disciples' wish to copy Him.

Early in the morning, while still dark, He got up in order to pray (Mark 1:35; Luke 4:42–43). As we remember His constant busyness, He must have been tired at the end of each day. Nevertheless, He looked for a place of quietness in those early hours of the morning before the crowds gathered with their urgent needs and requests.

As Jesus prayed, He found guidance. After prayer, He determined to move on to other places, much as people wanted Him to stay (Mark 1:35–39).

Jesus' decisions came to birth in prayer. He spent a night in prayer before calling and appointing the apostles (Luke 6:12–13). The decision to question the disciples about their understanding of His messiahship and sonship was likewise preceded by prayer (Luke 9:18; cf. Matt. 16:13).

Jesus' Compassion

Nowhere are we told in the Gospels what Jesus looked like, but everywhere His character stands out. He met people where they were, and He took them as He found them. Society's outcasts found in Him their best friend. He treated everyone alike and made plain God's unfailing love.

Jesus' compassion stands out. Looking at the crowds, He saw them "weary and scattered, like sheep having no shepherd" (Matt. 9:36). In answering a request for wholeness from a man with leprosy, rather than simply speaking a word of healing as He easily might have done, "Jesus put out His hand and touched him" (Matt. 8:3).

When the crowds pursued Him relentlessly, even though He needed peace for a while to instruct His disciples privately, at the sight of their need, "He was moved with compassion for them, and healed their sick" (Matt. 14:14). No needy individual stood before Jesus and doubted His loving concern for his or her total well-being.

In viewing people as sheep and as a harvest to be reaped (Luke 10:2), Jesus underlined the value of every individual. He, the Good Shepherd, was to lay down His life for the sheep. He is the Good Shepherd who was prepared to leave the ninety-nine for the one sheep that was lost (Luke 15:3–7). His death was to be the seed sown to produce a great harvest of redeemed men and women (John 12:24). His concern for their salvation caused Him never to be content with the proclamation of the good news in one place while people in other places had not heard (Mark 1:33–39; Luke 4:42–43).

Misconceptions About Jesus' Ministry

Preoccupation with Jesus' acts of power, and false understanding of what the Messiah was supposed to do, contributed to the crowds' misconceptions of His work. His popularity reached an all-time peak at the feeding of the five thousand. It is the only miracle recorded by all four gospel writers, but John brings to the surface the basic issue in his more detailed account (John 6:1–59).

The people rightly recognized Jesus as the promised Prophet and Messiah, but they wrongly looked for a political Savior. When they witnessed Jesus' ability to provide bread, they identified Him as the revolutionary leader for whom they were looking (John 6:15). One of Satan's early temptations repeated itself—that Jesus should be a Messiah who satisfied people's economic needs (Matt. 4:3).

The possible infection of the disciples by the crowds' misconceptions was a serious danger (Matt. 14:22–23), and Jesus took appropriate counteraction by sending the disciples to the other side of the lake and giving Himself to prayer. As the crowds continued to pursue Him (John 6:25–59), Jesus pointed out the mistake they were making about His mission (vv. 26–27). He stressed the priority of faith in Himself (vv. 28–29), although that provoked the request for yet another sign (vv. 30–31). In answer He used the picture of Himself as the true Bread from heaven, employing daring language to describe His death for our salvation (vv. 53–58). Food and drink are necessary for physical life. Jesus used the picture they provide to convey a spiritual lesson: apart from the sacrifice of His body and blood, and our eating His flesh and drinking His blood (John 6:51, 53–58), there is no possibility of spiritual life for us.

To eat the flesh of Jesus and to drink His blood are to come to Him, believing that He gave Himself for our sins on the cross, and putting our trust in Him to bring us back to God and to give us everlasting life.

Jesus' teaching—while it put the record straight—offended most of His hearers (v. 66). They wanted Jesus, but for the wrong reasons.

Increasing Opposition

After the feeding of the five thousand, opposition to Jesus grew. The warnings He gave His critics, His amazing works, and the authority of His teaching all seemed to increase the antagonism of the religious teachers and authorities. They were jealous of Jesus (Matt. 27:18) because of the popular following He had obtained.

Jesus could not go anywhere without being watched (Luke 14:1). The Pharisees made outrageous claims against Him, aiming to discredit Him in every way they could think of, including the accusation that He cast out demons by the devil's power. The mounting opposition was to reach its climax when He raised Lazarus from the dead (John 11:46–53). Evidences were there early on that His own people were on the threshold of rejecting Him (John 1:11).

M E D I T A T I O N

1. Jesus' experience of testing and temptation makes Him the perfect High Priest to help us: "For we do not have a High Priest who cannot sympathize with our weaknesses, but was in all points tempted as we are, yet without sin. Let us therefore come boldly to the throne of grace, that we may obtain mercy and find grace to help in time of need" (Heb. 4:15–16).

2. Jesus' miraculous signs revealed His glory, a glory we need to see by the miraculous working of God's Spirit in our hearts: "For it is the God who commanded light to shine out of darkness, who has shone in our hearts to give the light of the knowledge of the glory of God in the face of Jesus Christ" (2 Cor. 4:6).

3. Jesus "went about doing good and healing all who were oppressed by the devil, for God was with Him" (Acts 10:38).

4. "My food," said Jesus, "is to do the will of Him who sent Me, and to finish His work" (John 4:34). Paul's message to Archippus has relevance to all Christians: "Take heed to the ministry which you have received in the Lord, that you may fulfill it" (Col. 4:17).

5. "Who touched Me?" Jesus asked. Then the woman "saw that she was not hidden"; she "came trembling" and fell at His feet (Luke 8:45, 47). We never put out the hand of faith to Jesus unnoticed and unrewarded.

6. Who is my neighbor? "As we have opportunity, let us do good to all, especially to those who are of the household of faith" (Gal. 6:10).

7. No matter how Jesus' critics watched Him, they could find no legitimate excuses for criticizing Him: He "committed no sin, nor was deceit found in His mouth" (1 Pet. 2:22).

Q U E S T I O N S

1. What relevance does Jesus' temptation have to us in our temptations?

2. What was the significance of Jesus' miracles, and what place should they have in our witness to others about Jesus?

3. By what different means did Jesus make plain that His healing work was secondary to His teaching ministry? What does this teach us about our priorities in serving Him in the world?

4. Are there present-day misconceptions about what Jesus came to do? If so, identify them, and suggest ways of correcting them.

5. What were the likely reasons for Jesus' instruction to Jairus and his wife that they should not publicize their daughter's resurrection from the dead?

6. What is the relationship between our loving God and our loving our neighbor? What practical illustrations can you give of the difference our love for God should make in our attitude toward our neighbor?

7. How do you explain contemporary opposition to Jesus?

Chapter Four

JESUS THE MESSIAH

People looked for clues to Jesus' identity. Two stood out. We consider now the first—His identity as the Messiah. That one title—more than any other—explains the Jewish response to Jesus and His own understanding of His mission. Handel entitled his magnificent summary of Jesus' life the *Messiah*, and he could not have chosen a better title.

The Jews awaited the coming of a Great One whom they called the Messiah, our translation of a Hebrew word meaning "anointed." Translated into Greek, it becomes *Christos*, from which we get "Christ."

Matthew begins his gospel, "The book of the geneal-ogy of Jesus Christ, the Son of David" (Matt. 1:1). Mark's first words are, "The beginning of the gospel of Jesus Christ" (Mark 1:1). The title "Christ" or "Messiah" is so fa-miliar that we may miss its fundamental significance.

The Background of the Title "Messiah"

The rite of anointing in the Old Testament period set in-dividuals apart for special functions. Priests and kings of Is-rael were consecrated by a holy unction or anointing with oil (Exod. 29:7, 21; 1 Sam. 10:1), and in some instances prophets, too.

Anointing conveyed the idea of consecration to God's service, of being chosen by God for a specific task and spe-cially endowed by Him with power to fulfill it (1 Sam. 10:1, 6; 16:13; Isa. 61:1)—and frequently, the Holy Spirit's power is mentioned.

The Old Testament focuses on God's preparations for the advent of His Messiah—through prophets, priests, kings, in-numerable promises and symbols. The Old Testament Scrip-tures as a whole—and in particular the messianic Scriptures —anticipated His coming.

The title "Messiah" points to Jesus as the fulfillment of the long succession of Israel's anointed prophets, priests, and kings. The latter's offices all come together in Jesus, and He was consecrated to them by a public and immeasur-able effusion of the Holy Spirit (Ps. 45:7; Luke 3:22; 4:18): "For He whom God has sent speaks the words of God, for God does not give the Spirit by measure" (John 3:34).

The Expectation That Was Present

Expecting the Messiah's arrival, Jews took note of the many Scriptures that anticipated His coming. After listening to Jesus preach during one of His visits to Jerusalem, some of the people said, "Truly this is the Prophet." Others said, "This is the Christ" (John 7:40–41). The woman of Samaria expressed a similar conviction when she said to Jesus, "'I know that Messiah is coming' (who is called Christ). 'When He comes, He will tell us all things'" (John 4:25). As Jesus showed her truths about herself she had not been prepared to face up to before, and gave the wonderful promise of the living waters of eternal life, she recognized Him as the Messiah and believed on Him (John 4:29, 39).

The most popular conception of the Messiah was as a ruler who would restore the kingdom to Israel with more than its former glory and prosperity. The Dead Sea Scrolls show that the men of Qumran, for example, lived in expectation of three messianic figures: a Prophet like Moses, an anointed Priest, and an anointed King. Those, they anticipated, would wind up the present unsatisfactory world order and bring in the golden age.

Living as we do centuries afterward, with our ability to survey so much of human history, we cannot but be impressed by the preparations made for the Messiah's coming, and His absolute and unique importance in God's purposes. Everything that has happened in the world has been subject to God's great plan of redemption through His Christ.

An Immediate Intimation of Jesus' Identity

Three events illustrate this preparation and expectation. The first was the immediate announcement at Jesus' birth of His identity as the Messiah.

Shepherds in the fields outside Bethlehem were told that the baby born in the city was none other than "Christ the Lord" (Luke 2:11). When the Magi came to Jerusalem asking, "Where is He who has been born King of the Jews?"

Herod and those with him significantly asked the chief priests and teachers of the law "where the Christ was to be born" (Matt. 2:2, 4). The chief priests and teachers of the law told Herod of Micah's prophecy about the Messiah's birth in Bethlehem (Matt. 2:5–6; Mic. 5:2).

There is no doubt that many Jewish people properly interpreted prophecies concerning the Messiah and were looking for Him. When Mary and Joseph took the child Jesus into the temple, for Him to be immediately recognized as the Messiah, Luke tells us that Simeon had been told that he would not die until "he had seen the Lord's Christ" (Luke 2:26). The appearance at Bethlehem of the Magi is a reminder that others, besides the Jews, were also anticipating the coming of God's Promised One.

John's Witness

The second important pointer to Jesus' identity was the direct relationship of John the Baptist's ministry to Jesus' messiahship, and John's careful preparing of the way for Jesus' work—as we saw in chapter 2.

The Significance of Jesus' Baptism

The third pointer to Jesus' messiahship was the circumstances surrounding His baptism, and the Spirit's descent upon Him: "When He had been baptized, Jesus came up immediately from the water; and behold, the heavens were opened to Him, and He saw the Spirit of God descending like a dove and alighting upon Him. And suddenly a voice came from heaven, saying, 'This is My beloved Son, in whom I am well pleased'" (Matt. 3:16–17).

The heavenly voice Jesus heard at His baptism brought together two passages of Old Testament Scripture—Psalm 2:7 and Isaiah 42:1. In interpreting Psalm 2, it was commonly agreed that the person addressed by God in the words, "You are My Son," was the future Messiah of David's line. To Jesus, born of Mary into the house of David, those words were a divine confirmation of His messiahship. But the words that followed pointed to the character of His messiahship. They come from the first of the great "Servant Songs" of the book of Isaiah, songs that speak of Him as the obedient and suffering Servant.

The Spirit's coming on Jesus at His baptism further indicated His messiahship: the Spirit's anointing marked Him out as the Christ.

The Declaration at Nazareth

The messianic declaration at Nazareth that soon followed should not therefore take us by surprise. Luke records,

> He came to Nazareth, where He had been brought up. And as His custom was, He went into the synagogue on the Sabbath day, and stood up to read. And He was handed the book of the prophet Isaiah. And when He had opened the book, He found the place where it was written:

> "The Spirit of the LORD is upon Me,
> Because He has anointed Me
> To preach the gospel to the poor;
> He has sent Me to heal the brokenhearted,
> To proclaim liberty to the captives
> And recovery of sight to the blind,
> To set at liberty those who are oppressed;
> To proclaim the acceptable year of the LORD" (Luke 4:16–19).

The congregation's breath was taken away when He said, "Today this Scripture is fulfilled in your hearing" (v. 21).

The opening words—"The Spirit of the LORD is upon Me, because He has anointed Me" (Luke 4:18)—point to the close involvement of God the Holy Spirit in Jesus' life and ministry. A degree of mystery surrounds it that we cannot explore.

The Spirit brought about Jesus' physical conception in Mary's womb (Matt. 1:18, 20; Luke 1:35). The same Spirit equipped Him for His work (Matt. 3:16; Mark 1:10; Luke 3:22; John 1:32–33). The Spirit directed Jesus in the course and program of His ministry (Matt. 4:1; Mark 1:12; Luke 4:1).

The Lord Jesus Christ is described as having been full of the Spirit and having gone about in the Spirit's energy (Luke 4:1, 14). He spoke of His miracles being performed by the Spirit's power (Matt. 12:28).

A Complete Confirmation of Identity

Taking Luke 4:18–19 as our guide, we see how perfectly Jesus demonstrated His messiahship and fulfilled God's promises given through the prophet Isaiah.

First, the Holy Spirit anointed Jesus "to preach the gospel to the poor" (v. 18). The verb *preach* points to what we have noticed earlier: Jesus' primary task, prior to His going to Jerusalem to die as the Lamb of God, was to teach the Word of God, the message of the kingdom. He proclaimed the good news to the poor both in the literal sense and in the spiritual sense. Throughout these words quoted in the synagogue at Nazareth, the spiritual application is uppermost, but the physical or social aspects are not to be neglected.

People of humble circumstances were made aware of how rich they could be toward God as they put their faith in Jesus. "Do not fear, little flock," He said, "for it is your

Father's good pleasure to give you the kingdom" (Luke 12:32). In particular Jesus preached the good news to those aware of their spiritual poverty. "Blessed are the poor in spirit," He declared, "for theirs is the kingdom of heaven" (Matt. 5:3). He proclaimed the good news to those convicted of their sin and in need of salvation—people like the woman of Samaria, an adulteress (John 4:10, 18), Zacchaeus, the cheat (Luke 19:9), and the penitent thief, a man of violence (Luke 23:43).

Second, the Holy Spirit anointed Jesus to "proclaim liberty to the captives" (v. 18). Here the spiritual sense is especially to the fore. By nature men and women everywhere are slaves to sin and Satan. When they see the truth about themselves, Paul's words become theirs: "I see another law in my members, warring against the law of my mind, and bringing me into captivity to the law of sin which is in my members" (Rom. 7:23). By the power of the forgiveness He can give, Jesus brought—and brings—men and women release from the bondage of their sins. He said, "Whoever commits sin is a slave of sin. . . . If the Son makes you free, you shall be free indeed" (John 8:34, 36).

Third, the Holy Spirit anointed Jesus "to proclaim . . . recovery of sight to the blind" (Luke 4:18). He literally healed blind people (Luke 7:21–22), and this powerful physical act symbolized the far greater gift of spiritual sight He gives through the gift of His Spirit (John 9:35–41).

Fourth, the Holy Spirit anointed Jesus "to release the oppressed, to proclaim the year of the Lord's favor" (Luke 4:18–19 NIV). "Come to Me," He invited, "all you who labor and are heavy laden, and I will give you rest. Take My yoke upon you and learn from Me, for I am gentle and lowly in heart, and you will find rest for your souls. For My yoke is easy and My burden is light" (Matt. 11:28–30).

Oppressed over the years by disastrous circumstances, people accumulated debts they could never repay. "The year of the Lord's favor" (v. 19 NIV) has behind it the picture of the year of Jubilee, the fiftieth year, when a trumpet was sounded and liberty proclaimed throughout the land (Lev. 25:8–55). Fields lay fallow, people returned to their own homes, debts were blotted out, and slaves were set free.

The year of Jubilee provides a delightful picture of the messianic age, the era of salvation, and the glorious spiritual benefits Jesus brings. Jesus fulfilled all the promises made concerning Him.

A Deliberate Policy

Initially, Jesus sought to keep His messianic identity secret. His claims were more implicit than explicit. He never rejected the title, but apart from this messianic declaration at the beginning of His ministry, He made no public claims to be the Messiah. He let His works speak for themselves.

Jesus' reluctance to use the title was due in part at least to His recognition of the serious limitations of contemporary messianic hopes. He knew Himself to be the Christ in a very different manner from the Messiah popularly expected.

Evil spirits in particular recognized Him as God's Anointed One and declared Him such. Consistently, Jesus rebuked them and commanded them to be silent (Luke 4:41).

The Use of Messianic Titles

Nevertheless, messianic titles were used, descriptions that indicated Jesus' identity without immediately precipitating a crisis that might lead to His crucifixion before the appropriate time.

Jesus' favorite self-description was "Son of man." It always occurs on His lips in the Gospels, and it does so more than eighty times. The prophet Daniel had a vision of

One like the Son of Man,
Coming with the clouds of heaven!
He came to the Ancient of Days,
And they brought Him near before Him.
Then to Him was given dominion and glory and a
  kingdom,
That all peoples, nations, and languages should serve
  Him.
His dominion is an everlasting dominion,
Which shall not pass away,
And His kingdom the one
Which shall not be destroyed (Dan. 7:13–14).

With the benefit of hindsight, that is obviously a messianic passage. But it does not seem to have been prominent among the Jews. Furthermore, the title "Son of man" seemed to emphasize Jesus' humanity, and that put them off the scent. It was an ideal title for Jesus to use since it declared His identity to those with spiritual insight, but it did not encourage those who had false political aspirations for the Messiah.

"Son of David" was another title given to Jesus. Matthew begins his gospel, "The book of the genealogy of Jesus Christ, the Son of David, the Son of Abraham" (1:1). After Jesus' dramatic healing of a demon-possessed man who could not see or speak, the people asked, "Could this be the Son of David?" (Matt. 12:23). Blind Bartimaeus showed spiritual discernment when he cried out, "Jesus, Son of David, have mercy on me!" (Mark 10:47), and the crowds used the title as Jesus made His triumphal entry into Jerusalem (Matt. 21:9, 15).

Jesus' identity as the Son of David provides one of the reasons for the provision of the genealogies in Matthew and Luke (Matt. 1:1–17; Luke 3:23–38). The Messiah was expected to be of David's line (Luke 1:32; cf. 2 Sam. 7:12; Ps. 89:29). We may wonder how that fits in with Jesus being born of Mary rather than of Joseph, although there is no doubt that Mary and Joseph belonged to the same tribal clan. Two possible explanations may be given. Matthew carefully expresses Jesus' relationship to Joseph and Mary when he writes, "Joseph the husband of Mary, of whom was born Jesus who is called Christ" (1:16). In the physical sense it was "of Mary" and not of Joseph that Jesus was born. Joseph was Jesus' father in the legal sense alone, but that legal sense was important because among the Jews, recognition by the father determined the succession. Through Joseph, a son of David, the right to David's throne was transferred to Mary's child, Jesus. The other possibility is that Luke's genealogy is more that of Mary than of Joseph. This would make sense if Mary's father was the Heli mentioned in Luke 3:23 and had no sons, since Joseph would have become son of Heli on his marriage to preserve the family name and inheritance (Num. 27:1–11; 36:1–12, and especially v. 8).

Jesus showed Himself to be more than David's Son but also David's Lord in the question He addressed to the Pharisees in the final Jerusalem period of His ministry:

> While the Pharisees were gathered together, Jesus asked them, saying, "What do you think about the Christ? Whose Son is He?" They said to Him, "The Son of David." He said to them, "How then does David in the Spirit call Him 'Lord,' saying:

> 'The LORD said to my Lord,
> "Sit at My right hand,
> Till I make Your enemies Your footstool"'?

> If David then calls Him 'Lord,' how is He his Son?" And no one was able to answer Him a word, nor from that day on did anyone dare question Him anymore (Matt. 22:41–46).

The title "the Prophet" was also given to Jesus. God promised Moses, "I will raise up for them a Prophet like you from among their brethren, and will put My words in His mouth, and He shall speak to them all that I command Him. . . . Whoever will not hear My words, which He speaks in My name, I will require it of him" (Deut. 18:17–19; cf. Acts 3:22–23).

The messianic prophecies described the Christ as the tender Prophet (Isa. 42:1–4; cf. Matt. 12:18–21). It was a title soon given to Jesus. He was called "the prophet from Nazareth" on occasion (Matt. 21:11), and the people recognized Him as such (Matt. 21:46).

The manner in which the disciples consistently called Jesus "Teacher" was another way of calling Him "Prophet." The two disciples on the Emmaus Road at the time of Jesus' resurrection spoke of Him as "a Prophet mighty in deed and word before God and all the people" (Luke 24:19).

This identification of Jesus as a prophet, therefore, was a further pointer to His messiahship. After His rejection at Nazareth, Jesus said, "A prophet is not without honor except in his own country, among his own relatives, and in his own house" (Mark 6:4).

Other titles such as "Shepherd," "Bridegroom," and "King" were also used of Jesus. The Messiah was promised to be the Shepherd (Isa. 40:11), and Jesus delighted in that picture of Himself (John 10). He referred to Himself as the Bridegroom (Mark 2:19–20), a term used in the Old Testament of God's covenant relationship with His people (Isa. 62:5). The title "King of Israel" was more or less synonymous with "Messiah" (Matt. 27:42; cf. Mark 15:32). Pilate had some feeling of Jesus' identity when he asked, "Are You the King of the Jews?" (Matt. 27:11; Mark 15:2; Luke 23:3).

Controversy

The Pharisees demanded miraculous signs as further evidence of Jesus' messiahship. But Jesus declined to give them, in that they had sufficient signs already if they really wanted to believe (Matt. 12:38–42; 16:1–4; Mark 8:11–13; Luke 11:29–32).

The people were confused about Jesus' messianic identity at one point because of His Galilean associations (John 7:41–42). Controversy and conflict were inevitable since Jesus did not fit into contemporary and popular expectations.

At that stage in their history, the Jews had begun to look for the expected Messiah to lead Jewish armies against their hated Roman overlords, and to establish such a powerful empire that it would more than rival any empire there had ever been. The capital would be at Jerusalem, and the world would be the scope of the kingdom.

Jesus' teaching about the Messiah was altogether different from that, especially His destiny to be the Servant of the Lord whose unique task was to suffer to ransom many (Mark 10:45; Luke 22:37). But some people—although still a minority—did believe, and in particular His disciples, although not just by chance.

Spiritual Enlightenment

True awareness of Jesus' messiahship was—and remains—a matter of spiritual illumination and enlightenment. After an incident that showed the Pharisees and Sadducees were not going to believe in Jesus and His message without further signs, Jesus withdrew with His disciples into the region of Caesarea Philippi. He asked the disciples, "Who do men say that I, the Son of Man, am?" (Matt. 16:13). They replied, "Some say John the Baptist, some Elijah, and others Jeremiah or one of the prophets." "But who do you say that I am?" He asked. Peter answered for them all, "You are the Christ, the Son of the living God" (Matt. 16:14–16).

Jesus then made a most telling statement: "Blessed are you, Simon Bar-Jonah, for flesh and blood has not re-

vealed this to you, but My Father who is in heaven"
(Matt. 16:17).

Peter's confession of Jesus as the Messiah and the Son of
God was of crucial importance. Jesus had allowed time for
this accurate conviction to surface. From that moment on,
He spoke of His impending death—a truth that Peter re-
sisted, and for which he was severely rebuked (Matt. 16:23).

Jesus followed the first prediction of His death to His disciples (Matt. 16:13–23; Mark 8:27–33; Luke 9:18–22) with at
least two others soon afterward (Matt. 17:22–23; 20:17–19;
Mark 9:30–32; 10:32–34; Luke 9:43–45; 18:31–34).

The disciples found Jesus' declaration of His immediate
future hard to accept. Their understanding of Jesus' messiahship, while true, needed clarifying. Mark indicates that the
questions asked at Caesarea Philippi were immediately preceded by the healing of the blind man of Bethsaida, the man
who at first saw men only as if they were trees walking. Jesus
completed the healing by laying His hands on the man a
second time when he then saw everything clearly (Mark
8:22–26). That miracle may serve as a parable—and perhaps
an intended parable as well as a miracle—to show where the
disciples were regarding their "seeing" Jesus' messiahship
properly.

Disappointment's Climax

The crowds' disappointment at Jesus' nonpolitical but
spiritual stance as the Messiah reached a climax in the feeding of the five thousand. John describes the miracle in the
most detail and makes the comment: "Then those men,
when they had seen the sign that Jesus did, said, 'This is
truly the Prophet who is to come into the world.' Therefore
when Jesus perceived that they were about to come and take
Him by force to make Him king, He departed again to the
mountain by Himself alone" (John 6:14–15).

When they pursued Him to the other side of the lake, Jesus gave the strongest possible teaching about the necessity of His death. John records, "From that time many of His disciples went back and walked with Him no more" (John 6:66).

The explanation of Judas's later action is that he almost certainly shared the crowds' disappointment, but perhaps determined not to give up easily, he tried to force Jesus' hand (Matt. 26:14–16; Mark 14:10–11; Luke 22:3–6).

Opposition's Climax

Opposition reached its climax in Jesus' final visit to Jerusalem. His triumphal entry into the city, riding on a donkey, communicated a conception of messiahship very different from that of the crowds (Matt. 21:1–9; Mark 11:1–10; Luke 19:28–38; John 12:12–15; cf. Zech. 9:9). The second cleansing of the temple was also a messianic act (Matt. 21:12–13; Mark 11:15–19; Luke 19:45–48; cf. Mal. 3:1).

Pointed parables, spoken in Jerusalem, further indicated His messiahship. The parable of the wicked tenants showed how the Jewish people were to treat the Messiah (Matt. 21:33–46; Mark 12:1–12; Luke 20:9–19). The parable of the marriage feast pictured the Messiah as the Bridegroom whom the Jewish people rejected (Matt. 22:1–14; Luke 14:16–24).

Jesus' arrest became inevitable. At His trial, He was directly asked, "If You are the Christ, tell us" (Luke 22:67; Matt. 26:63; Mark 14:61). His accusers, however, did not ask to discover the truth, but so as to have reason to put Him to death. The accusation the Jewish authorities made to Pilate was, "We found this fellow perverting the nation, and forbidding to pay taxes to Caesar, saying that He Himself is Christ, a King" (Luke 23:2).

And so He was crucified, with a messianic title above His head—"JESUS OF NAZARETH, THE KING OF THE JEWS"—a title to which the Jews rigorously objected, but which Pilate refused to change (John 19:19–22). Wonderfully, it was "by the determined purpose and foreknowledge of God" (Acts 2:23) that His Son was allowed to be put to death. The suffering Servant, the true Messiah, gave His life a ransom for many. At the Resurrection, the disciples were going to be enlightened, and they were then no longer like those who saw "men as trees walking" but those who saw everything clearly.

John's Declared Emphasis

John tells us that he wrote his gospel to help us believe that Jesus is the Messiah. Throughout his gospel, that is the underlying emphasis (John 1:41, 45, 49; 3:28–30; 4:25, 29, 42; 5:45–46; 6:14; 7:26–27, 31, 40–42; 9:22; 10:25–26; 11:27; 12:34; 17:3; 20:31). He brings his twentieth chapter to a close with the statement: "Jesus did many other signs in the presence of His disciples, which are not written in this book; but these are written that you may believe that Jesus is the Christ" (John 20:30–31).

The Scriptures bear united testimony to Jesus' messiahship: the Old Testament anticipates it, and the New Testament proclaims its reality. God the Father, by His Spirit, shines into men's and women's hearts to show them the truth of Jesus' messiahship, and when that happens, they rejoice in Him as their Prophet, Priest, and King—the wonders of which never pale and will not do so for eternity!

M E D I T A T I O N

1. John the Baptist said, "One mightier than I is coming, whose sandal strap I am not worthy to loose" (Luke 3:16).

John is an example to us in his humility and in his goal: "He must increase, but I must decrease" (John 3:30).

2. The Lord Jesus, the Messiah, is the Father's delight: "A voice came from heaven, saying, 'This is My beloved Son, in whom I am well pleased'" (Matt. 3:17).

3. "The Spirit of the Lord GOD is upon Me, because the LORD has anointed Me" (Isa. 61:1).

4. "A bruised reed He will not break, and smoking flax He will not quench" (Matt. 12:20). "Take My yoke upon you and learn from Me, for I am gentle and lowly in heart, and you will find rest for your souls. For My yoke is easy and My burden is light" (Matt. 11:29–30).

5. Jesus is David's Lord and ours.

6. "I am the living bread which came down from heaven. If anyone eats of this bread, he will live forever; and the bread that I shall give is My flesh, which I shall give for the life of the world" (John 6:51).

7. To recognize and confess Jesus as Messiah and Lord is a gracious gift from God: "Blessed are you, Simon Bar-Jonah, for flesh and blood has not revealed this to you, but My Father who is in heaven" (Matt. 16:17).

Q U E S T I O N S

1. How did John the Baptist express the superiority of Jesus' ministry to his own?

2. In what ways was the Holy Spirit involved in Jesus' ministry? (See, for example, Matt. 1:18, 20; 3:16; 4:1; 12:18, 28; Luke 3:22; 4:1, 14, 18; 10:21.)

3. What did Jesus' declaration of His messiahship at Nazareth indicate about His priorities (Luke 4:16–19)?

4. Which are the principal Old Testament messianic Scriptures? To which of them in particular did Jesus refer in the Gospels?

5. What clues did Jesus give to His identity as the Messiah?

6. Why did the Jews find what Jesus said about His death such a "hard teaching" (John 6:60 NIV)?

7. What may we learn about our own confession of Christ from Peter's?

Chapter Five

JESUS' LORDSHIP

Names reveal identity. If the title "Messiah" was the first clue to Jesus' identity, that of "Lord" is the second. The latter was used in a variety of contexts in the first century. It was the name often given to Jesus (Matt. 8:6, 8, 21, 25). Without the definite article, it simply meant something like "sir." In a culture where slavery was acceptable, it was the way a slave most naturally addressed his master. His master was his lord (Luke 12:45).

There were religious uses of the term. Among the Greeks, worshipers employed it to describe their god. In particular it was the title given to Roman emperors if they were deified or regarded as gods. A typical affirmation of allegiance to Caesar was the declaration "Caesar is Lord." So—at the very least—giving the title to Jesus raises Him above humankind.

The most significant use of *Lord* in relation to Jesus is that it is the Greek word that substitutes for *Jehovah* or *Yahweh* in the Greek translation of the Old Testament (the Septuagint). In the New Testament, *Lord* is uniquely employed to describe God, and it is regularly used of Jesus.

John the Baptist applied the title to Jesus in his early witness to Him. Challenged as to whether or not he was the Messiah, John the Baptist said, "I am 'the voice of one crying in the wilderness: "Make straight the way of the LORD"'" (John 1:23).

John's identification of Jesus in relation to Old Testament prophecies indicated Jesus' lordship as well as messiahship. John heard the Father's attestation to Jesus' divine sonship as he baptized Him in the river Jordan: "John bore witness, saying, 'I saw the Spirit descending from heaven like a dove, and He remained upon Him. I did not know Him, but He who sent me to baptize with water said to me, "Upon whom you see the Spirit descending, and remaining on Him, this is He who baptizes with the Holy Spirit." And I have seen and testified that this is the Son of God'" (John 1:32–34).

Old Testament prophecies pointed to the divine nature of the Messiah who was also to be a man among men—in fact, "a Man of sorrows" (Isa. 53:3). One reason later on for the Jews' opposition to Jesus was that they recognized that if He claimed to be the Messiah, He was also laying claim to deity.

Five evidences of Jesus' lordship stand out.

1. Jesus' Authority

The Authority of Jesus' Teaching

The initial reaction of the crowds to Jesus' teaching was to be amazed "at the gracious words which proceeded out of

His mouth" (Luke 4:22). The people "were astonished at His teaching, for He taught them as one having authority, and not as the scribes" (Mark 1:22; Matt. 7:28–29; Luke 4:32). His teaching differed completely from that of the professional teachers who merely followed the teaching traditions handed down to them. Jesus spoke with the authority of the Son who alone knows the Father and can reveal Him (Matt. 11:27).

Gospel writer John records how "the Jews marveled, saying, 'How does this Man know letters, having never studied?'" (John 7:15). If they had followed that crucial question through with honesty, they would probably have arrived at the answer. But they did not do so. John adds the helpful and telling comment that Jesus answered, "My doctrine is not Mine, but His who sent Me. If anyone wills to do His will, he shall know concerning the doctrine, whether it is from God or whether I speak on My own authority" (John 7:16–17).

Jesus' authoritative teaching impressed His hearers right up to the conclusion of His ministry. The Pharisees and the chief priests sent temple guards to arrest Jesus. The guards discovered the crowds surrounding Him, and they found themselves compelled to listen to what He said. All thought of arresting Him disappeared: "Then the officers came to the chief priests and Pharisees, who said to them, 'Why have you not brought Him?' The officers answered, 'No man ever spoke like this Man!'" (John 7:45–46).

Alongside the authority of Jesus' teaching, and as part of it, went His amazing ability to deal with every question put to Him, especially questions intended to test or trip Him up. None succeeded.

Jesus' Authority to Cast Out Evil Spirits

Evil and unclean spirits recognized Jesus' deity (Mark 1:23–24; 5:7–8; cf. Acts 19:15). His powerful acts of deliverance showed that He had come to establish God's rule over all the forces of evil (Luke 11:14–20).

There was a uniqueness about Jesus' casting out of evil spirits that would have come across to first-century observers and that we may miss because of our unfamiliarity with such practices. Whereas exorcists used techniques and aids, like burning incense, playing music, and wearing charms, Jesus commanded, "Come out!" (Mark 1:25; 9:25). Furthermore, Jesus is not reported to have used prayer beforehand or to have invoked any power. The power to deliver was in Himself—His source of power was the Holy Spirit given to Him without limit (Matt. 12:28; Luke 11:20; John 3:34).

Jesus' Authority to Forgive Sins

The first recorded occasion that Jesus displayed His power to forgive sins was the healing of a paralyzed man whose four friends lowered him through the roof (Mark 2:1–12; Matt. 9:1–8; Luke 5:17–26). The teachers of the law who were present immediately recognized that Jesus' granting of forgiveness was a claim to deity: "Why does this Man speak blasphemies like this? Who can forgive sins but God alone?" (Mark 2:7; Matt. 9:3; Luke 5:21).

To a sinful woman who anointed His feet with her tears and then with valuable ointment, Jesus said, "Your sins are forgiven. . . . Your faith has saved you. Go in peace" (Luke 7:48, 50).

Jesus' Authority to Judge

Jesus was unambiguous in His claim to be the divine Judge. He said, "I say to you, the hour is coming, and now is, when the dead will hear the voice of the Son of God; and those who hear will live. For as the Father has life in Himself, so He has granted the Son to have life in Himself, and has given Him authority to execute judgment also, because He is the Son of Man" (John 5:25–27; cf. Matt. 7:22–23; 13:24–30; 25:31–46).

It must have been the sense of Jesus' authority that prompted men and women to kneel before Him instinctively (Matt. 8:2; Mark 1:40; Luke 5:12).

2. Jesus' Life and Character

A second evidence of Jesus' lordship was His unique life and character.

Jesus' Knowledge

We commonly speak of God's omniscience—that is to say, His knowledge of everything and, therefore, everything about us. At the beginning of his gospel, John explains, "Jesus did not commit Himself to them, because He knew all men, and had no need that anyone should testify of man, for He knew what was in man" (John 2:24–25).

Sitting at the well with a Samaritan woman, Jesus did not need her to tell Him of her disreputable reputation. He already knew all about her private life (John 4:16–18). As she said, "He told me all that I ever did" (John 4:39).

In preparation for His final entry into Jerusalem, Jesus told His disciples that they would find a colt tied up for Him, awaiting them (Matt. 21:2; Mark 11:2; Luke 19:30). Although other explanations are possible, His supernatural knowledge is the most obvious.

Jesus' Sinlessness

But the outstanding feature of Jesus' life and character was His sinlessness. His enemies accused Him of various crimes and offenses—usually because of their envy of His popularity—but the accusations never stuck.

Pilate could find no wrong in Jesus when he put Him on trial. No doubt used to making criminal charges stick against prisoners, he could not do so with Jesus. Pilate stressed his personal convictions about Jesus' blamelessness by washing his hands publicly before the Jews to underline that the decision to crucify Jesus was more theirs than his. His wife urged him, "Have nothing to do with that just Man, for I have suffered many things today in a dream because of Him" (Matt. 27:19).

The penitent thief had discernment to say to his companion in crime, as together they died by crucifixion, "We [are punished] justly, for we receive the due reward of our deeds; but this Man has done nothing wrong" (Luke 23:41).

The Roman soldier in charge of Jesus' execution, who witnessed His death, said, "Certainly this was a righteous Man!" (Luke 23:47).

The apostle Peter's testimony carries even greater weight: "[He] committed no sin, nor was deceit found in His mouth" (1 Pet. 2:22; cf. Isa. 53:9). Peter had lived with Jesus for three years and observed Him closely. His pinpointing of Jesus' blameless speech is significant in that James says, "If anyone does not stumble in word, he is a perfect man, able also to bridle the whole body" (3:2). Jesus totally fulfilled that telling criterion.

Jesus never once needed to confess sin or to pray for forgiveness. When we remember that men and women who have been outstanding for their desire to please God have always been most aware of their sinfulness, Jesus' awareness of His sinlessness becomes all the more impressive. "Which of you convicts Me of sin?" He asked (John 8:46).

3. Jesus' Miracles

Jesus' miracles were a third evidence of His lordship. His power to heal and to meet people's physical and material needs endorsed the authority of His teaching.

Miracles That Were Signs

John employs the interesting word *signs* to describe Jesus' miracles. His gospel differs from the other three in its approach to the miracles. He is concerned from the start to establish the truth of Jesus' lordship—the certainty that Jesus is the Son of God.

He indicates Jesus' lordship from the outset by proclaiming Him to be the Word—the eternal Word of God (John 1:1–5). Instead of recording many of Jesus' miracles, John selects seven, and he applies the term *signs* to describe them (John 2:11; cf. 20:30). It is a fascinating selection, for whether John intended it or not, they perfectly illustrate Jesus' deity and also His power in areas where men and women are accustomed to helplessness.

Jesus changed water into wine at the wedding in Cana of Galilee (John 2:1–11): He is Lord over quality—it was the best wine the wedding guests had ever tasted. Everything He gives is of superlative value—His peace, His grace, His love, and His gift of eternal life.

Jesus healed the royal official's son at Capernaum without leaving Cana (John 4:46–54): He is Lord of space. There is no place to which His power does not extend. He has but to speak the word, and what He commands is done.

Jesus healed a paralyzed man who had been unable to walk for thirty-eight years (John 5:1–15): He is Lord of time. What the passing of the years seems to make increasingly impossible, Jesus can undo in a moment.

Jesus fed five thousand people with a boy's lunch (John 6:1–15): He is Lord of quantity as well as of quality. His resources are unlimited in every sphere.

Jesus walked on the water (John 6:16–21): He is Lord over natural law, since He created everything (John 1:3).

Jesus healed a man who was born blind (John 9:1–12): He is Lord over misfortune. He can transform tragedies into triumphs.

Jesus raised Lazarus from the dead (John 11:1–46): He is Lord over death.

Put together, these seven miracles—or signs—point conclusively to Jesus' deity.

4. Jesus' Statements Concerning His Lordship

Jesus' clear statements of His deity were a fourth evidence of His lordship. From His earliest years, His unique consciousness of divine sonship came to light.

At the age of twelve, He asked Mary and Joseph, when they had lost Him for a while in Jerusalem, "Why did you seek Me? Did you not know that I must be about My Father's business?" (Luke 2:49).

He spoke of God in a unique sense as His Father, and He spoke of Himself as equal with Him. The latter practice was one of the grounds of the Jewish leaders' persecution of Him (John 5:18). "I and My Father," He said, "are one" (John 10:30). He never gave the impression that God was the disciples' Father in exactly the same way as God is His Father. He would say, for instance, "My Father" (Matt. 11:27; Luke 2:49) or "your Father" (Matt. 5:16; Luke 12:30; cf. John 20:17). But He never identified Himself with the disciples by saying "our Father."

He explained that to receive Him is to receive the Father (Matt. 10:40), that to reject Him is to reject the Father (Luke 10:16), and that to see Him is to see the Father (John 14:9).

He sometimes spoke of Himself as "the Son" (Matt. 11:27; Mark 13:32), and at least two of the parables identified Him as the Son of God—the parable of the tenants and the vineyard (Mark 12:1–11, especially v. 6), and that of the marriage of the king's son (Matt. 22:1–14, especially v. 2).

He referred to Himself as "Lord of the Sabbath" (Mark 2:28; Matt. 12:8; Luke 6:5). His claims are set forth most forcibly and clearly in the seven I am's found in John's gospel: Jesus describes Himself as the bread of life (6:35), the light of the world (8:12; 9:5), the door of the sheep (10:7), the good shepherd (10:11, 14), the resurrection and the life (11:25–26), the way, the truth, and the life (14:6), and the true vine (15:1).

The uniform introduction to these statements—that is, the "I am"—bears the marked ring of the Lord Jehovah's authority as He revealed Himself in the Old Testament (Exod. 3:14). John 18 provides an instance of this at the time of Jesus' betrayal when soldiers came to arrest Him: "Jesus therefore, knowing all things that would come upon Him, went forward and said to them, 'Whom are you seeking?' They answered Him, 'Jesus of Nazareth.' Jesus said to them, 'I am He.' And Judas, who betrayed Him, also stood with them. Now when He said to them, 'I am He,' they drew back and fell to the ground" (vv. 4–6).

Jesus claimed to meet men's and women's deepest needs (Matt. 11:28–30; John 6:35), as God alone can. These claims were the claims either of an impostor or of the Son of God. The Jews recognized His assertions were either a matter of blasphemy or truth (John 19:7)—and they came to the wrong conclusion. Jesus' miracles backed up what He said; they authenticated His claims.

5. *Jesus' Resurrection*

The fifth evidence of Jesus' lordship was His resurrection from the dead. He spoke about it beforehand: "My Father loves Me, because I lay down My life that I may take it again. No one takes it from Me, but I lay it down of Myself. I have power to lay it down, and I have power to take it again. This command I have received from My Father" (John 10:17–18).

The Resurrection was the most telling evidence of Jesus' authority and lordship. When He cleansed the temple at the beginning of His ministry, the Jews demanded of Him, "What sign do You show to us, since You do these things?" (John 2:18). Jesus answered, "Destroy this temple, and in three days I will raise it up" (John 2:19). His questioners did not understand His answer, but as John comments, "He was speaking of the temple of His body" (John 2:21).

Living as we do after the event, we are perhaps inclined to take for granted the truth of the Resurrection. But we only have to ponder the disciples' reaction upon Jesus' death—their utter dejection and despondency—to see how dramatic and transforming an event it was.

The testimony of the Resurrection is that "God has made this Jesus . . . both Lord and Christ" (Acts 2:36). The evidences that Jesus is Lord are powerful and convincing. His lordship is an essential part of Christian faith, and the New Testament wants to bring us to where Thomas had to come, so that we cry out with absolute conviction, "My Lord and my God!" (John 20:28), only for us without first seeing the risen Lord with our physical eyes.

"Jesus is Lord!" was the earliest Christian profession of faith or creedal statement. To call Jesus "Lord" is to acknowledge His deity. His lordship—His deity—gives value to His death. On the cross it was God Himself shedding His blood for us—a mind-boggling assertion (Acts 20:28). Jesus' lordship is the ground of His ability to be our Savior. The angel significantly proclaimed at His birth, "For there is born to you this day in the city of David a Savior, who is Christ the Lord" (Luke 2:11).

Had Jesus been a mere creature, He could never have accomplished all that was necessary for our salvation. As God, He was able to perform what He undertook. His atonement is sufficient to expiate the sins of the whole world; His righteousness is adequate to justify all who trust in it for acceptance with God; and His grace is more than enough for all believers to conquer all their enemies.

As Lord, He is able to provide the abundant life He promises. His lordship explains the amazing allegiance He both demands and receives (Mark 8:34–35).

To call Jesus "Lord" is to surrender ourselves to His authority. It is to pledge ourselves to His obedience. Our confession of Him must be genuine—that is the thrust of the challenging parable with which the Sermon on the Mount concludes (Matt. 7:21–27).

Jesus "is Lord of all" (Acts 10:36). Napoleon is reputed to have said, "If Socrates would enter the room we should rise and do him honor, but if Jesus Christ came into the room we should fall down on our knees and worship Him!"

MEDITATION

1. "They were astonished at His teaching, for His word was with authority" (Luke 4:32). "The Pharisees and the chief priests sent officers to take Him. . . . Then the officers came to the chief priests and Pharisees, who said to them, 'Why have you not brought Him?' The officers answered, 'No man ever spoke like this Man!'" (John 7:32, 45–46).

2. "Son, your sins are forgiven you." "Who can forgive sins but God alone?" (Mark 2:5, 7). "In Him we have redemption through His blood, the forgiveness of sins, according to the riches of [God's] grace" (Eph. 1:7).

3. Jesus knew their thoughts (Luke 11:17). Jesus knows everything about us: "Lord, You know all things; You know that I love You" (John 21:17).

4. Judgment is God's unique prerogative: that prerogative belongs to Jesus.

5. Jesus' miracles were signs revealing His glory: "The Word became flesh and dwelt among us, and we beheld His glory, the glory as of the only begotten of the Father, full of grace and truth" (John 1:14): He "manifested His glory; and His disciples believed in Him" (John 2:11).

6. "I am the vine, you are the branches. He who abides in Me, and I in him, bears much fruit; for without Me you can do nothing" (John 15:5).

7. Jesus, the Son of God, is the only One who can reveal the Father to us: "All things have been delivered to Me by My Father, and no one knows the Son except the Father. Nor does anyone know the Father except the Son, and the one to whom the Son wills to reveal Him" (Matt. 11:27).

Q U E S T I O N S

1. What marked out Jesus' teaching as authoritative, and how does it differ from all other teaching?

2. How do we show men and women the relevance of the forgiveness Jesus alone makes possible?

3. What illustrations do the Gospels provide of Jesus' knowledge of men and women without their providing Him with information?

4. What may we learn about the judgment from Jesus? (See, for example, Matt. 7:1–2, 21–27; 11:20–24; 12:33–42; 25:31–46; John 5:16–30.)

5. How does the raising of Lazarus in John 11 fulfill John's declared purpose in John 20:30–31 in recording Jesus' miraculous signs?

6. What do the seven I am's of Jesus (John 6:35; 8:12; 9:5; 10:7, 11, 14; 11:25–26; 14:6; 15:1) show to be our crucial needs, and how is He uniquely equipped to meet them?

7. What do we know about God through Jesus' coming that otherwise we would not have known?

Chapter Six

JESUS' MESSAGE

It almost appears presumptuous to attempt to summarize Jesus' message in that no one ever spoke as He did, and He perfectly expressed all He said. Fortunately, the New Testament solves the dilemma: it records Jesus' summary of His message, and it also gives the apostles' account of what Jesus proclaimed.

Mark's words early in his gospel provide a clear starting point: "After John was put in prison, Jesus came to Galilee, preaching the gospel of the kingdom of God, and saying, 'The time is fulfilled, and the kingdom of God is at hand. Repent, and believe in the gospel'" (Mark 1:14–15).

1. It Is God's Message

Jesus came "proclaiming the good news of God" (Mark 1:14 NIV). The source of the message was God Himself. Gospel writer John in particular records a number of Jesus' statements in which He made plain that all that He said was on His Father's authority. Jesus' words are best left to speak for themselves:

> For He whom God has sent speaks the words of God, for God does not give the Spirit by measure (John 3:34).

> My doctrine is not Mine, but His who sent Me (John 7:16).

> If anyone wills to do His will, he shall know concerning the doctrine, whether it is from God or whether I speak on My own authority (John 7:17).

> When you lift up the Son of Man, then you will know that I am He, and that I do nothing of Myself; but as My Father taught Me, I speak these things (John 8:28).

> I speak what I have seen with My Father (John 8:38).

> For I have not spoken on My own authority; but the Father who sent Me gave Me a command, what I should say and what I should speak (John 12:49).

> The words that I speak to you I do not speak on My own authority; but the Father who dwells in Me does the works (John 14:10).

> For I have given to them the words which You have given Me; and they have received them (John 17:8).

At every opportunity Jesus explained that it was God's message He proclaimed—in fact, He Himself embodied the message as the Living Word of God (John 1:1).

2. It Is God's Long-Awaited Message

Jesus began by saying, "The time is fulfilled" (Mark 1:15). What the Jews in particular had been waiting for was about to happen. It was the "time" to which the prophets had looked forward, and which they had promised with excitement (1 Pet. 1:10–12).

This sense of divine fulfillment predominates as a theme of the apostolic preaching after Jesus' resurrection and ascension. Addressing his fellow Jews, Paul stated, "We declare to you glad tidings—that promise which was made to the fathers. God has fulfilled this for us their children, in that He has raised up Jesus" (Acts 13:32–33). In Jesus, God brought to completion His Old Testament promise to bring peace to His people (Pss. 29:11; 85:8; Isa. 9:6–7; 53:5). The phrase Paul uses to describe his handing on of the gospel to others fits in here: everything happened "according to the Scriptures" (1 Cor. 15:3–4).

3. It Is Good News

"After John was put in prison, Jesus went into Galilee, proclaiming the good news of God. 'The time has come,' he said. 'The kingdom of God is near. Repent and believe the good news!'" (Mark 1:14–15 NIV).

Good news is one word in the Greek. We may be inclined to overlook how surprising its use is because we are so accustomed to the term. Men and women—because of sinful rebellion against God—deserve only bad news. But Jesus came with a message of hope for the hopeless, strength for the weak and, above all, salvation for the lost.

4. It Is Good News of the Kingdom of God

Jesus said, "The time is fulfilled, and the kingdom of God is at hand" (Mark 1:15). God's kingdom is both a present reality and a future event. It is spoken of in three ways in Jesus' teaching and that of the apostles: first, in terms of God's rule; second, of Jesus Christ, the King, actively ruling in our hearts (a fruit of the new birth); and third, as a future inheritance.

It is a logical concept in view of the manner in which God is often spoken of in the Old Testament as the King of Israel (Pss. 68:24; 74:12; 84:3; 95:3; 145:1; Jer. 10:10). Even when the Jews had kings, those with discernment recognized that any human king ruled in God's name. The ideal future for Israel was pictured as a time when God's reign would be fully acknowledged.

Whenever men and women met Jesus, they were confronted by God's kingdom: He was—and is—the way into it. As we acknowledge Him, and He then reigns in our lives, so we are assured of a place in God's eternal kingdom.

The parables Jesus told about God's kingdom underline its importance. The parable of the sower describes how we enter it and how God's rule in our lives begins: we must respond with obedience to Jesus' message (Mark 4:1–12). The parable of the weeds (Matt. 13:24–30, 36–43) shows that the kingdom of God does not grow without opposition from Satan. The parables of the mustard seed and the yeast illustrate the growth and penetration of the kingdom (Matt. 13:31–35). Its beginnings may be small, but its growth is irresistible.

The parables of the treasure and the pearl point to the incalculable worth of the kingdom (Matt. 13:44–46), since finding it is finding Jesus. None can measure the value of this discovery (Phil. 3:7–9). The parable of the ten virgins looks forward to the great day of the kingdom when Jesus returns (Matt. 25:1–13); and the two parables of the talents and of the mina coins indicate the kingdom's rewards (Matt. 25:14–30; Luke 19:12–27). The latter have nothing to do with earning salvation, since it is a free gift. But when we have received God's gift of salvation, Jesus chooses to reward faithful service.

5. It Is a Message That Requires a Definite Response

"Repent, and believe in the gospel" Jesus said (Mark 1:15). He never left men and women in doubt about what was required of them. He called for a change of mind about sin and a radical change of direction of life—that is what repentance is. In giving forgiveness to a woman taken in adultery, He also said, "Go and sin no more" (John 8:11).

Zacchaeus, a dishonest tax collector, knew he could not welcome Jesus without making a clean break with all he knew to be wrong in his life (Luke 19:1–10). God sent Jesus to bless us by turning us from our wicked ways (Acts 3:26).

Along with repentance goes faith—faith in Jesus Himself. All invitations to come to Him are invitations to exercise faith. "Come to Me," He said, "all you who labor and are heavy laden, and I will give you rest. Take My yoke upon you and learn from Me, for I am gentle and lowly in heart, and you will find rest for your souls. For My yoke is easy and My burden is light" (Matt. 11:28–30).

Jesus looked for faith in Himself as the vital evidence that men and women understood His message and had entered God's kingdom. As John 3:16 succinctly puts it: "For God so loved the world that He gave His only begotten Son, that whoever believes in Him should not perish but have everlasting life."

Jesus always commended faith, no matter how feeble its exercise or small its beginnings. Perceiving the faith of four men and their paralyzed friend, who had overcome great difficulties to get to Jesus, He gave forgiveness first and then healing (Mark 2:5, 11). A woman who touched Him in the crowd, whose physical need was healing from a continual bleeding, was commended for her faith (Mark 5:34), as was the Roman soldier whose servant was seriously ill and about to die (Luke 7:9).

6. It Is a Message for All

Jews tended to imagine that the good news of the Messiah was exclusively for them, but Jesus taught otherwise. In the gospel records we have evidence of non-Jews—that is to say, Gentiles—hearing the gospel and believing. I have mentioned already the faith of a Roman army officer (Luke 7:1–10). A Greek woman, born in Syrian Phoenicia, came to Jesus and was likewise rewarded for her faith in Him (Mark 7:24–30).

John records, with an obvious eye to its significance, that some Greek converts to Judaism, in Jerusalem for the Passover, made the request to Philip, "Sir, we wish to see Jesus" (John 12:21).

Later Jesus was to command His disciples to "go therefore and make disciples of all the nations" (Matt. 28:19), to "preach the gospel to every creature" (Mark 16:15). He instructed them to be His witnesses "in Jerusalem, and in all Judea and Samaria, and to the end of the earth" (Acts 1:8).

Peace

Peace is a word above all others that sums up Jesus' message. He came to preach peace to those who were far away like the Gentiles, and peace to those who were near like the

Jews (Eph. 2:17). The first time Peter shared the gospel with a Gentile, a Roman centurion called Cornelius, he began, "The word which God sent to the children of Israel, preaching peace through Jesus Christ—He is Lord of all" (Acts 10:36).

Zacharias, the father of John the Baptist, made a prophecy about Jesus at the time of John's birth; he declared that Jesus would "guide our feet into the way of peace" (Luke 1:79). When angels sang God's praise to the shepherds at the birth of Jesus, they declared, "Glory to God in the highest, and on earth peace, goodwill toward men!" (Luke 2:14). When as a young child, Jesus was taken to the temple in Jerusalem, Simeon took Him in his arms, recognizing that he held the promised Savior, and declared, "Lord, now You are letting Your servant depart in peace, according to Your word" (Luke 2:29).

Peace of Forgiveness

Jesus proclaimed the peace of forgiveness because as sinners, in a wrong relationship with God, we have that as our primary need. Away from God, we are like sons and daughters away from a father—it is as if we were dead (Luke 15:24, 32). Forgiveness demands a central place in gospel preaching because it is the means by which men's and women's relationship with God is restored.

Jesus' open and loving attitude to notorious sinners confirmed the peace of forgiveness He came to bring (Luke 19:1–10). His enemies muttered, "This Man receives sinners and eats with them" (Luke 15:2), and what they said was true. Responding to a woman's faith—a woman who had been a notorious sinner—Jesus gave her the assurance of forgiveness by saying, "Go in peace" (Luke 7:36–50).

The fundamental nature of forgiveness as Jesus' message was further established in His commission to the apostles on the evening of His resurrection: "'As the Father has sent Me, I also send you.' And when He had said this, He breathed on them, and said to them, 'Receive the Holy Spirit. If you forgive the sins of any, they are forgiven them; if you retain the sins of any, they are retained'" (John 20:21–23). This commission must be read in the context of all Jesus had already said and taught. He was not saying that the power to forgive sins was invested in them because they were apostles. Rather, He was declaring that as they preached the good news—the message of peace through forgiveness in His name—they could assure all who believed the message, and who gave proper evidence of repentance, that God's forgiveness was theirs.

Peace of Reconciliation

Linked with the peace of forgiveness is the peace of reconciliation. Peace in its full sense is identical with salvation. All through the Old Testament, and especially in the book of Psalms, God is the unique Giver of peace (Ps. 4:8). Those who are blessed, guarded, and treated graciously by God possess His peace (Num. 6:24–26).

Jesus is the sole Mediator of God's peace. He told the simple yet telling story of the Pharisee and the tax collector (Luke 18:9–14). Of the tax collector, who "would not so much as raise his eyes to heaven, but beat his breast, saying, 'God, be merciful to me a sinner!'" Jesus said, "This man went down to his house justified" (Luke 18:13–14)—that is to say, he went on his way reckoned as righteous. He was not only forgiven, but he was put right with God. God's perfect records no longer contained any evidence of the man's sins. God's favor rested on him, and he had peace with God—the great benefit of salvation (Luke 2:14).

As Paul explains, "Having been justified by faith, we have peace with God through our Lord Jesus Christ" (Rom. 5:1).

The message of the apostles was, "Be reconciled to God" (2 Cor. 5:20). God does not impose reconciliation on sinners, but He waits for them to "come to their senses" (Luke 15:17 NIV) and then grants it as a gift through faith in His Son. The peace of forgiveness and reconciliation surpasses all other experiences of peace.

Peace at a Price

Basic to Jesus' message was His emphasis that peace could be obtained only at a price to Himself. Anointed by the Spirit to preach the good news to the poor, to proclaim freedom for the prisoners and recovery of sight for the blind, to release the oppressed, to proclaim the year of the Lord's favor, He had to fulfill other prophecies relating to the Messiah, prophecies of suffering, culminating in death.

His death alone could make peace with God possible for sinners. He explained to His disciples, "The Son of Man did not come to be served, but to serve, and to give His life a ransom for many" (Matt. 20:28; Mark 10:45). The Lord Jesus saw Himself as the exchange price on the grounds of which freedom may be granted. His death was the price of sinners' release. Only as He offered Himself in our place, as the propitiation for our sins, could He become the one Mediator between God and humankind. He is the Good Shepherd, who laid down His life for His sheep (John 10:11, 14–15).

At the Last Supper, He spoke of the reconciling effect of His death when, taking the cup, He declared, "This is My blood of the new covenant, which is shed for many for the remission of sins" (Matt. 26:28). No relationship between God and sinful men and women is possible apart from Jesus Christ and His death: "For there is one God and one Mediator between God and men, the Man Christ Jesus, who gave Himself a ransom for all" (1 Tim. 2:5–6).

There is an implied, although not stated, relationship between Jesus' first words to His disciples in the Upper Room on the day of His resurrection and His first action afterward. He said, "Peace be with you." After He said that, He showed them His hands and side (John 20:19–20). The peace of forgiveness into which we enter as we are reconciled to God is through Jesus' wounds, His atoning sacrifice.

Peace of God's Rule

Jesus taught that forgiveness and reconciliation bring the peace of God's rule to our lives. Peace—in one of its aspects—is a state of law and order, which gives rise to the blessings of prosperity. Where, for instance, leaders of nations have the true interests of their citizens at heart, to be under their rule is synonymous with peace and well-being. It is far more wonderful to be under the rule of the sovereign Lord, whose love and concern for His people are perfect.

Reconciled to God, we are born again of His Spirit, who takes up residence within us to assure us that we have become God's children and to make God's rule effective in our hearts. God's reign in our lives brings peace: that was Jesus' message. In the Sermon on the Mount, He taught that if we follow God's instructions and obey His laws, we may leave to Him all the practical matters of life that so easily produce worry, such as what we are going to eat, what we are going to wear, or how long we are likely to live. If we make God's rule in our lives our preoccupation, then all these things will be taken care of by our heavenly Father who knows our needs perfectly (Matt. 6:32–33).

Handing over the reins of life's control to God, we discover His peace. We may have to do this time and time again because we so often take back what we hand over to Him. Prayer enables us to keep giving the control back to Him.

Zacchaeus's conversion is illuminating at this point (Luke 19:1–10). He was wealthy as a chief tax collector because he had, among other things, cheated. To all appearances, he might have seemed a happy individual, but he was not, since self ruled his life. Despite all he possessed, his life was basically empty. After he met Jesus, Zacchaeus's life was transformed as God's kingdom was established within him. Zacchaeus vacated the throne of his heart, and God reigned instead. In his giving half of his possessions to the poor, and repaying four times over anyone he had cheated, some might have considered him mad, but in place of unrest, discontent, and emptiness, Zacchaeus knew the peace of God's rule and the ability to enjoy all God gave him through living righteously rather than unrighteously.

Peace of Right Relationships

The urgent peace all need is peace with God. That peace has relevance to every aspect of daily life. Peace pervades human relationships when they are as they ought to be. Out of harmony with God, we find ourselves out of harmony with others. In harmony with God, we soon become committed to aiming at peace in all our relationships, as part of God's rule in our lives.

Peace, in the biblical sense of wholeness, renews human relationships. Right with God, we feel bound to make every effort to live in peace with everyone (Heb. 12:14). Take, for example, Jesus' stress on forgiveness. He was always utterly down-to-earth in His teaching. Things do go wrong in our relationships with one another, as they do in the relationship with God through our sin. First we need God's forgiveness, and then we need to forgive one another. We are taught to pray, therefore, "Forgive us our debts, as we forgive our debtors" (Matt. 6:12). This is the one petition of the Lord's Prayer—as we now call it—that Jesus chose to amplify: "For if you forgive men their trespasses, your heavenly Father will also forgive you. But if you do not forgive men their trespasses, neither will your Father forgive your trespasses" (Matt. 6:14–15). The principle is plain: "Forgive, and you will be forgiven" (Luke 6:37).

Prizing God's forgiveness, we aim at always forgiving those who hurt or offend us. That is an effective key to peace in human relationships, although it is not always easy; nevertheless, it is an approach to be persisted in. "If your brother sins against you," Jesus said, "rebuke him; and if he repents, forgive him. And if he sins against you seven times in a day, and seven times in a day returns to you, saying, 'I repent,' you shall forgive him" (Luke 17:3–4).

Peter found this a hard principle to accept at first. He asked, "Lord, how often shall my brother sin against me, and I forgive him? Up to seven times?" Jesus answered, "I do not say to you, up to seven times, but up to seventy times seven" (Matt. 18:21–22). He followed up this instruction by the telling parable of an unmerciful servant who having received mercy from his master, then failed to show similar mercy to his fellow servant who owed him much less than he had owed his master (Matt. 18:23–35).

Peaceableness is part of God's Spirit's fruit, and it indicates God's rule in our lives. "Salt is good," Jesus said, "but if the salt loses its flavor, how will you season it? Have salt in yourselves, and have peace with one another" (Mark 9:50). He also said, "Blessed are the peacemakers, for they shall be called sons of God" (Matt. 5:9).

The Sermon on the Mount guides those who delight in God's rule in their lives. Its instruction was given not to the crowds but to disciples. It sets a much higher standard of behavior than even the Ten Commandments, and it is impossible to achieve without God's Spirit's power. It sums up Jesus' message concerning God's rule and the peace it brings to human relationships. It begins with the beatitudes, which set forth the nature of true happiness (Matt. 5:1–12)—a happiness quite different from the world's. That happiness depends on the right attitudes, which God's rule in the human heart brings.

Jesus speaks pointedly about anger and murder (Matt. 5:21–26). When anger is dealt with, human relationships are well on the way to being safeguarded. His words on adultery are searching (Matt. 5:27–30), but the benefits of heeding His instructions are obvious. If adultery is checked in the heart, it is then cut out of the life, and marriages are held together in peace. Jesus does not suggest that we will not sometimes have enemies (Matt. 5:38–48), but if we actively strive to love them, we will know peace within ourselves whatever their attitude.

Jesus' emphasis on prayer is important (Matt. 6:5–15; 7:7–12), since praying about everything that troubles us is one of God's special means of providing us with His peace (Phil. 4:6–7). He also gives specific instruction about seeking treasure in heaven and adopting a Christian lifestyle that trusts God for everything. Seeking first God's kingdom and doing what is right in His sight are to be practiced priorities (Matt. 6:19–34). Knowing that God is our Father and recognizing that He may be completely trusted to provide for us are glorious grounds of peace.

Jesus warns against deliberate faultfinding and speedy judgment of others simply on the basis of how things may appear (Matt. 7:1–6). People critical of others, who sit in judgment on them, seldom, if ever, know peace within themselves. But learning not to judge brings peace to our own minds and to our relationships.

The Sermon on the Mount ends significantly with the story of two builders (Matt. 7:24–27), demonstrating that those who obey—rather than those who only listen—provide proof of their reconciliation to God and their acceptance of His rule in their lives. This accords with the Old Testament principle, often expressed, "Great peace have those who love Your law, and nothing causes them to stumble" (Ps. 119:165). Jesus taught that under God's rule, we find God's peace.

Peace That Does Not Originate in This World

The peace Jesus taught, proclaimed, and promised is His own peace: "Peace I leave with you, My peace I give to you; not as the world gives do I give to you. Let not your heart be troubled, neither let it be afraid" (John 14:27); "These things I have spoken to you, that in Me you may have peace. In the world you will have tribulation; but be of good cheer, I have overcome the world" (John 16:33).

The peace Jesus gives is the pledge and foretaste of the ultimate experience of peace we shall have in God's everlasting kingdom. Peace in heaven is part of our expected salvation (Luke 19:38). God's kingdom here and now in our lives means righteousness, peace, and joy in the Holy Spirit, but how much more in the life to come (Rom. 14:17)!

Peace We Dare Not Neglect

Jesus' peace is a peace we dare not neglect. Wherever we turn in His teaching, we find Him emphasizing the positive reasons for His coming, but always accompanied with the mention of the serious consequences of refusing His message. We find this particularly expressed in John 3:16–19:

For God so loved the world that He gave His only begotten Son, that whoever believes in Him should not perish but have everlasting life. For God did not send His Son into the world to condemn the world, but that the world through Him might be saved. He who believes in Him is not condemned; but he who does not believe is condemned already, because he has not believed in the name of the only begotten Son of God. And this is the condemnation, that the light has come into the world, and men loved darkness rather than light, because their deeds were evil.

If men and women reject His message of peace with God, Jesus taught that they must face Him as their Judge; and this prior notice of judgment is just as much part of His message as His message of peace. Throughout His ministry, He displayed His character as the Judge in perfect consistency with His character as the Savior. He cleansed the temple, and He uttered severe woes on the hypocrisy of many of the Pharisees (Matt. 23:1–36). He explained that the Father has committed all judgment to Him: "For as the Father has life in Himself, so He has granted the Son to have life in Himself, and has given Him authority to execute judgment also, because He is the Son of Man" (John 5:26–27). God has appointed Jesus the "Judge of the living and the dead" (Acts 10:42).

All need to hear and heed Jesus' message of peace—of peace with God through the merits of His atoning sacrifice. That peace opens our lives to God's rule and the peace His rule then brings. Jesus Christ has committed this message of peace to His people so that they may proclaim it. No one else can bring it to the world but them.

M E D I T A T I O N

1. "The Word became flesh and dwelt among us, and we beheld His glory, the glory of the only begotten of the Father, full of grace and truth" (John 1:14). "For the

law was given through Moses, but grace and truth came through Jesus Christ" (John 1:17). "The law was our tutor to bring us to Christ, that we might be justified by faith" (Gal. 3:24).

2. "But other seed fell on good ground and yielded a crop that sprang up, increased and produced: some thirtyfold, some sixty and some a hundred" (Mark 4:8). The greatest threats to fruitfulness are the "thorns" of "the cares of this world, the deceitfulness of riches, and the desires for other things" (Mark 4:18–19). We need to guard against all such "thorns" taking root.

3. "There is another king—Jesus" (Acts 17:7). "And He has on His robe and on His thigh a name written: KING OF KINGS AND LORD OF LORDS" (Rev. 19:16). "In your hearts set apart Christ as Lord" (1 Pet. 3:15 NIV). "Let the peace of God rule in your hearts" (Col. 3:15).

4. Jesus' message is for the lost: "The Son of Man has come to seek and to save that which was lost" (Luke 19:10).

5. Jesus showed for whom His message was intended by the company He kept: "This Man receives sinners and eats with them" (Luke 15:2).

6. "The word which God sent to the children of Israel, preaching peace through Jesus Christ—He is Lord of all" (Acts 10:36). Jesus' gift of forgiveness is the way to peace: "Your sins are forgiven. . . . Go in peace" (Luke 7:48, 50).

7. "We declare to you glad tidings—that promise which was made to the fathers. God has fulfilled this for us their children, in that He has raised up Jesus" (Acts 13:32–33). "For I delivered to you first of all that which I also received: that Christ died for our sins according to the Scriptures, and that He was buried, and that He rose

again the third day according to the Scriptures" (1 Cor. 15:3–4). "God . . . cannot lie" (Titus 1:2).

Q U E S T I O N S

1. In what ways was Jesus Himself the embodiment of the message He came to proclaim?

2. What significance may be read into the fact that the parable of the sower is the first recorded parable of Jesus?

3. How does Jesus' rule in our lives as King display itself in practice?

4. In what ways do men and women show themselves to be lost? What are the consequences if men and women remain lost?

5. In what ways is Zacchaeus's reception of Jesus typical of the response of all who obey His message?

6. What are the implications for local church evangelism and personal witness that the message of Jesus is for everyone?

7. How important are the Scriptures in our conveying the gospel message, and how should we use them?

THE WITNESSES

A single word sums up the function of the first disciples and, in particular, the apostles. They were to be *witnesses*. Jesus' priority task in the early days of His ministry was the call He gave them with that end in view.

First and foremost, they were to "be with Him" (Mark 3:14). Later, they were recognized to be distinctive because they "had been with Jesus" from the beginning to the end of His ministry (Acts 4:13; cf. 1:21–22). He carefully showed them more and more of His glory, leading them to a deeper and more assured faith in Him (John 2:11; 20:30–31).

He called them that they might receive a unique message to pass on to others (1 John 1:1–3). Following a period of instruction, He sent them out "to preach, and to have power to heal sicknesses and to cast out demons" (Mark 3:14–15). His ultimate purpose—after their three years of training—was to send them into the world as He had been sent by the Father (John 17:18).

The Call of the First Disciples

The disciples' call is described in Mark 1:14–20. Peter and Andrew answered the call to discipleship as they cast their nets into the Sea of Galilee, and James and John as they mended their nets close by. Their response to Jesus' invitation was immediate (vv. 18, 20). The calling of Levi, or Matthew, the tax collector, followed soon afterward (Mark 2:13–17). Matthew was later to become the writer of the gospel that bears his name.

Jesus' call was not a total surprise to them (John 1:35–43). John the Baptist taught his disciples to look for another teacher, one greater than himself—the Messiah, the Lamb of God. Jesus' first disciples had almost certainly been disciples of John the Baptist—part of the latter's assigned task to prepare the way for the Lord.

The more detailed account in John's gospel of the first disciples' call indicates that at least Andrew and Peter had already made contact with Jesus after John the Baptist's witness to Him (1:40–42). John's gospel also records that Philip was summoned to discipleship the day after Andrew and Peter met Jesus (1:43).

Disciples First

These men—who later became witnesses—were called first to be *disciples*, the latter being a familiar term in the first century. Disciples bound themselves to a teacher in order to acquire theoretical and practical knowledge. They may have been apprentices in a trade, students of medicine, or members of a school of thought or philosophy. The key feature was that to become a disciple, a person needed a special relationship with a master or teacher.

Jesus' call was, "Follow Me" (Mark 1:17). He demanded instant obedience. Following Him meant going wherever He went and sharing His hardships. "Foxes have holes and birds of the air have nests," Jesus said, "but the Son of Man has nowhere to lay His head" (Matt. 8:20).

As disciples, they were under discipline and instruction. They accepted Jesus' yoke and learned from Him (Matt. 11:29–30). There was no escaping His yoke—although once accepted, it proved to be easy and His burden light.

A Call to Serve

The call to discipleship was a call to service. Above all else, Jesus taught His disciples to be servants. He instructed them that service would lead them into similar dangers to those to which He Himself was exposed. The disciple was—and is—to expect no better treatment than his Master received (Matt. 10:24–26; 16:24–28; cf. 10:38). Following Jesus as a disciple implies the unconditional sacrifice of the whole of a person's life for the whole of his or her life (Matt. 10:37–39; Luke 14:26–33; cf. Mark 3:31–35; Luke 9:57–62; John 11:16). Jesus said, "He who loves father or mother more than Me is not worthy of Me. And he who loves son or daughter more than Me is not worthy of Me. And he who does not take his cross and follow after Me is not worthy of Me. He who finds his life will lose it, and he who loses his life for My sake will find it" (Matt. 10:37–39).

Discipleship is different from a relationship with any other teacher or master. Greek pupils or Jewish disciples bound themselves personally to their master and put themselves under his teaching so that in due course they might become teachers or rabbis. Jesus explained, however, "A disciple is not above his teacher, nor a servant above his master. It is enough for a disciple that he be like his teacher, and a servant like his master" (Matt. 10:24–25). Jesus' call to discipleship did not mean that a disciple was put in a learning situation from which he could depart as a master: "But you, do not be called 'Rabbi'; for One is your Teacher, the Christ, and you are all brethren" (Matt. 23:8). Discipleship is a life-long commitment to walk in Jesus' footsteps—and no one knows where that may lead.

The Twelve

The call was also given to the Twelve to apostleship. Jesus appointed them only after prayer to His Father (Mark 3:13; cf. Luke 6:12), and Mark 3:13–19 describes their appointment. He "called to Him those He Himself wanted. And they came to Him" (Mark 3:13).

We may perhaps wonder, why twelve? The choice may be a symbolic representation of the twelve tribes of Israel, and thus of the whole people of God.

More of some disciples' background is told us than of others. Peter's original name was Simeon, a Hebrew name (Acts 15:14; 2 Pet. 1:1), and perhaps like many Jews, he adopted also "Simon," used in the New Testament as a Greek name of similar sound. We sometimes adopt this habit with people from other countries whose names are difficult to pronounce. His father's name was Jonah (Matt. 16:17), and he was married (Mark 1:30). He spoke Aramaic with a strong north country accent (Mark 14:70). A man of impulsive devotion (Matt. 14:28; Mark 14:29; Luke 5:8; John 21:7), he was the regular spokesman (Matt. 15:15; 18:21; Mark 1:36–37; 8:29; 9:5; 10:28; 11:21; 14:29; Luke 5:5; 12:41).

James is always mentioned next—James, the son of Zebedee. He and John, his brother, were nicknamed "Boanerges, that is, 'Sons of Thunder'" (Mark 3:17). He was to die later by the sword of Herod Agrippa (Acts 12:2). John, his brother, was probably the younger of the two. They seem to have come from a well-to-do family since their father had "hired servants" working for him (Mark 1:20).

On three important occasions Peter, James, and John are mentioned together, to the exclusion of the other disciples: (1) at the raising of Jairus's daughter (Mark 5:37), (2) at the Transfiguration (Mark 9:2), and (3) in the Garden of Gethsemane (Mark 14:33).

Andrew was the brother of Simon Peter. He first brought Peter to Jesus (John 1:42). It seems probable that Andrew was later crucified in Achaia. Philip came from Bethsaida of Galilee (John 12:21), the home of Andrew and Peter. Bartholomew is someone we know little about, although we do know more if he is to be identified with Nathanael, but that identification cannot be proved. Matthew, as we have noted, has his call described in the Gospels. Thomas's background is not known, except that he was a twin. James, son of Alphaeus, is usually identified as James the younger, being younger than James, the son of Zebedee. Thaddaeus's name appears only in the list of the apostles, and nothing more is known of him.

Two remain: first, Simon the Zealot. We do not know whether he was a zealot in the religious or the political sense. Political zealots had led a revolt against Rome in A.D. 6. Judas Iscariot always appears last in the list of the apostles, and usually with the description "who betrayed Jesus." He was the treasurer (John 13:29).

The Twelve were not a particularly outstanding group of men. Many of them, like Peter and John, were unschooled, ordinary men (Acts 4:13). In His choice of disciples, Jesus showed the principle by which God often chooses to work, outlined in 1 Corinthians 1:26–29:

For you see your calling, brethren, that not many wise according to the flesh, not many mighty, not many noble, are called. But God has chosen the foolish things of the world to put to shame the wise, and God has chosen the weak things of the world to put to shame the things which are mighty; and the base things of the world and the things which are despised God has chosen, and the things which are not, to bring to nothing the things that are, that no flesh should glory in His presence.

Jesus saw not what the men were, but what they could become and what He could make of them. When Andrew brought Simon to Jesus, Jesus looked at him and said, "'You are Simon the son of Jonah. You shall be called Cephas' (which is translated, A Stone)" (John 1:42).

This group of men received Jesus' call to be "sent ones" or "apostles." As the Father sent the Son, so He was to send them. They were to be His messengers to bring others to faith in Him (John 17:20).

Fishermen and Harvesters

Fishers of men and harvesters are two other descriptions Jesus gave of their task. Like fishermen, the apostles were to "catch" men and women for God's kingdom by preaching the gospel. The daily work of the first four disciples was a picture of the spiritual task upon which they were about to enter. Jesus' promise that they were to be fishers of men received dramatic fulfillment on the day of Pentecost and afterward (Acts 2:41; 6:7).

So far as the spiritual harvest was concerned, Jesus spoke about that early on in His ministry, too. The woman of Samaria was an example and proof of a potential harvest, and a reminder that the reaping was not to be only from among the Jews. Having told His disciples, "My food is to do the will of Him who sent Me, and to finish His work," Jesus went on to say, "Do you not say, 'There are still four months and then comes the harvest'? Behold, I say to you, lift up your eyes and look at the fields, for they are already white for harvest!" (John 4:34–35). Matthew records, "When He saw the multitudes, He was moved with compassion for them, because they were weary and scattered, like sheep having no shepherd. Then He said to His disciples, 'The harvest truly is plentiful, but the laborers are few. Therefore pray the Lord of the harvest to send out laborers into His harvest'" (Matt. 9:36–38).

Jesus trained the apostles to be undershepherds, for that was another vital aspect of their calling (John 21:15–17). Their further task, although they were unaware of it at the time, was to be pillars of the church—a title Paul gave to James, Peter, and John when he wrote of a meeting with them (Gal. 2:9). In their testimony to Jesus, the apostles were to be part of the foundation of His church (Eph. 2:20; cf. Matt. 16:18).

The Training of the Witnesses

Jesus devoted three years to instructing and equipping the apostles. It was in-service training. They watched Him at work and received constant instruction as they went everywhere with Him.

Jesus' prayer in John 17 provides insight into His purpose: their training was part of the work the Father had given Him to do (John 17:4). He taught them as He taught no one else, as in John 14—16. He gave them direct and formal instruction, as in the Sermon on the Mount. He also used the opportunities incidents provided. He taught them an important lesson, for example, when His family tried to restrain Him from teaching the people (Mark 3:31–35). He instructed the apostles spontaneously, for instance, when they commented on the magnificence of the temple structure in Jerusalem (Matt. 24:1–2).

The apostles also had the special privilege of asking Jesus questions. They sought detailed explanation of the parables—an opportunity not open to others. When they saw a man born blind, they asked, "Rabbi, who sinned, this man or his parents, that he was born blind?" (John 9:2), and they received an answer that corrected their mistaken ideas about suffering.

He constantly instructed them by example, sometimes indicating this to be the case as when He washed their feet in the Upper Room (John 13:1–17). In the Garden of Gethsemane, He taught the principle of nonviolence, no matter how greatly provoked we may be (John 18:11). He turned even their mistakes to their good as He drew lessons from them (Mark 9:28–29; John 21:15–17).

They were specially privileged in the spiritual understanding He entrusted to them. Truths were explained to them, and to them alone, as the explanation of what we now call the Lord's Supper (Mark 14:12–26). He gave them the Father's words, and they accepted them (John 17:8, 14). They came to understand that all He said came from the Father (John 17:7). He made the Father known (John 17:26; cf. John 14:8–9); He revealed the Father's character to them (John 17:6).

A crucial point in His teaching and instruction of the apostles was His question at Caesarea Philippi. "Who do you say that I am?" He asked (Matt. 16:15). After Peter, speaking on behalf of all the others, declared, "You are the Christ, the Son of the living God" (Matt. 16:16), Jesus carefully prepared them for the dreadful shock that awaited them in Jerusalem (Matt. 16:21–28). Peter's words were profoundly significant. They first came to believe on Jesus as Messiah (John 1:40–41); they then came to believe on Him as the Son of God. Their ultimate confession was that of Thomas: "My Lord and my God!" (John 20:28).

As their insight concerning Jesus' identity grew, so they received the predictions concerning His death (Matt. 16:21). Approaching His betrayal and crucifixion, Jesus said, "The hour has come that the Son of Man should be glorified. Most assuredly, I say to you, unless a grain of wheat falls into the ground and dies, it remains alone; but if it dies, it produces much grain" (John 12:23–24).

As the time grew closer to His departure, Jesus warned the disciples of dangers ahead (Matt. 10:16–42; cf. John 14–16). An essential part of their training was their being prepared to face the difficulties that come to genuine disciples. He did not minimize the opposition they would encounter. He encouraged them, nevertheless, to witness fearlessly (Matt. 10:26–33). He warned that a most unpleasant experience in some cases would be division within families (Matt. 10:21, 34–36). At the same time, He taught that victory would be ultimately His (Matt. 16:27–28), and that they need not be afraid (Luke 12:4–12, 32–34). Some disciples were to witness to Jesus by martyrdom.

Training accompanied instruction, as Jesus sent them out (Mark 6:7–13). Their preaching trips were minimissions, and they reported back afterward. Jesus provided basic missionary principles to guide them (Matt. 10:1–15). They were to recognize evangelistic priorities—spiritual need alone does not provide guidance as to where to go. They were to trust God for the supply of their material needs. They were to preach in both cities and rural areas, working in partnership with others. They were to see themselves as representatives of the Great Shepherd of the flock. Opposition was not to stop them from persevering in their task, and dependence on God was to mark all they did. No delay was to be permitted in getting on with the affairs of God's kingdom. The conversion of whole families was to be their goal. Giving themselves to the work of the gospel, they had a right to earn their living through the gospel. They were to show concern for the whole person, and to see their task as carrying on Jesus' work.

Slow to Understand

The disciples were not quick to understand Jesus' message (Matt. 13:36; Mark 4:10). That was particularly the case with regard to His teaching about the necessity of His death (Mark 8:27–30). When He spoke about His impending crucifixion, they seemed especially blind—perhaps almost stubborn (Matt. 16:22; Luke 18:34).

At the critical moment at Caesarea Philippi, Peter represented all the disciples in the answer he gave, for Jesus' question was directed at them all (Mark 8:27, 29), and all were included in the look that went with the reprimand given to Peter (Mark 8:33).

They were backward in appreciating the nature of their work. For example, they rebuked those who brought young children to Jesus (Mark 10:13–16). They were slow to grasp the goal of discipleship (Mark 10:35–45), as witnessed in James's and John's request for prominence in the kingdom of God. And yet in spite of all their slowness, Jesus persevered.

Witnesses

The apostles were to be Jesus' *witnesses.* The latter is the term that they used subsequently, and that Jesus chose to describe their ministry as He spoke to them immediately prior to His ascension: "You shall receive power when the Holy Spirit has come upon you; and you shall be witnesses to Me in Jerusalem, and in all Judea and Samaria, and to the end of the earth" (Acts 1:8).

Witnesses must be faithful above all to facts, and to their understanding of their meaning and significance. The apostles knew exactly the content of the gospel they had to deliver (1 Cor. 15:1–4). Witnesses to the truth as it is in Jesus are passionately involved in the case they seek to present. They have been apprehended by it and have an inner compulsion to plead its merits to others. The apostles urged men and women, exhorted them, and pleaded with them in Christ's name to be reconciled to God (Acts 2:38–40; 2 Cor. 5:20).

Witnesses are accountable for the truthfulness of their testimony. The apostles were aware of their solemn responsibility to deliver faithfully what the Lord had given them. They established a strategic pattern: what Jesus had done with them, they did in turn with others, and that is how the gospel has come down to us. As Paul put it to Timothy, "The things that you have heard from me among many witnesses, commit these to faithful men who will be able to teach others" (2 Tim. 2:2). The apostles received the gospel—the whole will of God (Acts 20:27)—that they might pass it on (1 Cor. 15:1–4), and this they did and turned the world upside down (Acts 17:6).

As witnesses, the apostles had personal knowledge of what they affirmed. They witnessed all or most of Jesus' miracles, whereas the crowds witnessed only some. They experienced firsthand Jesus' holiness. Peter was compelled to exclaim, "Depart from me, for I am a sinful man, O Lord!" (Luke 5:8). They were left in no doubt as to His sinlessness. Peter wrote, "[He] committed no sin, nor was deceit found in His mouth" (1 Pet. 2:22). They saw how full He was of grace and truth (John 1:14).

Three of them witnessed Jesus' glory at the Transfiguration. They all observed His amazing patience and trust in God when suffering. As Peter testified, "When He was reviled, [He] did not revile in return; when He suffered, He did not threaten, but committed Himself to Him who judges righteously" (1 Pet. 2:23). They saw the glory of the one and only Son of the Father, and they knew with certainty that He came from the Father (John 17:8).

Above all, they understood that God Himself had come among them. "The Word became flesh and dwelt among us," they explained (John 1:14). The apostles were able to give witness of what they had seen and heard:

> That which was from the beginning, which we have heard, which we have seen with our eyes, which we have looked upon, and our hands have handled, concerning the Word of life—the life was manifested, and we have seen, and bear witness, and declare to you that eternal life which was with the Father and was manifested to us—that which we have seen and heard we declare to you, that you also may have fellowship with us; and truly our fellowship is with the Father and with His Son Jesus Christ (1 John 1:1–3).

"We are witnesses," they declared (Acts 3:15). "We are witnesses of all things which He did both in the land of the Jews and in Jerusalem" (Acts 10:39). Preeminently, they were witnesses of His resurrection: "This Jesus God has raised up, of which we are all witnesses" (Acts 2:32).

The Relevance of Their Witness

The apostles' function as witnesses is of fundamental importance. We have every reason to believe the testimony of genuine eyewitnesses. The apostles underlined this truth as they proclaimed the good news of Jesus. Peter wrote,

> We did not follow cunningly devised fables when we made known to you the power and coming of our Lord Jesus Christ, but were eyewitnesses of His majesty.

For He received from God the Father honor and glory when such a voice came to Him from the Excellent Glory: "This is My beloved Son, in whom I am well pleased." And we heard this voice which came from heaven when we were with Him on the holy mountain (2 Pet. 1:16–18).

From the apostles' witness has come the priceless treasure of the four Gospels, which proclaim the gospel itself—the unsearchable riches of Jesus Christ. What they passed on is in our hands today to pass on to others. When Jesus Christ brings us into a relationship with Himself, it is always His intention that we should be committed to the work and growth of His kingdom, witnessing first and foremost to the truth of the gospel, and doing so from the reality of our personal experience of Him, the risen Lord. We then become His witnesses.

M E D I T A T I O N

1. Jesus' call to come to Him is a call to discipleship: "Come to Me, all you who labor and are heavy laden, and I will give you rest. Take My yoke upon you and learn from Me, for I am gentle and lowly in heart, and you will find rest for your souls. For My yoke is easy and My burden is light" (Matt. 11:28–30).

2. Jesus showed for whom His message was intended by the company He kept: "This Man receives sinners and eats with them" (Luke 15:2).

3. The principle by which Jesus chose the Twelve holds true for all His people: "For you see your calling, brethren, that not many wise according to the flesh, not

many mighty, not many noble, are called. But God has chosen the foolish things of the world to put to shame the wise, and God has chosen the weak things of the world to put to shame the things which are mighty . . . that no flesh should glory in His presence" (1 Cor. 1:26–27, 29).

4. "These twelve Jesus sent out" (Matt. 10:5). "As the Father has sent Me, I also send you" (John 20:21). Jesus' commission has been handed down to us (Matt. 28:18–20). As we are obedient, so we know His presence and power.

5. To confess Jesus as Christ, the Son of God, is a gift from God: "Truly You are the son of God" (Matt. 14:33). "Blessed are you, Simon Bar-Jonah, for flesh and blood has not revealed this to you, but My Father who is in heaven" (Matt. 16:17).

6. I pray also "for those who will believe in Me through their word" (John 17:20). Jesus interceded for us, and does so still: "He is also able to save to the uttermost those who come to God through Him, since He always lives to make intercession for them" (Heb. 7:25).

7. Our preoccupation must not be with the time or date the Father has set for His Son's coming; rather, we should focus on obedience to Him until He comes.

Q U E S T I O N S

1. What may we learn of the character and background of the men and women God uses from those of Jesus' first disciples?

2. Who are contemporary equivalents of the "sinners" and "tax collectors" who might not feel the good news is for them unless we take trouble to share it with them?

3. "He appointed twelve—designating them apostles—that they might be with him" (Mark 3:14 NIV). How do you think this unique experience of three years with Jesus influenced the rest of their lives?

4. In what ways should all Christians regard themselves as those "sent out" by Jesus Christ into the world?

5. What will lead us to confess our faith in Jesus Christ? How may we best confess our faith in Him to the world? To whom in particular may we look for help in this, and how?

6. What were Jesus' principal requests for all disciples in His prayer recorded in John 17, and what obligations do these requests place on us?

7. In what ways did the apostles bear witness to Jesus?

Chapter Eight

JESUS' MINISTRY IN JERUSALEM

Jesus followed a careful program, determined by His Father, for the salvation of men and women. From the beginning, by His name "Jesus," He had been announced as the "Savior." John the Baptist's identification of Jesus as the Lamb of God pinpointed the unique purpose for which He had come into the world.

The atoning sacrifice He was to make as the Lamb of God was to be at God's appointed time in Jerusalem. Although an experience of unspeakable sorrow and desolation, paradoxically, it was to be Jesus' "exodus" and moment of glorification (John 12:23). Jesus did not go up to Jerusalem, therefore, by accident. Essential to the Father's plan, it was Jesus' deliberate purpose.

Once the disciples were clear as to His identity, Jesus told them plainly of the necessity of the Cross. The Transfiguration conversation between Moses, Elijah, and Jesus was all "about his departure [the Greek word for 'exodus'], which he was about to bring to fulfillment at Jerusalem" (Luke 9:31 NIV). The Transfiguration signaled that Jesus' death was imminent. Luke tells us, "As the time approached for him to be taken up to heaven, Jesus resolutely set out for Jerusalem" (9:51 NIV). It required resolution since He knew what awaited Him there.

The exact course of Jesus' journey to Jerusalem cannot be traced, although the Gospels provide considerable information (Matt. 19—20; Mark 10; Luke 9:51—19:27). We cannot be sure where all the events John alone records fit in with the details the other three Gospels provide.

Luke has a unique teaching section in his gospel (Luke 9:51—18:14), and it seems that this instruction was given on the way to Jerusalem. If that is the case, some of the most familiar parables, such as the good Samaritan, the rich fool, and the three concerning the lost sheep, the lost coin, and the lost son, belong to this period.

As Jesus drew closer to Jerusalem, questions about marriage and divorce were asked (Matt. 19:1–12; Mark 10:1–12). The disciples mistakenly turned parents and children away from Jesus and consequently received His strong rebuke (Matt. 19:13–15; Mark 10:13–16; Luke 18:15–17).

Jesus also met the rich young man who decided against discipleship when he discovered the cost (Matt. 19:16–30; Mark 10:17–31; Luke 18:18–30).

Jesus predicted His death for the third time as they approached the city. Matthew relates,

Now Jesus, going up to Jerusalem, took the twelve disciples aside on the road and said to them, "Behold, we are going up to Jerusalem, and the Son of Man will be betrayed to the chief priests and to the scribes; and they will condemn Him to death, and deliver Him to the Gentiles to mock and to scourge and to crucify. And the third day He will rise again" (Matt. 20:17–19; cf. Mark 10:32–34; Luke 18:31–34).

The immediate request of the mother of James and John—prompted by the men themselves—that they might obtain prominent positions in Jesus' kingdom demonstrated that His real mission had not really been understood (Matt. 20:20–28; Mark 10:35–45; cf. Luke 22:24–27).

During this period, we must also include the raising of Lazarus, which John records (John 11). Lazarus's resurrection before so many witnesses caused many of the Jews to believe in Him (John 11:45), and the news quickly reached the authorities in Jerusalem.

At a meeting of the chief priests and the Pharisees in the Sanhedrin, Caiaphas, the high priest, made a prophetic statement without appreciating the deep significance of what he said: "You know nothing at all, nor do you consider that it is expedient for us that one man should die for the people, and not that the whole nation should perish" (John 11:49–50). "From that day on, they plotted to put Him to death" (John 11:53). Jesus had to watch His movements carefully, therefore, in order not to precipitate His arrest before other necessary events preceded it (John 11:54).

Much speculation in Jerusalem occurred as "many went from the country up to Jerusalem before the Passover, to purify themselves. Then they sought Jesus, and spoke among themselves as they stood in the temple, 'What do you think—that He will not come to the feast?'" (John 11:55–56). Huge crowds thronged Jerusalem, and Jesus' entry into the city stimulated considerable interest.

To give some idea of the size of the crowds, thirty years after this event a Roman governor took a census of the number of lambs slaughtered in Jerusalem and discovered that it was not far off a quarter of a million. Passover regulations demanded a minimum of ten people for each lamb. Therefore, there could have been about 2.5 million people crowding into Jerusalem at Passover time. Every adult male within a radius of twenty miles had to be there, and Jews from all over the then known world converged on the city. The people were keyed up with expectation anyway, and Jesus' anticipated arrival increased that sense of expectancy.

For no other part of Jesus' ministry have we greater detail than this last week. We should not lose sight of the profound significance of this: Jesus' death was the culmination of all He had come to do, and it is the heart of the good news. As we understand His death, so we understand His work. It was the most momentous week in the world's history.

John records that it was six days before the Passover that "Jesus came to Bethany, where Lazarus was who had been dead, whom He had raised from the dead" (John 12:1). There, the memorable anointing of Jesus took place (Matt. 26:6–13). John identifies the woman as Mary, the sister of Martha and Lazarus. She appears to have had some clear idea of what was before Jesus. John tells us that Judas asked, "Why wasn't this perfume sold and the money given to the poor? It was worth a year's wages" (John 12:5 NIV).

Initially, we may be puzzled by Matthew's and Mark's mention of the anointing later (Matt. 26:6–13; Mark 14:3–9 NIV). But there is no contradiction. Matthew writes, "*While* Jesus was in Bethany." At this point in his gospel, Matthew wants to indicate when Judas first decided to make contact with the Jewish authorities to set up his act of betrayal, and so he has to go back a few days, which explains why he and Mark use the word *while*.

The Triumphal Entry

The next day—Sunday—witnessed Jesus' triumphal entry (Matt. 21:1–9; Mark 11:1–10; Luke 19:28–38; John 12:12–15). Mounted on a young donkey, He rode into Jerusalem to the applause and delight of the great crowd that had come for the Feast. They cried, "Hosanna to the Son of David! 'Blessed is He who comes in the name of the LORD!'" (Matt. 21:9). Matthew quotes Zechariah's prophecy concerning the coming of the Messiah as being fulfilled by this act (Matt. 21:5; Zech. 9:9).

The gospel writers see the whole course of Jesus' ministry following a definite plan, to the fulfillment of which in every detail Jesus set Himself. Everything the prophets said would happen did happen. Nevertheless, what took place was not always in the manner the Jews expected. Jesus entered Jerusalem in connection with His kingdom but not to enter at that time into its triumph. Rather, He came to enter on His sufferings, which had to precede the triumph (cf. 1 Pet. 1:11), and which were essential if His work was to achieve salvation.

Matthew and Mark indicate that the acclamation was not universal, although the majority entered into the enthusiastic reception. Luke makes the point that the *disciples* began to rejoice and praise God with a loud voice for the miracles they had seen (Luke 19:37). John adds the comment that the disciples did not understand the real significance of Jesus' entry into Jerusalem until after His death and resurrection (John 12:16). Then it dawned on them as they understood what had been written beforehand in the Old Testament (Luke 24:25–27).

Fearful probably of the political repercussions of such an entry from the point of view of the Roman authorities, the Pharisees urged Jesus to silence His disciples and to curb their enthusiastic praise (Luke 19:39–40). The whole city was stirred to ask, "Who is this?" (Matt. 21:10), and the Pharisees were compelled to say to one another, "See, this is getting us nowhere. Look how the whole world has gone after him!" (John 12:19 NIV). Luke relates that as Jesus drew near to the city, He wept over it and predicted its sad destruction (Luke 19:41–44).

Jesus' first call, the day He entered into Jerusalem, was at the temple (Matt. 21:12–17; Mark 11:11; Luke 19:45–46). Mark's record is especially helpful because he relates, "When He had looked around at all things, as the hour was already late, He went out to Bethany with the twelve" (Mark 11;11). Reading the other accounts in Matthew and Luke, we might think that Jesus acted impetuously in His cleansing of the temple. But He never acted hastily; His actions were always under perfect control.

Jesus did not spend the night in Jerusalem, crowded as it was with pilgrims and with His enemies. Rather, He stayed out at Bethany, almost certainly at the home of Mary, Martha, and Lazarus.

The Cursing of the Fig Tree

The following morning the cursing of the fig tree took place (Matt. 21:18–19; Mark 11:12–14). Hungry, Jesus went to the fig tree, which was in leaf, looking for fruit. He found nothing but leaves, and He condemned it with the words, "Let no one eat fruit from you ever again" (Mark 11:14).

The condemning and withering of the fig tree were an acted parable in which Jesus set forth the judgment that was about to come on Jerusalem. The people of Israel honored

God with their lips, but their hearts were far from Him. They bore all "the leaves" of religious activity, but beneath them there was no fruit. The temple itself was full of human activity, but spiritual fruit was absent.

The Cleansing of the Temple

Jesus' first act after the cursing of the fig tree was the cleansing of the temple. He drove out those who sold and bought in the temple, and He overturned the tables of the money changers and the seats of those who sold pigeons. Greek and Roman money was unacceptable to the temple, and all dues had to be paid in the Tyrian coinage, the Tyrian shekel. Money-changing facilities were necessary, therefore, but the exchange rate was such that extortionate profit was exacted, and the same was true of other selling activities within the temple precincts.

While in His first coming Jesus had not come to judge the world, occasions of judgment were inevitable when He was confronted by sin. By such judgments, promise was made of the judgment yet to come.

Although Jesus had come to save first His own people, the Jews, His concern was also for Gentiles (John 10:16). The commerce that took place in the court of the Gentiles hindered prayer and worship in the one area of the temple open to them.

The clearing of the temple aroused the fury of the Jewish leaders more than any other action of Jesus. Having cleansed the temple, Jesus taught the crowds there and said, "Is it not written, 'My house shall be called a house of prayer for all nations'? But you have made it a 'den of thieves'" (Mark 11:17). Mark comments, "The scribes and chief priests heard it and sought how they might destroy Him; for they feared Him, because all the people were astonished at His teaching" (Mark 11:18).

These events took place on Monday. As before, Jesus and His disciples went out of the city for the night (Mark 11:19).

The next morning, Tuesday, the disciples noticed the fig tree had withered away to its roots—a sign of Jerusalem's impending destruction (Mark 11:20–21).

A Question of Authority

Inevitably, the main issue was Jesus' authority. "By what authority are You doing these things?" they asked. "And who gave You this authority to do these things?" (Mark 11:28).

The religious leaders sensed messianic claims were being made, but they could not pinpoint them. They sought to draw Jesus out so that somehow or other they might condemn Him. Jesus perfectly anticipated their attack, and as so often was the case, He asked a question to counter a question. He asked, "The baptism of John—was it from heaven or from men? Answer Me" (Mark 11:30). They were completely floored by the question since either response created difficulties for them.

Jesus demonstrated that the religious leaders did not really want to know the answer to their questions. Consequently, He refused to answer them. With the victory so clearly His, antagonism increased.

The Week in Brief

Luke provides a summary of this last week in Jerusalem: "And in the daytime [Jesus] was teaching in the temple, but at night He went out and stayed on the mountain called Olivet. Then early in the morning all the people came to Him in the temple to hear Him" (Luke 21:37–38). This does not contradict what I suggested about Jesus staying in the home of Mary, Martha, and Lazarus, since Bethany was a village on the slopes of the Mount of Olives.

Jesus filled the last days with giving Himself to the crowds and His disciples in teaching. Three parables belong to this period, and they all relate to the Jewish leaders' challenging of Jesus' authority and their tragic rejection of Him.

The first followed immediately after their question, "By what authority are You doing these things?" and it was the parable of the two sons. "What do you think?" Jesus asked.

> "A man had two sons, and he came to the first and said, 'Son, go, work today in my vineyard.' He answered and said, 'I will not,' but afterward he regretted it and went. Then he came to the second and said likewise. And he answered and said, 'I go, sir,' but he did not go. Which of the two did the will of his father?" They said to Him, "The first" (Matt. 21:28–31).

Jesus had in view the contrasting approach of the Jewish leaders to that of the tax collectors and prostitutes. The Jewish leaders were full of empty assurances that they wanted to do God's will. Despised sinners of society—like tax collectors and prostitutes, who had lived in open disobedience to God—were the ones turning to God to give Him the kind of obedience He really wants.

Jesus immediately followed this parable with another that was even more pointed—that of the vinedressers:

> A man planted a vineyard and set a hedge around it, dug a place for the wine vat and built a tower. And he leased it to vinedressers and went into a far country. Now at vintage-time he sent a servant to the vinedressers, that he might receive some of the fruit of the vineyard from the vinedressers. And they took him and beat him and sent him away empty-handed. Again he sent them another servant, and at him they threw

stones, wounded him in the head, and sent him away shamefully treated. And again he sent another, and him they killed; and many others, beating some and killing some. Therefore still having one son, his beloved, he also sent him to them last, saying, "They will respect my son." But those vinedressers said among themselves, "This is the heir. Come, let us kill him, and the inheritance will be ours." So they took him and killed him and cast him out of the vineyard. Therefore what will the owner of the vineyard do? He will come and destroy the vinedressers, and give the vineyard to others. Have you not even read this Scripture:

"The stone which the builders rejected
Has become the chief cornerstone.
This was the LORD's doing,
And it is marvelous in our eyes"? (Mark 12:1–11; cf. Matt. 21:33–42; Luke 20:9–19).

Jesus took up a familiar picture to the Jews, since the Old Testament likened Israel to God's vineyard (Isa. 5:1–7). Throughout the centuries, God explained His purposes for His chosen people through the teachings of the prophets. But God's people persistently ill-treated His messengers, and Israel's rebellion came to a head in their crucifying God's own Son.

Nevertheless, through their rejection of Jesus, the good news was to be proclaimed to the Gentiles so that they, too, might be given the opportunity of becoming part of God's vineyard. This parable finds its summary in John's words concerning Jesus: "He came to His own, and His own did not receive Him" (John 1:11). The chief priests and the Pharisees were in no doubt as to the thrust of what Jesus said (Matt. 21:45–46; Mark 12:12).

The third parable—that of the wedding banquet—followed immediately and had the same message (Matt. 22:1–14; cf. Luke 14:16–24). Those originally invited to the feast—the Jews—refused to come when the time arrived. The king who had invited them was angry, and he sent his troops to destroy them and their city. We cannot fail but see a reference here to the impending destruction of Jerusalem. The rejection of the invitation by those invited did not mean, however, that the feast was abandoned. Rather, the invitation was widened—in fact, extended to all.

Traps and Snares

Such direct teaching from Jesus inevitably prompted many schemes to trip Him up. Since the Jewish leaders refused to listen to Him and to believe the evidences of His messiahship, they could only be increasingly committed to getting rid of Him. They tried first to discredit Him before the crowds. But they were never to succeed.

The intense seriousness of the opposition is seen in that it brought together groups that normally had little to do with one another—the Pharisees, the Herodians, and the Sadducees. They combined forces against the One whom they regarded as their common enemy.

Three main issues—the paying of taxes to Caesar, the question of marriage at the resurrection, and the definition of the greatest commandment—dominated.

The question, "Should we pay taxes to Caesar or not?" was an obvious trap. If Jesus said yes, He would alienate the ordinary people. If He said no, He could be denounced to the Romans as subversive of their government. Mark explains that Jesus discerned their hypocrisy (Mark 12:15), Matthew their evil intent (Matt. 22:18), and Luke their duplicity (Luke 20:23). Jesus' answer, "Render therefore to Caesar the things that are Caesar's, and to God the things that are God's," completely foiled His questioners (Luke 20:25–26).

That same day the Sadducees brought their question about a woman who had married in turn seven brothers of one family (Mark 12:18–27; cf. Matt. 22:23–33; Luke 20:27–40): "In the resurrection, when they rise, whose wife will she be? For all seven had her as wife" (Mark 12:23). The question was important for the Sadducees because they denied immortality, resurrection, angels, and spirits. Used to arguing these issues, they felt themselves a match against Jesus. But Jesus' answer so defeated them that they did not dare to ask Him any more questions (Luke 20:39–40).

The final trick question came from a Pharisee, a lawyer, who asked Jesus, "Which is the first commandment of all?" (Mark 12:28; cf. Matt. 22:34–36). Jesus did what He did more than once. He joined together two Old Testament passages, demonstrating that true religion demands a positive attitude both to God and to people (Deut. 6:4–5; Lev. 19:18): "'You shall love the LORD your God with all your heart, with all your soul, with all your mind, and with all your strength.' . . . And the second, like it, is this: 'You shall love your neighbor as yourself.' There is no other commandment greater than these" (Mark 12:29–31). The expert in the law felt compelled to express his admiration of Jesus' answer (Mark 12:32–33), and from that point on "no one dared question Him" (Mark 12:34).

The Pattern

The pattern of this last week in Jerusalem was symbolic action (the cursing of the fig tree and the cleansing of the temple) followed by questions from the authorities, leading to clear teaching about Jesus' identity and mission. That, in turn, led to increasingly furious opposition, coming to a head in the proposal to put Jesus to death.

Apocalyptic Teaching

We have concentrated on the public reaction to Jesus in this period and the teaching He gave to the crowds. But Jesus' disciples were not neglected, and to this week in His ministry, there belongs His apocalyptic teaching—that is to say, instruction relating to the end of all things and the Final Judgment.

As so often happened, a question on the part of the disciples prompted it: "As He went out of the temple, one of His disciples said to Him, 'Teacher, see what manner of stones and what buildings are here!'" (Mark 13:1). It was a justifiable comment. The third temple ranked as one of the architectural wonders of the Roman world, and it was not even complete at the time of its destruction. Jesus replied, "Do you see these great buildings? Not one stone shall be left upon another, that shall not be thrown down" (Mark 13:2). His response prompted Peter, James, John, and Andrew to ask Jesus privately, "Tell us, when will these things be? And what will be the sign when all these things will be fulfilled?" (Mark 13:4).

The instruction that followed is almost a summary of what we find expressed in symbolic form in greater detail in the book of Revelation. Jesus spoke first of the signs of His coming (Matt. 24:4–8; Mark 13:5–8; Luke 21:8–11). Many will be led astray by false Christs. Wars and rumors of wars, nation rising against nation, famines, and earthquakes will mark the beginning of the sufferings that will come.

Jesus then spoke of the beginnings of the troubles (Matt. 24:9–14; Mark 13:9–13; Luke 21:12–19). Christians will be persecuted and betrayed. False prophets will increase, and wickedness will multiply. He predicted "the abomination of desolation" (Matt. 24:15–22; Mark 13:14–20; Luke 21:20–24)—the great and final violation by the Antichrist of all that is sacred.

Interwoven with predictions of future history right up to the end of time are references to the fall of Jerusalem in A.D. 70 when the temple was to be desecrated by the Roman legions. In such circumstances, the people of God would naturally look for the Messiah to return, and there would be a danger of overeager identification of an impostor as the returning Messiah (Matt. 24:23–25; Mark 13:21–23). Believers are warned not to listen to every rumor, since the Lord's coming is to be sudden and as dramatic as lightning (Matt. 24:26–28; cf. Luke 17:23–24). At the time of His coming, He will gather His elect from every place (Matt. 24:29–31; Mark 13:24–27; Luke 21:25–28).

Jesus emphasized that the day and the hour of His coming are unknown either to the world at large or to His privileged people, His church:

> But of that day and hour no one knows, not even the angels in heaven, nor the Son, but only the Father. Take heed, watch and pray; for you do not know when the time is. It is like a man going to a far country, who left his house and gave authority to his servants, and to each his work, and commanded the doorkeeper to watch. Watch therefore, for you do not know when the master of the house is coming—in the evening, at midnight, at the crowing of the rooster, or in the morning —lest, coming suddenly, he find you sleeping. And what I say to you, I say to all: Watch! (Mark 13:32–37).

Matthew records two parables Jesus then told indicating the priority of watchfulness—the parable of the ten virgins (Matt. 25:1–13) and the parable of the talents (Matt. 25:14–30; cf. Luke 19:12–27). Matthew indicates that Jesus concluded His teaching about His return by reminding the disciples that it would also be the occasion of the Last Judgment (Matt. 25:31–46).

Just One Week

This final visit to Jerusalem, and all we see recorded of it in the Gospels, took place in the space of a week. We cannot help being amazed at Jesus' energy, His determination to complete the tasks the Father had given Him, and His set purpose to go to the cross.

He knew all that was before Him, and He did not allow it for a moment to hinder His obedience to the Father. Everything He did hastened the train of events that was going to lead to His arrest, unjust condemnation, and death.

Already He had His eyes fixed upon His future triumph and the joy of His disciples sharing it with Him—hence, His teaching about His return. He "endured the cross," the writer to the Hebrews tells us, "for the joy that was set before Him" (Heb. 12:2). His call to His disciples today, as in that last week of His earthly life, is, "Be on guard! Be alert! . . . Watch!" (Mark 13:33, 37 NIV).

Life in this world will not just go on and on. We are not to be lulled into the world's sleep: "As long as it is day, we must do the work of him who sent" Jesus (John 9:4 NIV).

M E D I T A T I O N

1. The way in which Jesus entered Jerusalem illustrates an aspect of the profound mystery of His person: He is the King of kings, yet humble and gentle (Matt. 21:5; cf. Zech. 9:9; Matt. 11:29; Phil. 2:8).

2. Mark makes plain that Jesus' clearing of the temple was not an impetuous act in the heat of the moment but a considered action (Mark 11:11, 15–19). Wherever we turn in the Gospels, we see Jesus' perfect self-control, and herein the difficult task of judgment.

3. Jesus' authority, once recognized and understood, must lead us to worship and obey Him (Matt. 28:18).

4. "He came to His own, and His own did not receive Him. But as many as received Him, to them He gave the right to become children of God, to those who believe in His name: who were born, not of blood, nor of the will of the flesh, nor of the will of man, but of God" (John 1:11–13).

5. Jesus is the only man who has perfectly fulfilled both the first great commandment and the second: this qualified Him to be the Savior we, as transgressors of God's law, need (Matt. 5:17; Gal. 3:13; 4:4–5).

6. Jesus was the perfect Teacher—in contrast to the teachers of the law and the Pharisees—in that He always practiced what He taught and preached.

7. Jesus' coming will be the revelation of His power and glory (Matt. 24:30) and the gathering together of His people.

Q U E S T I O N S

1. In what ways is Jesus our King, and how is His kingship different from any other?

2. In view of Jesus' reference to Isaiah 56:7 and God's house being called "a house of prayer," can we identify hindrances to worship and prayer when God's people today meet together to worship Him?

3. By what authority did Jesus clear the temple? Who gave Him that authority?

4. What do Jesus' parables in Matthew 21:28—22:14 have in common, and what do they teach about God's saving purposes in the world?

5. What is the purpose of the law for humankind in general? What place should the Ten Commandments have in a Christian's life?

6. What was Jesus' main criticism of the teachers of the law and the Pharisees? Which of those areas of failure are dangers for us, and how may we avoid them?

7. What did Jesus teach about His coming again? What are the practical implications of His coming for Christians?

Chapter Nine

JESUS' CRUCIFIXION

More space is given in the Gospels to Jesus' death than to any other event. The conclusion is inescapable: His death was the main purpose of His coming. The Gospels show us how the early Christians preached the gospel—everything led up to the Cross and the Resurrection.

All that we have considered so far indicates that we have now arrived at the most important point in Jesus' earthly life. To be our Savior from sin's guilt, condemnation, and penalty, He had to die in our place. Only then could He fulfill the promise contained in His name. The moment for which all the prophets had looked and longed, when reconciliation between God and people was to be accomplished, had come.

Two Initiatives

Two initiatives were taken. First, Judas set in motion his act of betrayal (Matt. 26:14–16; Mark 14:10–11; Luke 22:3–6). The chief priests received Judas gladly, changing their minds about the decision they had earlier made to delay their attempt on Jesus' life.

No real explanation is provided for Judas's action. Some have thought it was his greed for money, bearing in mind, for example, that he had been frustrated on the occasion of the anointing at Bethany from gaining possession of the expensive ointment. Others have suggested that, believing Jesus to be a political Savior and Messiah, Judas tried to force Jesus to take action by handing Him over to the authorities, never expecting that Jesus would allow Himself to be crucified. Luke's explanation is the true one, however we try to understand Judas's action: "Satan entered Judas, surnamed Iscariot, who was numbered among the twelve" (Luke 22:3).

Second, Jesus began the preparations for the disciples' celebration of the Passover (Matt. 26:17–19; Mark 14:12–16; Luke 22:7–13). His words indicate the urgency with which He gave His instructions: "My time is at hand" (Matt. 26:18).

That there was a room already prepared for them suggests Jesus had made arrangements beforehand. On the other hand, His divine foreknowledge is apparent in the manner in which He told them of the man they would meet and they were to follow (Mark 14:13–15; Luke 22:10).

The Last Supper

Jesus earnestly anticipated eating the Passover meal with His disciples on the day before His crucifixion (Matt. 26:26–29; Mark 14:17–25; Luke 22:14–23). The Old Testament memorial feast was merged into the New Testament feast of remembrance and communion.

Distress filled the disciples as Jesus foretold the betrayal. Quoting Psalm 41:9, He interpreted God's dealings with Him in the light of the Scriptures (Matt. 26:23–24; Mark 14:18). Disturbed at the thought of any one of them betraying Jesus, the disciples asked Him one after another, "Is it I?" and Judas was the last one to ask the question. John tells us that Jesus then told Judas to do what he had to do quickly, although the others did not understand what He was talking about (John 13:27–28).

The words that accompanied their eating of the bread and drinking of the wine emphasize the substitutionary nature of Jesus' death as, for example, in His words about the cup: "Drink from it, all of you. For this is My blood of the new covenant, which is shed for many for the remission of sins" (Matt. 26:27–28; Mark 14:24; cf. 1 Cor. 11:24–25).

Once Judas had left the room, Jesus spoke His most intimate words to the remaining eleven (John 13:31). It would seem that He delayed saying them until Judas had gone. Jesus' determination and complete confidence about what He was going to accomplish by His death shone through all He said:

Now the Son of Man is glorified, and God is glorified in Him. If God is glorified in Him, God will also glorify Him in Himself, and glorify Him immediately. Little children, I shall be with you a little while longer. You will seek Me; and as I said to the Jews, "Where I am going, you cannot come," so now I say to you (John 13:31–33).

John alone records Jesus' moving conversations with the disciples at the table (John 14—16). Jesus spoke of the assurance of heaven He wanted the disciples to possess (John 14:1–4), and the sure knowledge they had of the Father because they had seen Him, the visible image of the invisible God (John 14:5–14). Although Jesus knew they were all going to forsake Him, He nevertheless gave all those encouragements since never for a moment did He stop loving them (John 13:1).

From the Upper Room, they went to the Garden of Gethsemane. On the way Jesus spoke about the disciples' falling away (Matt. 26:30–35; cf. Mark 14:26–31; Luke 22:31–34). He interpreted their imminent desertion of Him in the light of the Old Testament Scriptures (Matt. 26:31; Mark 14:27; cf. Zech. 13:7), His constant guide and comfort. Although the spotlight was on Peter, because of his forceful protest as the spokesman, all the disciples objected to the suggestion that they were to deny Jesus (Matt. 26:35).

At Gethsemane (Matt. 26:36–46; Mark 14:32–42; Luke 22:40–46), Jesus withdrew from the main group of disciples and took Peter, James, and John with Him. The name Gethsemane implies it was an olive orchard. Jesus went through great agony of soul, not only because of the physical sufferings that were before Him, but also because of the prospect of His bearing the whole weight of human sin. He was to be made sin for us; He was to bear our sins in His own body (2 Cor. 5:21; 1 Pet. 2:24). The Father's face was to be hidden from Him—something He had never known before. The Cross was like a cup of bitter wine He was compelled to drink if He was to do the Father's will and obtain eternal salvation for men and women.

The temptations Satan threw at Jesus at the beginning of His ministry, he presented again, no doubt with even greater force. But through prayer, Jesus was victorious (Matt. 26:36).

We may draw considerable encouragement that Jesus found it necessary to pray the same words again to renew and maintain His submission to His agonizing path of duty (Matt. 26:39, 42, 44). The company of others as we pray is often helpful (Matt. 26:37), but the three disciples were little encouragement to Jesus (Matt. 26:40, 43, 45). Luke, however, tells us that an angel appeared from heaven, strengthening Him (22:43)—an illustration of 1 Corinthians 10:13.

The events that followed the hours in the Garden of Gethsemane underline the humiliation Jesus suffered as He made His way to the cross. First, He was betrayed by Judas and taken captive (Matt. 26:47–56; Mark 14:43–52; Luke 22:47–53, cf. John 18:2–11). A great sense of sadness surfaces when the gospel writers record, "While He was still speaking, behold, Judas, *one of the twelve*, . . . came" (Matt. 26:47, emphasis added). That a man could have lived so close to Jesus, and then betray Him, demonstrates the inborn sinfulness of the human heart.

John records that Peter impulsively drew his sword and slashed at the high priest's servant, cutting off his ear (John 18:10). Jesus allowed no room for personal retaliation, even when wrongly treated, and He rebuked Peter and healed the servant (Luke 22:51).

Jesus' humiliation went a step further because "then all the disciples forsook Him and fled" (Matt. 26:56; Mark 14:50).

Jesus was humiliated once more as He was first brought before the Sanhedrin (Matt. 26:57–75; Mark 14:53–72; Luke 22:54–71). To their own condemnation, they found making up false evidence extremely difficult, and what they eventually produced did not sound at all convincing (Mark 14:55–59). Both Matthew and Mark draw attention to Jesus' silence, something especially telling in view of the prophecy of Isaiah 53:7:

> He was oppressed and He was afflicted,
> Yet He opened not His mouth;
> He was led as a lamb to the slaughter,
> And as a sheep before its shearers is silent,
> So He opened not His mouth.

Jesus showed by His example that silence is often the best response to false accusation. When it came to direct questions, which did not involve self-defense, Jesus gave appropriate answers, answers that brought serious consequences (Luke 22:67–71).

When morning came, the chief priests, the elders, the teachers of the law, and the whole council determined to hand Jesus over to Pilate (Matt. 27:1–2; Mark 15:1; Luke 23:1; cf. John 18:28–32).

Pilate's interrogation of Jesus and ultimate crucifixion of Him are events anchored in history. Josephus, the Jewish historian whose *Antiquities* were published in A.D. 93, writes,

> And there arose about this time [i.e., Pilate's time, A.D. 26–36], Jesus, a wise man, if indeed we should call him a man; for he was a doer of marvelous deeds, a teacher of men who receive the truth with pleasure. He won over many Jews and also many Greeks. This man was the Messiah. And when Pilate had condemned him to the cross at the instigation of our own leaders, those who had loved him from the first did not cease (18.3.3).

In 1961 in Caesarea, an inscription providing archaeological evidence of Pilate's governorship came to light when a stone slab was unearthed bearing the Latin names *Pontius Pilatus* and *Tiberius.*

Jesus was tried before Pilate at a place called The Pavement or, in Hebrew, Gabbatha (John 19:13). For years no one knew anything about this pavement; and it seemed to be an unnecessary detail in the account of Jesus' trial. In the 1930s, however, the French archaeologist Père Vincent excavated what is thought to be the place. If so, it measures fifty yards square, and it was the pavement of the Roman barracks. There are marks on the stones indicating a game the Roman soldiers played. But we cannot be dogmatic about this site's identification.

The Jewish leaders knew how to manipulate Pilate to do what they wanted, for, as Luke tells us, they began by saying, "We found this fellow perverting the nation, and forbidding to pay taxes to Caesar, saying that He Himself is Christ, a King" (Luke 23:2). Evidence points to Pilate having made mistakes in his administration, and he would have been sensitive to any bad reports going back to his masters in Rome. Such an accusation was one he could not afford to ignore.

When Pilate learned that Jesus was a Galilean, he sent Him to Herod (Luke 23:6–12). He hoped Herod would pass judgment on Jesus, thus letting Pilate himself off the hook. Jesus, however, made no answer either to Herod's request for a miracle or to his questions. Herod had had his opportunity of listening to God when he had been faced earlier by John the Baptist.

The responsibility for action then lay fairly and squarely on Pilate again (Matt. 27:15–26; Mark 15:6–15; Luke 23:13–25; cf. John 18:38–40; 19:4–16). He made three attempts to escape the pressures toward what he knew to be a false judgment, but the crowd—at the prompting and bribing of the Jewish authorities—demanded Barabbas instead.

Pilate's ultimate decision was to yield to human pressures rather than to follow his conscience. He was as much on trial as Jesus was. Mark provides a pointed comment on Pilate's whole attitude: "Pilate, wanting to gratify the crowd, released Barabbas to them; and he delivered Jesus, after he had scourged Him, to be crucified" (Mark 15:15).

Crucifixion was practiced first by the Phoenicians and the Carthaginians. Then the Romans used it as a punishment. Only slaves, the lowest types of criminals, and people living outside Italy were crucified, and so it rarely happened to Roman citizens. Criminals were not crucified alive in the Old Testament, although dead bodies were sometimes hung on a tree as a warning—this explains why the New Testament speaks sometimes of Jesus' cross as a tree (Acts 5:30; 10:39; 13:29; 1 Pet. 2:24).

Crucifixion was widespread in some periods of ancient history. Josephus records that in 4 B.C. the Roman general Varus crucified two thousand rebels. During the siege of Jerusalem by Titus (A.D. 70), so many were crucified that there was a shortage of wood for the crosses.

Matthew, Mark, and Luke mention Simon of Cyrene being seized upon to carry the cross that Jesus initially carried to His place of execution (Matt. 27:32; Mark 15:21; Luke 23:26; cf. John 19:17).

The last days Jesus spent in Jerusalem had been crammed full of activity, with tremendous demands made on Him by the crowds. To that were added a night without sleep and a dreadful beating. It was the custom, after sentence had been passed, for the victim to be flogged by a whip of leather thongs with small pieces of metal or bone tied to them. Little wonder that Jesus became weak and exhausted.

As for Simon who carried the cross, the reference to his family in Mark 15:21 may indicate that carrying Jesus' cross led to his conversion and then in turn to his sons' (cf. Rom. 16:13).

Although Pilate's behavior and decision cannot be excused, the real blame must be placed on those who handed Jesus over to him. The gospel writers indicate that crucifixion was not Pilate's wish for Jesus (John 19:15). The chief priests are shown to have been behind it (John 19:6, 15–16).

When the apostles later proclaimed the gospel—the record of which we have in the Acts of the Apostles—they placed the responsibility on the Jews rather than the Romans (Acts 10:39). As Peter put it to the crowds who listened to him in the temple precincts, "You handed him over to be killed, and you disowned him before Pilate, though he had decided to let him go. You disowned the Holy and Righteous One and asked that a murderer be released to you. You killed the author of life" (Acts 3:13–15 NIV). Stephen likewise said to the Jews, "You now have become the betrayers and murderers" (Acts 7:52).

Crucifixion was an agonizing way to die (Matt. 27:33–44; Mark 15:22–32; Luke 23:33–43; John 19:17–27). Nailing the victim to the cross caused excruciating pain. Considerable suffering occurred because of the abnormal position of the body. Any movement, no matter how slight, brought additional torture. There was also the strong possibility of a fever brought on by the wounds inflicted. Cicero, a Roman writer, described it as "the most cruel and revolting punishment," and Josephus as "the most pitiable of deaths." It was not a pleasant sight, with its pain and indignity intensified by the burning sun and inquisitive crowds.

None of the gospel writers dwells on the physical details of the Crucifixion, and they all, like Mark, simply record: "And they crucified him" (Mark 15:24 NIV). While Jesus' physical sufferings were great, His spiritual sufferings were greater. The sufferings of Jesus' soul were the most terrible part of His agony. He experienced in His inner man the fearful torments and inexpressible anguish of the full weight of God's anger against sin.

A most significant event was the darkness that came over the whole land at the time of Jesus' death (Matt. 27:45; Mark 15:33; Luke 23:44–45), a symbol of the world's darkness when men and women reject light and truth.

The extraordinary sweat "like great drops of blood" (Luke 22:44) and the heart-rending cry, "My God, My God, why have You forsaken Me?" (Matt. 27:46), point to the extreme nature of Jesus' spiritual sufferings as He "who knew no sin" was made "to be sin for us, that we might become the righteousness of God in Him" (2 Cor. 5:21).

Jesus' physical sufferings on the cross underline His real humanity. By His incarnation, He took upon Himself a human body. As a consequence, He suffered and knew pain like us. And yet the mystery was that it was the crucifixion of God since Jesus was no mere man—He was the Son of God. Paul spoke to the Ephesian elders of "the church of God which He purchased with His own blood" (Acts 20:28). Christ "has redeemed us from the curse of the law, having become a curse for us (for it is written, 'Cursed is everyone who hangs on a tree')" (Gal. 3:13).

God's Control

Some aspects of the Crucifixion require special attention. Throughout we see evidences of God's sovereignty—His overruling control of events. Peter declared on the day of Pentecost: "This man was handed over to you *by God's set purpose and foreknowledge*; and you, with the help of wicked men, put him to death by nailing him to the cross. But God raised him from the dead" (Acts 2:23–24 NIV, emphasis added).

Pilate became an unconscious proclaimer of Christ when he declared, "Behold your King!" (John 19:14), even as Caiaphas had been His prophet when he said, "It is expedient . . . that one man should die for the people, and not that the whole nation should perish" (John 11:50). And both of them did not realize the true meaning of what they said.

Seven Statements from the Cross

Jesus' words from the cross are commonly known as the seven words. First, they were words of intercession: "Father, forgive them, for they do not know what they do" (Luke 23:34). Second, they were words of assurance: "Assuredly, I say to you, today you will be with Me in Paradise" (Luke 23:43). Third, they were words of provision and responsibility: "He said to His mother, 'Woman, behold your son!' Then He said to the disciple, 'Behold your mother!'" (John 19:26–27). Fourth, they were words of separation: "My God, My God, why have You forsaken Me?" (Matt. 27:46). Fifth, they were words of suffering: "I thirst!" (John 19:28). Sixth, they were words of completion: "It is finished!" (John 19:30). Finally, they were words of confidence: "Father, into Your hands I commit My spirit" (Luke 23:46).

A Torn Curtain and Open Graves

The temple's curtain was torn in two as Jesus cried, "It is finished!" (Matt. 27:51; Mark 15:38; Luke 23:45; John 19:30). This curtain separated men and women from the Most Holy Place, and the high priest alone could go beyond it, and then only on the Day of Atonement. By the symbolic tearing of the curtain, God symbolized the glorious assurance that Jesus' death has opened the way for us into God's presence.

Matthew records a strange and remarkable happening as the curtain of the temple was torn: "The earth quaked, and the rocks were split, and the graves were opened; and many bodies of the saints who had fallen asleep were raised; and coming out of the graves after His resurrection, they went into the holy city and appeared to many" (Matt. 27:51–53).

We have no further details, and Matthew makes no comment. Two questions arise: What was the meaning of this event? And what happened to these people afterward? The point must be that Jesus' resurrection is the promise of the resurrection of the believing dead, and that was visual proof and confirmation of Christian hope. Jesus is the firstfruits of those who sleep. It was an evidence, therefore, of Jesus' victory over death.

As to what happened afterward, we cannot say. Either they rested again in their graves, or they shared in some way—not described—in our Lord's experience of ascension. The latter seems more probable since if the life they were given had been only mortal, it would not have been a genuine share in our Lord's resurrection. He rose again to die no more, and the promise He makes to us is that we shall share in His resurrection.

An Illustrative Substitution

Pilate regularly released a prisoner at the time of the Feast of Passover. In the hope that it might provide a way out for him to release Jesus, he offered the crowd the opportunity to choose a prisoner to be released: Barabbas or Jesus. But to his dismay, the crowd cried out for the release of Barabbas, a notorious prisoner who had committed murder in an insurrection (Matt. 27:15–26; Mark 15:6–15).

The cross upon which Jesus died, therefore, was originally prepared for Barabbas—it had his name on it. As Barabbas looked up at Jesus dying on the cross, he could truthfully say, "That cross ought to be mine. He's dying in my place." In a far deeper way, every Christian may say that.

Testimonies

Remarkable testimonies were given to Jesus' innocence and character. Pilate's wife sent a message to her husband: "Have nothing to do with that just Man, for I have suffered many things today in a dream because of Him" (Matt. 27:19). Pilate said to the Jews, "Having examined Him . . . I have found no fault in this Man concerning those things of which you accuse Him" (Luke 23:14). The centurion in charge of the crucifixion, on hearing Jesus' cry at His death and seeing the manner in which He died, said, "Truly this Man was the Son of God!" (Mark 15:39). His words may not have had the full content we are able to read into them, but we cannot doubt that his understanding was God-given.

Certified Dead

And so Jesus died. Certified dead by the centurion on duty at Calvary and by the soldiers under his command (John 19:31–34), He was buried. Joseph of Arimathea, a respected member of the council and a rich man, took courage and asked Pilate for Jesus' body. Permission granted, he laid Jesus' body in his own new tomb. Once again, the Scriptures were fulfilled: "They made His grave with the wicked—But with the rich at His death" (Isa. 53:9).

That was the end, so far as the world was concerned. But it was not! Really it was only the beginning. Jesus had fulfilled God's plan. Before the world was made, the Father and the Son had entered into an agreement and a covenant: the Son was to accomplish the work given to Him (John 12:27; 17:2, 4), and the Father promised that as a result, a great number of men and women from all nations would be given to Him as His inheritance (Ps. 2:7–8), and He should be supreme Head of the church (Eph. 1:22; Phil. 2:9–11; Heb. 12:2).

Things would never be the same again. No more sacrifices for sin were necessary—all the Old Testament types and symbols found their crowning fulfillment at Calvary. An eternal sacrifice for sins had been offered: the punishment Jesus suffered was sufficient to satisfy God's just anger against sin because He who had suffered was not only man but God. He was of infinitely more value than all transgressors (Rom. 5:8; Heb. 9:13–14). His sacrifice was final—once and for all—and utterly sufficient for all time (Heb. 9:26; 10:11–14; 1 Pet. 3:18). The message of the New Testament—the heart of the gospel—is this: we preach Jesus Christ and Him crucified (1 Cor. 2:2).

Jesus seldom spoke about His cross without linking it with His disciples' obedience to His example in cross bearing. Our taking up the cross is not a matter of bearing some particular hardship or difficult task. Rather, it is accepting the principle that guided Jesus' life—obedience to the Father's will. The Lord Jesus lived by the principle of "no suffering, no glory." He calls His disciples to do the same. The call to cross bearing becomes all the more imperative as we view and understand the Cross and respond to Him in gratitude.

M E D I T A T I O N

1. The betrayal of Jesus by one of His close disciples should prompt us to examine our profession of loyalty to Him (cf. 1 Cor. 11:23, 28).

2. The Lord's Supper is intended to keep ever before us the death of Jesus and all that He achieved by it so that, with Paul, we may say from the heart, "God forbid that I should boast except in the cross of our Lord Jesus Christ" (Gal. 6:14).

3. Jesus' repeating of His prayer to His Father in the Garden of Gethsemane indicates the overwhelming bitterness of the cup of God's wrath against sin that He had to drink in order to save us.

4. Jesus' immediate reaction upon His arrest was to be concerned for the best interests of His disciples (John 18:4–9). This same Jesus lives to intercede for us (Heb. 7:25).

5. All the efforts of the religious authorities to find fault in Jesus fell to the ground, bearing unspoken testimony to the truth of 1 Peter 2:22: "[He] committed no sin, nor was deceit found in His mouth."

6. Although Jesus was put to death by demand of the people (Luke 23:23–24), it was also by God's set purpose and foreknowledge for our salvation (Acts 2:23).

7. "There they crucified Him" (Luke 23:33). The gospel writers do not provide a commentary on the sufferings of Jesus, but the Old Testament does:

> See
> If there is any sorrow like my sorrow,
> Which has been brought on me,
> Which the LORD has inflicted
> In the day of His fierce anger (Lam. 1:12).

Q U E S T I O N S

1. What do you think were Judas's reasons for betraying Jesus? What does the underlying reason (Luke 22:3) tell us about Satan?

2. What do we proclaim about Jesus' death as we share in the Lord's Supper (1 Cor. 11:26)?

3. What does Jesus' experience in Gethsemane tell us about the Cross?

4. How did Jesus show Himself in complete command of all that happened, even when arrested in the garden?

5. On what two aspects of Jesus' identity did the Sanhedrin's questions center? To what extent did they already have the answers to their questions?

6. What indications did Pilate's words and behavior give of his conviction concerning Jesus' innocence of the charges brought against Him?

7. What was the significance of the darkness that came on the whole land and the tearing of the curtain of the temple (Mark 15:33, 38)?

Chapter Ten

JESUS' RESURRECTION, ASCENSION, AND PRESENT POSITION

Good Friday and Easter Day are not two separate events —they belong together. Jesus Christ died for our sins. If, however, He had not risen from the dead, we would have no assurance that He had achieved salvation for all who trust in Him. Furthermore, He promised that He would rise again. His claims to deity and messiahship rest finally on His resurrection.

At the beginning of His ministry, Jesus said, "Destroy this temple, and in three days I will raise it up" (John 2:19). Urged by the Pharisees to provide a sign, He replied, "No sign will be given . . . except the sign of the prophet Jonah. For as Jonah was three days and three nights in the belly of the great fish, so will the Son of Man be three days and three nights in the heart of the earth" (Matt. 12:39–40).

The inseparability of Good Friday and Easter Day is illustrated in Paul's declaration to the Corinthians that the message of the gospel is "Jesus Christ and Him crucified" (1 Cor. 2:2). "Crucified" is a perfect participle, meaning "having been crucified," and it points to two further truths.

First, Jesus is not now crucified—the Crucifixion is past, and He is risen. But, second, He continues in the character of the Crucified One since His death was perfect in its effects and will always be the focus of His people's praise and thanksgiving.

The Crucifixion was people's act; the Resurrection was God's! The emphasis of the New Testament is that "God raised [Him] from the dead" (Acts 3:15; 4:10; Rom. 4:24; 8:11; 10:9; 1 Cor. 6:14; 1 Cor. 15:15; 2 Cor. 4:14; 1 Pet. 1:21). By the Resurrection, God totally reversed the judgment people had made on His Son by their crucifying Him. People said, "Jesus is not who He says He is." God declared, "He is all that He said He is—and more!"

The Disciples' Lack of Expectation

The disciples were unprepared for the Resurrection. They were not expecting it to happen as it did. But that was not because Jesus had not told them about it beforehand.

Once they made their declaration of His messiahship at Caesarea Philippi, He "began to show to His disciples that He must go to Jerusalem, and suffer many things from the elders and chief priests and scribes, and be killed, and *be raised the third day*" (Matt. 16:21, emphasis added; cf. Mark 8:31).

The disciples failed to understand what Jesus said and were afraid to ask Him about it (Mark 9:32). But He continued to tell them what was going to happen (Matt. 17:23; 20:18–19; Mark 9:31; 10:33–34; Luke 9:22; 13:32–33; 18:31–33), for although they did not take it in at the time, the truth of what He said was going to dawn upon them powerfully once the event took place.

Having deliberately shut their minds to the thought of Jesus dying, they had not been able to anticipate the joy of His rising again. They allowed themselves to be influenced, perhaps unconsciously, by false views of Jesus' messiahship that focused on immediate political power, and such a preoccupation gave no place to a crucified Messiah.

They had not understood the Old Testament Scriptures and the teaching Jesus had given them about Himself (Luke 24:27). Their understandings were not yet fully opened. Prior to the event, the Scriptures had not fitted into place in their minds, but at the Resurrection, they did.

The Jewish authorities, however, did take seriously what He had said about His rising again (Matt. 27:62–66). Having accused Jesus of being an impostor, the chief priests and Pharisees spoke together of His declaration that He would rise again after three days. They urged Pilate, therefore, to provide a guard of soldiers to keep watch over the tomb to prevent the disciples from stealing Jesus' body and then claiming that He had risen from the dead.

Once more God's control of all the circumstances surrounding Jesus' death and resurrection is evident. Pilate's agreement to the Jewish authorities' request only added confirmation to the Resurrection's reality.

The Empty Tomb

The careful guard by the soldiers makes the empty tomb all the more impressive. On the first day of the week, the tomb was empty (Matt. 28:1–10; Mark 16:1–8; Luke 24:1–12).

Matthew, in common with all the New Testament writers, encourages close examination of the evidences of the Resurrection: for example, first, the rolled-back stone (v. 2); second, the presence of the angel (v. 2); third, the clear identification of the tomb as the one in which Jesus had been laid (v. 6); and, fourth, the actual emptiness of the tomb (v. 6).

John provides additional information (John 20:1–10). He records how Peter and he responded to Mary's message that she and the other women had found the tomb empty (v. 2). They set off at once, John arriving first, but not attempting to go inside the tomb until Peter caught up with him. When Peter arrived, he went straight inside. The first things they both noticed were the linen cloths lying there, and the handkerchief that had been around Jesus' head was not lying with the linen cloths but was rolled up by itself, a little way apart. At that point, John declares that he believed (v. 8). The sight of the graveclothes, lying still in their original folds, yet untouched by human hands, indicated a supernatural event.

If we are surprised at the amount of convincing the disciples needed to be sure that the Resurrection had really happened, we must remember its almost unbelievable nature before it took place. We look at it in a completely different light: we live *after*, whereas they lived *before* it. This background of initial unbelief makes all the more impressive the disciples' subsequent wholehearted testimony to the reality of Jesus' resurrection.

The empty tomb does not stand on its own as proof of Jesus' resurrection. More important still were His resurrection appearances. The early Christians believed in the Resurrection not because they could not find Jesus' body but because they saw the risen Lord. The appearances were made not to people in general but to those who had a long association with Jesus.

God allowed His Son to be seen by a select group of witnesses whom He chose. The details of these personal encounters are found, first, in the four Gospels, second, in Paul's statement in 1 Corinthians 15:1–8 and, third, in the apostles' speeches in the Acts of the Apostles.

Paul's list, coming from one of the earliest New Testament documents, may be the first written record we possess of the Resurrection appearances. He indicates that Jesus "was seen by [Peter], then by the twelve. After that He was seen by over five hundred brethren at once, of whom the greater part remain to the present, but some have fallen asleep. After that He was seen by James, then by all the apostles" (1 Cor. 15:5–7). Paul does not try to provide an exhaustive list of the Resurrection appearances, but he gives these as illustrations of those that took place. The Gospels provide a more detailed account of some of them.

An attempt is sometimes made to provide a time sequence of Jesus' appearances and to use the gospel narratives to this end. It can be done, but the initial problems in piecing them together are exactly the difficulties we would expect with eyewitness accounts.

Suppose a few people were asked to describe an event they all saw. If they used the same words and provided identical descriptions, they would be immediately suspect. We would say, "Someone put them up to this and got them together so that they agree perfectly." But if they all told the truth with varying descriptions and different emphases, we would say, "And *now* we have the truth!"

The gospel narratives are all the more to be trusted because they are not exactly the same. Having said that, it is possible to build up a reasonable and consistent narrative of the events, but insofar as the New Testament does not strive to do this, it may not be a necessary exercise, much as it is helpful to know that it can be done.

Mary Magdalene first met the risen Lord (John 20:10–18), and her experience was repeated in the company of other women later in the day (Matt. 28:8–10).

The next appearance took place in the late afternoon on the Emmaus Road (Luke 24:13–35). The narrative is so vivid that the unnamed disciple could have been Luke himself, but we have no means of knowing. If so, it would doubly underline the significance of Luke's later writing of Jesus showing Himself alive by "many infallible proofs" (Acts 1:3).

The two disciples' conversation clearly shows how their ideas of Jesus' messiahship were materialistic and political rather than spiritual (v. 21). That, to varying degrees, had been a common failing of the disciples. They expressed their honest amazement at the Resurrection (v. 22), even though Jesus had spoken plainly of it beforehand.

Several explanations may be given for their initial failure to recognize the risen Jesus: they had certainly not expected to meet Him; and perhaps His resurrection body was not so immediately recognizable because of its now heavenly nature. But the main reason must have been that Jesus did not want them to recognize Him until He had shown them from the Old Testament Scriptures how essential to God's plan of redemption had been the events they had recounted (vv. 19–27). What the Lord Jesus did for those two disciples He now does through the teachers and preachers He gives by His Spirit (see, for example, Acts 8:26–35; 18:26).

When the two disciples returned to Jerusalem to share their wonderful experience, they in turn received the news that the risen Jesus had appeared to Peter (Luke 24:33–34; cf. 1 Cor. 15:5).

Understandably, great prominence is given to the Lord's appearance on the evening of the day of His resurrection when the disciples were together in the Upper Room (Luke 24:36–49; John 20:19–23). Luke makes the interesting point that the disciples disbelieved for joy and amazement (v. 41). He also shows how Jesus pointed out to them the physical nature of His resurrection: He encouraged them to touch Him and give Him food to eat (vv. 39, 41).

John's account of the same events records Jesus' significant words of greeting: "Peace be with you" (John 20:19, 21). The clue to their meaning is in the way in which Jesus then showed His disciples His hands and side (v. 20)—the evidences of His crucifixion and of His substitutionary death. It was through His death, as the atoning sacrifice for our sins, that we may now have peace with God (Eph. 2:13–18).

Jesus then commissioned them to be His witnesses, and the Holy Spirit was given with this purpose in view. "Ambassadors of peace" describes their task (cf. Acts 10:36; 2 Cor. 5:18–21)—especially in light of our understanding of Jesus' message.

Exactly a week later, Jesus appeared again to the disciples, when Thomas was present (John 20:24–31). The conditions Thomas laid down, of putting his finger where the nails were and his hand into Jesus' side, proved unnecessary because, on seeing the Lord, he cried, "My Lord and my God!" (John 20:28). Jesus used what had happened in Thomas's case to point out the happiness of those who believe without first seeing Him (John 20:29).

John also relates Jesus' appearance to the disciples in Galilee (John 21). He showed Himself to them on the shore of Lake Tiberias as they were fishing. At first they thought Him a stranger, until their obedience to His instruction about where they should fish produced an amazing catch. John was the first to recognize Jesus, and Peter the first to make for the shore to meet Him (v. 7).

At the breakfast that followed, Jesus addressed three questions to Peter about his love for Him (John 21:15–17), and Peter could not help but be reminded of his threefold denial of Jesus. Nevertheless, Peter was completely restored and recommissioned as a shepherd of Jesus' flock.

Final Instructions

Jesus gave His disciples His final instructions about their responsibilities for the furtherance of God's kingdom (Acts 1:3). Peter sums up those instructions in his words to Cornelius, recorded in the Acts of the Apostles:

> He was not seen by all the people, but by witnesses whom God had already chosen—by us who ate and drank with him after he rose from the dead. He commanded us to preach to the people and to testify that he is the one whom God appointed as judge of the living and the dead. All the prophets testify about him that everyone who believes in him receives forgiveness of sins through his name (Acts 10:41–43 NIV).

Jesus' commission to the apostles and disciples is found in all the Gospels as well as in the opening chapter of the Acts of the Apostles (Matt. 28:16–20; Mark 16:15–20; Luke 24:36–49; John 21:15–25; Acts 1:1–11). First and foremost, they were to proclaim the gospel of peace—the good news of peace with God through the forgiveness of sins Jesus makes possible by His death (Mark 16:15–16; Luke 24:47; John 20:23). They were to make disciples of those who believed on Him (Matt. 28:19), passing on all they had been taught. They were to be confident of their Lord's presence with them and, therefore, of their success (Matt. 28:20; Mark 16:20).

Luke tells us that it was over a period of forty days that Jesus appeared to His disciples. He summarizes the days like this: "After his suffering, he showed himself to these men and gave many convincing proofs that he was alive" (Acts 1:3 NIV).

Jesus' resurrection transformed the disciples. They were in no doubt that His resurrection was a physical reality. They spoke afterward of how they "ate and drank with Him after He arose from the dead" (Acts 10:41; cf. Luke 24:41–43). Jesus' body was the same, yet different. He could appear to them behind closed doors. They knew He was alive—and they were witnesses!

The only satisfactory explanation of the energy, drive, and enthusiasm of the early church is Jesus' resurrection. "This Jesus God has raised up, of which we are all witnesses," was Peter's testimony on the day of Pentecost (Acts 2:32). As Paul reminded Agrippa, "This thing was not done in a corner" (Acts 26:26).

A story is told of Auguste Comte, the French philosopher, and Thomas Carlyle, the Scottish writer. Comte declared that he was going to start a new religion that would supplant Christianity. It was to have no mysteries, and it was to be as plain as the multiplication table—its name was to be positivism. "Very good, Mr. Comte," Carlyle replied. "Very good. All you will need to do will be to speak as never a man spake, and live as never a man lived, and be crucified, and rise again the third day, and get the world to believe that you are still alive. Then your religion will have a chance to get on."

Christianity is unique because Jesus Christ is unique. When we understand that, we say with the first apostles, "Lord, to whom shall we go? You have the words of eternal life. Also we have come to believe and know that You are the Christ, the Son of the living God" (John 6:68–69).

Jesus' Ascension

The Ascension was the climax of the Resurrection appearances and marked the end of the forty days. Luke, both in his gospel and in his record of the early church, the Acts of the Apostles, describes Jesus' ascension at the Mount of Olives. Jesus led His disciples out as far as Bethany, and lifting up His hands, He blessed them. While He blessed them, He parted from them (Luke 24:50–51; cf. Mark 11:1; Acts 1:12).

His final words were words of commission: "It is not for you to know times or seasons which the Father has put in His own authority. But you shall receive power when the Holy Spirit has come upon you; and you shall be witnesses to Me in Jerusalem, and in all Judea and Samaria, and to the end of the earth" (Acts 1:7–8).

As Jesus was taken up out of their sight, the apostles were told that He will come back in the same way as they saw Him go into heaven, which—at least—must mean physically, visibly, and at a fixed point in history.

The Ascension was an act of God's power, the necessary completion of Jesus' death and resurrection. He was exalted to the place in the universe He had laid aside when He humbled Himself to assume our humanity. He carried our humanity with Him to heaven, and He has been highly honored and glorified in doing so. He prepares a place for His disciples (John 14:2).

His ascension was necessary, He explained, for the coming of the Holy Spirit (John 16:7). On the day of Pentecost, Peter declared, "Being exalted to the right hand of God, and having received from the Father the promise of the Holy Spirit, He poured out this which you now see and hear" (Acts 2:33). Jesus' ascension and the outpouring of the Spirit that followed have made possible the numerous gifts of the Spirit, which the church now enjoys (Eph. 4:8, 11–13).

The earthly life and ministry of Jesus end, therefore, with His ascension into heaven where He now governs the universe to the end that all God's purposes for the church may be carried out. As the church's Head, He rules and protects it, helps its members in need, and gives them power to do God's will. He is the explanation of the church's continuance.

The apostles must have cast their minds back many times to the parables Jesus told them that indicated something of how they were to view His ascension. Just before His triumphal entry, He told the parable of the ten minas—a mina was about three months' wages. It began like this: "A certain nobleman went into a far country to receive for himself a kingdom and to return. So he called ten of his servants, delivered to them ten minas, and said to them, 'Do business till I come'" (Luke 19:12–13).

Our Lord Jesus has gone to "a far country to receive for Himself a kingdom and to return." Meanwhile, until His return, He has given all His servants in every age and generation different responsibilities for His gospel and its proclamation.

Above all, Jesus Christ is the Savior. That is how we must first come to know Him. But once we know Him as Savior, He is also our primary example. As He gave Himself to the work of His Father, so we are to do the same. As the Father sent Him, so He sends us.

Luke begins the Acts of the Apostles with an interesting reference to his earlier work, his gospel: "The former account I made . . . of all that Jesus *began* both to do and teach, until the day in which He was taken up, after He through the Holy Spirit had given commandments to the apostles whom He had chosen" (Acts 1:1–2, emphasis added). The word *began* is significant. What Jesus *began* to do, His church *continues* to do. We are to continue Jesus' work, and for this reason He sent His Spirit.

The next part of God's great and glorious plan is Jesus' return, and to be ready for that we must be faithful stewards of the everlasting gospel He has placed in our hands.

M E D I T A T I O N

1. "Remember that Jesus Christ . . . was raised from the dead" (2 Tim. 2:8).

2. As soon as Jesus said "Mary," she recognized His voice. The good shepherd "calls his own sheep by name. . . . And the sheep follow him, for they know his voice" (John 10:3–4).

3. We are never more likely to find our hearts burning within us with the joy of fellowship with Jesus Christ than when we open the Scriptures and listen to Him.

4. "The disciples were glad when they saw the Lord" (John 20:20). Jesus' word to us is, "He who has My commandments and keeps them, it is he who loves Me. And he who loves Me will be loved by My Father, and I will love him and manifest Myself to him" (John 14:21).

5. Thomas said to Him, "My Lord and my God!" (John 20:28). Peter urges us, "Sanctify the Lord God in your hearts, and always be ready to give a defense to everyone who asks you a reason for the hope that is in you" (1 Pet. 3:15).

6. Again Jesus said, "Simon, son of Jonah, do you love Me?" He answered, "Yes, Lord; You know that I love You." Jesus said, "Tend My sheep" (John 21:16). Love for Jesus shows itself in our care of His people.

7. "We see Jesus, who was made a little lower than the angels, now crowned with glory and honor. . . . Fix your thoughts on Jesus" (Heb. 2:9; 3:1 NIV).

Q U E S T I O N S

1. Imagine the women reporting to the disciples their experience at the empty tomb and then of meeting Jesus. What do you think were the principal truths and evidences they shared?

2. What important lessons did Jesus teach Mary of Magdala when she sought to hold on to Him (John 20:17)?

3. Which passages from "Moses and all the Prophets" can you imagine Jesus referring to in His conversation with the two disciples on the Emmaus Road (Luke 24:27)?

4. How important were the actions and words of Jesus to His disciples on the evening of the Resurrection for their understanding of their new commission (John 20:19–23)?

5. Thomas's confession, "My Lord and my God," is the confession every Christian makes concerning Jesus (cf. Rom. 10:9; 1 Cor. 12:3). How would you explain that confession to someone who asks you what you mean by it?

6. Why was Peter singled out for a special conversation with Jesus, and what lessons may we draw from that conversation concerning all service for God (John 21:15–23)?

7. In the light of Acts 1:11, what does Jesus' ascension teach us about His return?

PART 2

AN A THROUGH Z OF BIBLE WORDS, NAMES, AND PLACES

This "A Through Z" is not intended to be comprehensive, in that the ground for inclusion of any subject is its mention in the preceding chapters concerning Jesus' life and ministry.

— A —

Abraham

Abraham, the son of Terah, brother of Nahor and Haran, uncle of Lot, and husband of Sarah, belonged originally to Ur of the Chaldeans (Gen. 11:26–29; 15:7), where he and his family worshiped heathen gods (Jos. 24:2).

With his wife, Sarah, he set out with his father to go from Ur to Canaan at the call of God (Acts 7:2), but for unknown reasons settled instead initially at Haran (Gen. 11:31).

At the age of seventy-five, he was instructed to leave his country, his people, and his father's household and go to the land God would show him (Gen. 12:1), with the promise that God would make him into a great nation and a blessing to all the peoples of the earth (Gen. 12:2–3; 18:18). Canaan was promised him as his descendants' inheritance (Gen. 13:14–17; Deut. 34:4).

When he and Sarah were old, Abraham was promised a son, and Abraham believed God and God credited it to him as righteousness (Gen. 15:5–6), being justified not by works but by faith (Rom. 4:1–25; Gal. 3:6).

Originally called Abram, his name was changed to Abraham (father of multitudes) because of God's promise to make him a father of many nations (Gen. 17:5; Neh. 9:7). When God called him, he was one, and God blessed him and made him many (Isa. 51:2).

Circumcision was the mark of the covenant God made with Abraham when he was ninety-nine years old (Gen. 17:23–24; Acts 7:8).

Two moral failures are recorded of Abraham, both relating to his instructions to Sarah to pretend to be his sister rather than his wife because of her beauty (Gen. 12:11–13; 20:1–13).

He was the father of Ishmael through Hagar (Gen. 16:1–16).

Abraham was peaceable (Gen. 13:8–9), loyal to his family (Gen. 14:12–16), ungrasping (Gen. 14:21–24), hospitable (Gen. 18:2–8), a faithful intercessor (Gen. 18:23–33), tested and proved faithful (Gen. 22:1–19), obedient (Gen. 12:1, 4; 15:7; 26:5), a man of faith (Heb. 11:8–12, 17–19). And he has the distinction of being known as "the friend of God" (2 Chron. 20:7; Isa. 41:8; James 2:23) and the spiritual father of all who believe and are justified (Rom. 4:12, 16; Gal. 3:9).

After Sarah's death, he married Keturah (Gen. 25:1), and he died at the age of 175 (Gen. 25:7).

Abraham anticipated Jesus' coming with joy (John 8:56).

Jesus, by His human birth, was a descendant of Abraham (Matt. 1:1, 17; Luke 3:34).

Jews tragically fell into the trap of relying on their relationship with Abraham rather than knowing God for themselves through faith as he did (Luke 3:8; John 8:39).

Achaia

Achaia is the smallest region of Greece, lying along the southern shore of the Corinthian Gulf.

The original inhabitants were Ionians who established twelve cities on the coast.

In Roman times, Achaia was the name used to describe practically the entire Roman province of Greece.

"Macedonia and Achaia" in the New Testament usually mean all of Greece (Acts 19:21; Rom. 15:26; 1 Thess. 1:8).

Gallio, mentioned in Acts 18:12, was "proconsul of Achaia."

Stephanas and Fortunatus were the first converts in Achaia (1 Cor. 16:15–17).

The churches of Achaia were commended for their generosity (2 Cor. 9:2, 13).

Adam

Adam—the name probably relates to the ruddiness of man's complexion—was the first man (1 Cor. 15:45; 1 Tim. 2:13). He was made in God's image and given rule over all God's creation (Gen. 1:26–27); he was formed from the dust of the ground, and God breathed into him the breath of life (Gen. 2:7).

Adam was put in the Garden of Eden to work it and to take care of it (Gen. 2:15).

Adam was entrusted with the task of naming the birds of the air and the beasts of the field (Gen. 2:19–20).

Eve was God's gift to be his companion (Gen. 2:20–24), and Adam named her Eve because she would become "the mother of all living" (Gen. 3:20).

He was given freedom to eat from any tree in the Garden of Eden except the tree of the knowledge of good and evil (Gen. 2:16–17), and he enjoyed fellowship with God (Gen. 3:8).

Adam ate from the tree that God had forbidden (Gen. 3:17): he thus broke God's covenant and was unfaithful to Him (Hos. 6:7). Because of his disobedience, Adam was driven out of the Garden of Eden (Gen. 3:24).

As a consequence of Adam's sin, death entered the world and reigned (Rom. 5:14). Identified with Adam in his sin, we, his descendants, die (1 Cor. 15:22).

Adam received the promise of the Savior (Gen. 3:15), so that as by his disobedience we were made sinners, so by the obedience of Jesus Christ, the last Adam, we may be made righteous and receive resurrection life (Rom. 5:19; 1 Cor. 15:45).

Agrippa, Herod. *See* Herod.

Andrew

Andrew, the son of Jonah and the brother of Simon Peter, came originally from Bethsaida, and he had his home in Capernaum (Mark 1:21, 29).

He brought Peter to Jesus (John 1:40–42).

He was one of the Twelve (Mark 3:18).

Tradition suggests that Andrew was crucified in Achaia.

Angels

Angels are created beings, who act as God's messengers (Acts 7:53; Gal. 3:19; Heb. 1:7) and heavenly servants (Heb. 1:14).

Their presence with God expresses His glorious nature (Rev. 5:11).

There are evidences of a fall among the angels, with Satan as their leader (Job 4:18; Matt. 25:41; 2 Pet. 2:4; Rev. 12:9).

The Gospels record the particular activity of angels at the time of Jesus' human birth and ministry (Matt. 1:20, 24; 2:13, 19; 28:2, 5; Mark 1:13; Luke 1:26–38; 2:9–10, 13; 22:43; John 20:12).

Anna

Anna was an older prophetess, the daughter of Phanuel, of the tribe of Asher, who identified the child Jesus as the promised Savior when Mary and Joseph brought Jesus to the temple to present Him to the Lord (Luke 2:36–38).

She was well over one hundred years old, since she had been a widow eighty-four years after a brief married life of seven years (Luke 2:36–37).

Her life was given over to worshiping God by fasting and praying (Luke 2:37).

She looked for spiritual deliverance through God's Messiah, and she bore witness to Jesus as such (Luke 2:38).

Antichrists

Antichrists are opponents or adversaries of the Messiah who appear in the last days.

They are individuals who put forth teaching that fundamentally opposes and denies Christ (1 John 2:18, 22; 4:3).

Such teaching may be deceitful in that it pretends to be true Christian teaching (2 John 7).

Apocalyptic

The term comes from the Greek word *apokalupsis*—found in Revelation 1:1—meaning "uncovering" or "revelation."

Apocalyptic teaching reveals what is going to happen in the future, and particularly at the end of the world.

The New Testament contains a number of apocalyptic passages besides the book of Revelation (Matt. 25:31–46; John 14–16; 1 Cor. 15:25–28; 2 Pet. 3:1–13).

Apostle, Apostolic, Apostleship

The noun *apostle* comes from the verb *to send* and means "a person sent by another." The term can be used simply of messengers "sent" by the churches, but such apostleship is not in the same category as that of the Twelve, and Paul who joined their number later.

They were chosen, called, and sent forth by Christ Himself (John 6:70; 13:18; 15:16, 19; 1 Cor. 15:8–9; Gal. 1:15–17); they were His witnesses, especially of His resurrection (Acts 1:8, 22; 1 Cor. 9:1; 15:8; Gal. 1:12; Eph. 3:2–8; 1 John 1:1–3).

They knew in a special way the help of the Holy Spirit, who led them into all truth (Matt. 10:19–20; John 14:26; 15:26; 16:7–15; 20:22; 1 Cor. 2:10–13; 7:40; 1 Thess. 4:8).

God confirmed the value of their work by signs and miracles (Matt. 10:1, 8; Acts 2:43; 3:2–10; 5:12–16; Rom. 15:18–19; 2 Cor. 12:12; Gal. 2:8).

Aramaic

Technically the language of the Arameans, Aramaic is a Semitic language, with various dialects, closely related to Hebrew.

Although the Arameans had a long history, going back as far as the Hebrew patriarchs in Genesis, they never developed an empire.

Aramaic became an important trade language as well as a vernacular for ancient diplomacy, and the Jews translated their Scriptures into Aramaic.

It seems certain that Jesus spoke it, and some of His words in Aramaic are found in the Gospels (Matt. 27:46; Mark 5:41; 15:34).

Paul addressed his fellow Jews in Aramaic (Acts 21:40; 22:2), and he related how the Lord Jesus spoke to him on the Damascus road in that language (Acts 26:14; cf. Rom. 8:15; Gal. 4:6).

Arimathea

The exact location of Arimathea is not known.

It was a Judean town (Luke 23:51), and the home of Joseph, a prominent member of the Jewish council, who buried Jesus in his own tomb (Mark 15:43; John 19:38).

It is thought to be identified with Ramathaim Zophim, Samuel's birthplace, some twenty miles northwest of Jerusalem.

Ascension

The Ascension was a vital link in a chain of fulfilled prophecy, promised in the Old Testament (Ps. 110:1; Acts 2:32–36) and by Christ Himself (Matt. 26:64; John 6:62; 7:33; 14:28; 16:5; 20:17).

It took place forty days after the Resurrection (Acts 1:3)

at the Mount of Olives (Luke 24:50–51; cf. Acts 1:12). The apostles witnessed it after He had talked with them (Mark 16:19) and lifted up His hands to bless them (Luke 24:50).

It was an act of God's power (Eph. 1:19–23) and the necessary completion of Christ's death and resurrection. It proved the full acceptance by God of His single sacrifice for sins for all time (Heb. 10:12) and identified Christ as Lord, even as the Resurrection marked Him out as the Son of God (Phil. 2:9–11; cf. Acts 2:34–36; Rom. 1:4).

It indicated Christ's return to the Father who had sent Him into the world (John 6:62; 7:33; 14:28; 16:5; 20:17) and a further glorification of His human nature. He carried His humanity with Him back to heaven (Heb. 2:14–18; 4:14–16), and He was highly exalted and glorified in doing so (Acts 2:33; John 7:39; 1 Tim. 3:16), the Father honoring Him with the highest possible honor (Eph. 1:19–23).

Christ ascended to receive, as conqueror, the gifts promised Him for His church (Eph. 4:8; Ps. 68:18). He ascended to send forth the Holy Spirit (John 7:39; 16:7; Acts 2:33) with His special gifts to His people (Eph. 4:7–13).

In Christ's ascension, Christians have the assurance of a place in heaven (John 14:2, 19; 2 Cor. 4:14) and of their own future glorification (Phil. 3:20–21).

His ascension in power is the prelude to His coming in power as the divine Judge (Dan. 7:13–14; Matt. 26:64; John 14:28; Acts 10:42; 2 Thess. 1:6–10).

Atonement, Atoning Sacrifice (Propitiation)

Atonement is compensation or satisfaction of our penal debt to God by the actual punishment of our Substitute. Behind atonement is the truth of God's holy and righteous reaction to sin in wrath, displeasure, and vengeance. The purpose of propitiation—or an atoning sacrifice—is the removal of God's displeasure.

The need for atonement was taught by the Old Testament provision of sacrifices (Exod. 30:10, 16; 32:30; Lev. 1:4; 4:20, 26, 31) and the teaching that the shedding of blood was necessary for atonement to be achieved for sin (Lev. 17:11).

By His death upon the cross in our place, Jesus Christ made an atoning sacrifice for our sins (1 John 2:2). He propitiated the wrath of God and made God well disposed to His people—and this He did at the Father's initiative and as the provision of the Father's love for sinners (Rom. 3:25; 1 John 4:8–10).

The wonder of the Atonement is that God satisfied His own justice and wrath by substituting Himself in Jesus Christ for us (Acts 20:28; 2 Cor. 5:19, 21).

— B —

Baptism

The verb from which the noun *baptism* comes means "to dip, immerse, plunge, or overwhelm," and Jesus used it to describe the overwhelming experience of His death as the substitute for sinners (Mark 10:38).

Baptisms—or ritual washings—were practiced by the Jews in rites of initiation for those who abandoned paganism for Judaism.

John the Baptist's baptism symbolized cleansing through forgiveness, together with a commitment to righteousness (Matt. 3:2, 6; Mark 1:4).

Christ Himself was baptized, setting an example to all who would follow Him (Matt. 3:13–17; Mark 1:9–11; Luke 3:21–22).

Baptism is part of the Great Commission, given to the apostles after the Resurrection, to be the first subject in which believers are to be instructed of all that Christ commanded (Matt. 28:19–20; Mark 16:15–16).

It is administered in the name of the Trinity (Matt. 28:19).

It is a symbol of an individual's reception of the gospel

(Acts 16:14–15), of repentance (Acts 2:38), and faith in Jesus Christ (Acts 8:12–13, 37; 16:31–33).

It is a confession of Jesus' lordship (Acts 2:38; 8:37).

It symbolizes admittance into the family of God (Acts 9:18; 22:16; 1 Cor. 1:13–17) and the body of Christ (1 Cor. 12:13).

It expresses the union believers have with Christ in His death and resurrection, and all the benefits that flow from it (Acts 2:38; 22:16; Rom. 6:3–4; Col. 2:12; Heb. 10:22).

Barabbas

Barabbas was a notorious insurrectionist who, with others, had committed murder immediately prior to Jesus' crucifixion (Matt. 27:16; Mark 15:7; Luke 23:18; John 18:40).

Through the intrigue and conspiracy of the Jewish authorities, he, rather than Jesus, was released when Pilate offered to set free a prisoner, as was his custom, at the Feast of Passover (Matt. 27:15; Mark 15:6).

Bartholomew

Bartholomew is someone about whom little is known unless he is to be identified with Nathanael, but that cannot be proved. *See* Nathanael.

Bartimaeus

Bartimaeus (meaning "son of Timaeus"), a blind man, lived in Jericho (Mark 10:46).

On Jesus' last journey to Jerusalem, he recognized Jesus to be the Son of David, the Messiah. Refusing to be put off, he called out to Jesus for mercy and received his sight as the reward of his persistent faith (Mark 10:47–52).

Believe

Believe is the verb from which we obtain the noun *faith* expressing confidence in God.

It describes awareness of God's existence (Heb. 11:6), assurance as to His trustworthiness, active confidence in His help, and self-commital to His care (John 3:16; Acts 16:31, 34; 27:25; Rom. 10:9–10).

Believer

Believer is the most common description of Christians in the New Testament, and especially in the Acts of the Apostles (Acts 1:15; 2:44; 4:32; 5:12 NIV).

It is the name given to those who believe and trust in the Lord Jesus Christ as the only Savior and Lord, and who find themselves added to Him and to His church (Acts 2:38, 41, 44, 47; 5:14).

An essential characteristic of Christians is their clear and unreserved faith in the Lord Jesus Christ, the Son of God, and His finished work on their behalf (2 Tim. 1:12).

The Christian church is a family of believers (Gal. 6:10; 1 Pet. 2:17).

Bethany

Bethany, a village on the Mount of Olives, was nearly two miles from Jerusalem.

It was the last stopping place for pilgrims on the road from Jericho to Jerusalem.

The home of Simon the leper (Matt. 26:6; Mark 14:3), Mary, Martha, and Lazarus (John 11:1, 18; 12:1), it was also the area where the Ascension took place (Luke 24:50).

Bethlehem

Bethlehem means in the Hebrew "house of bread," and it was called Bethlehem Judah or Ephrathah to distinguish it from another town of the same name.

It is five miles southwest of Jerusalem on the main road to Hebron and Egypt.

The home of Boaz and Ruth (Ruth 2:4; 4:11), it was known later as "the city of David" since it was David's home (1 Sam. 16:1, 4, 18).

It was the promised birthplace of the Messiah (Mic. 5:2; Matt. 2:1–6; Luke 2:1–7).

Beth Nimrah

Beth—in Hebrew place-names—means "home" or "tent." *Beth Nimrah* is, therefore, "house of Nimrah."

It was a fortified city in the plain of Moab built by the Gadites (Num. 32:36; Josh. 13:27).

Bethsaida

Bethsaida means in Aramaic "house of fishing."

Not far from Capernaum, it was on the northern shores of the Sea of Galilee close to the Jordan.

It was the home of at least three of Jesus' disciples—Philip, Andrew, and Peter (John 1:44; 12:21).

Blasphemy

Blasphemy is an open insult to God's majesty.

At first, specific words of reviling and defamation were thought of as offending in this way (Lev. 24:16; Mark 2:7), but it came to be appreciated that words encroaching upon God's sole rights are also blasphemous. That explains the false charge the religious authorities made concerning Jesus when He spoke of His sitting at the right hand of the Mighty One (Mark 14:64).

Never a mark of the Holy Spirit's influence (1 Cor. 12:3), blasphemy characterizes the devil and his agents (Rev. 13:1, 5–6).

Blood of Christ

Blood is the symbol of life, and for this reason blood makes atonement (Lev. 17:11). Shed blood stands for bringing an end to a life in the flesh.

The principle God laid down from the beginning was that "without shedding of blood there is no remission" (Heb. 9:22).

"The blood of Christ" is a phrase often used in the New Testament to express the truth of Christ's death as a sacrifice for sins.

It is a particularly apt way of describing His death in view of the ceremonial offerings of the Old Testament, which prepared the way for it by their symbolism (Heb. 10:1–18). They were the shadows of which Jesus' sacrifice was the reality.

Drinking Christ's blood signifies appropriating the benefits of His life laid down for us (John 6:54).

His blood purges believers' consciences of moral guilt and provides redemption (1 Pet. 1:18–19), forgiveness and cleansing (Eph. 1:7; Heb. 9:13–14; 1 John 1:7), justification (Rom. 5:9), peace (Col. 1:20), and sanctification (Heb. 13:12).

— C —

Caesar

Caesar, a Latin word, was originally a Roman family name, the most famous of which was Julius Caesar, who became dictator with supreme power. It then became a title given to Roman emperors (Matt. 22:17, 21; Mark 12:14, 17). It is placed either before or after an emperor's name—for example, Caesar Augustus (Luke 2:1) and Tiberius Caesar (Luke 3:1).

Caesarea

Caesarea is to be distinguished from Caesarea Philippi. *See* Caesarea Philippi.

Caesarea was located south of Mount Carmel, on the Mediterranean coast, about sixty-five miles northwest of Jerusalem. It was built as a city and port (Acts 9:30; 18:22) between 25 and 13 B.C. by Herod the Great on the site of the great Tower of Strato, and named in honor of Caesar Augustus.

The ministry of Philip the evangelist, one of the Seven, extended as far as Caesarea (Acts 8:40), his home city, where a church was established (Acts 18:22; 21:16) and where he lived with his family (Acts 21:8).

Roman military headquarters were located at Caesarea (Acts 23:33), and Cornelius, the Roman centurion, was stationed there (Acts 10:1).

It was a seat of government for the Roman governors or procurators (Acts 23:33; 24:1), and the official residence of the Herodian kings (Acts 12:19).

Paul was held prisoner at Caesarea for two years (Acts 23:31—26:32).

Caesarea Philippi

On the northern boundary of Palestine, at the foot of the southern slopes of Mount Hermon, and at the main source of the Jordan, Caesarea Philippi once had the name of Paneas (because of the worship of the heathen god Pan there), and its present name is Banias (since there is no *p* in the Arabic language).

Given to Herod the Great by Augustus Caesar, it was rebuilt by Philip the tetrarch and named by him Caesarea Philippi to distinguish it from coastal Caesarea.

Caiaphas

Caiaphas was high priest from approximately A.D. 18 to 36, and Annas, a previous high priest, was his father-in-law (John 18:13).

Without realizing the full import of what he said, Caiaphas "prophesied that Jesus would die for the [Jewish] nation" (John 11:51).

He was high priest at the time of Jesus' betrayal and arrest (Matt. 26:3, 57).

Calvary. *See* Golgotha.

Cana

Cana, a village in Galilee, the exact location of which cannot be clearly established, was where Jesus' first recorded miraculous sign took place—the turning of water into wine—in which He revealed His glory, causing His disciples to believe in Him (John 2:1–11).

Cana was also the place where a royal official from Capernaum begged Jesus to heal his son, and Jesus healed him without leaving Cana to do so (John 4:46–54).

Nathanael, one of the apostles, came from Cana (John 21:2).

Capernaum

Capernaum was an important city on the northwest shore of the Sea of Galilee, with at least one centurion and a detachment of troops stationed there (Matt. 8:5–13) and a customs post (Matt. 9:9). Uncertainty exists as to its exact location, but the ruins at Tell Hum—two and a half miles southwest of the mouth of the Jordan—are the best-supported site.

Jesus made it His headquarters during His Galilean ministry (Matt. 4:13; Mark 2:1; Luke 7:1–10; 10:15).

Carthage, Carthaginians

Carthage was a great ancient city on the north coast of Africa, about twelve miles from modern Tunis.

It was originally a Phoenician settlement, important for trade, and had often been in conflict with Rome for control of the western Mediterranean.

Chief Priests

The plural is used in the New Testament to describe members of the Sanhedrin (*see* Sanhedrin) who belonged to high-priestly families and who themselves held priestly office. *See* Priesthood.

Christ

Christ is a Greek word meaning "Anointed One"—the explanation of the title "Messiah."

Anointing was a symbol of someone being set apart for a special task by God.

The Jews looked for the coming of a Great One, called the Messiah, who would accomplish God's purposes for His people.

Jesus' ministry clearly identified Him as the Messiah (Matt. 11:2–6; Luke 4:17–19), but He discouraged the public use of the title for the first and major part of His ministry because the Jews thought mainly of the Messiah as a political deliverer and Jesus had not come as such (Matt. 16:16–17; Mark 14:61–62; John 4:25–26; cf. Matt. 1:18; 2:4; Luke 2:11, 26).

Christian, Christians

Christians are people associated and united with Christ— Christ's men and women.

Believers were first called Christians in Antioch (Acts 11:26). It was initially a nickname.

To believe and obey the apostolic gospel is to become a Christian (Acts 26:28).

Although being known and recognized as a Christian may be a cause of persecution, the Christian is to rejoice at the privilege of bearing the name (1 Pet. 4:16).

Church

The word *church* is used in two principal ways. It refers first to the whole company of people redeemed through Christ (Matt. 16:18; Acts 20:28; Eph. 5:23–32).

It is used second of a company of professing Christians in a particular area or district (Matt. 18:17; 1 Cor. 1:2; 10:32; 11:16, 22; 15:9; 2 Cor. 1:1; Gal. 1:13; 1 Thess. 2:14; 2 Thess. 1:4; 1 Tim. 3:5, 15).

Circumcision

Circumcision, which means "a cutting around," was the sign of God's covenant with Abraham—an indication that he and his descendants were the people of promise (Gen. 17:11; Acts 7:8).

It did not originate with Moses, therefore, but it was through Moses that it was laid down as obligatory for the Jewish people (John 7:22).

It took place seven days after the birth of a male child—that is, the eighth day (Luke 1:59; 2:21; Acts 7:8).

It was intended to be an outward sign of dedication and love for God (Deut. 30:6) and a commitment of obedience to Him (Jer. 4:4; 9:25), so that true circumcision is of the heart and not of the flesh (Deut. 10:16; Rom. 2:28–29; Phil. 3:3).

Circumcision became a matter of controversy in the early church because the first Christians—who were Jews—required gentile believers to be circumcised (Acts 15:1). But the issue was resolved by the Council at Jerusalem (Acts 15:1–21), where it was determined that it should not be obligatory for Gentiles. However, there remained those of "the circumcision party," or Judaizers, who still hankered after such a requirement (Gal. 2:12; Titus 1:10).

The New Testament stresses that in Christ neither circumcision nor uncircumcision has any value. The only thing that matters is a right relationship with God through new birth and its fruits (Gal. 5:6; 6:15; cf. 1 Cor. 7:19; Col. 2:11).

Coming of Christ

It is appropriate to call Jesus Christ's return His second coming (Heb. 9:28).

The three words used to describe His coming indicate something of its character. First, it will be His *parousia*, the time of His presence or arrival (Matt. 24:3, 27; 1 Cor. 15:23; 1 Thess. 3:13).

Second, it will be His *apokalupsis*, an unveiling or revelation of His power and glory (1 Cor. 1:7; 2 Thess. 1:7; 1 Pet. 1:7, 13).

Third, it will be His *epiphaneia* (from which we get our English word *epiphany*), His appearing, a visible event (1 Tim. 6:14; 2 Tim. 4:1, 8; Titus 2:13), which all will see (Rev. 1:7).

His coming will be the gathering together of His people to be with Him (2 Thess. 2:1).

Christians are always to remember that the day of the Lord's coming is near (Phil. 4:5; James 5:8; Rev. 3:11; 22:7, 12, 20), and they are to wait for it with expectancy (1 Thess. 1:10), remembering its surprise element (Matt. 24:37; Mark 13:26; Rev. 16:15).

His coming will be the signal for the resurrection of the dead (1 Cor. 15:23). *See* Resurrection.

Conversion

Conversion is turning to God from sin with sincerity (Acts 14:15; 15:8; 1 Thess. 1:9).

It is possible because God sent His Son into the world so that sinners might be converted from their wickedness (Luke 24:46–47; Acts 3:26; 5:31).

Its negative aspect is repentance (Acts 3:19; 26:20; 1 Thess. 1:9), and its positive aspect is faith in Jesus Christ (Acts 11:21; Gal. 1:15–16; 1 Pet. 2:25).

It is a necessity for entry into the kingdom of heaven (Matt. 18:3), and it marks the beginning of the Christian life in a person's experience (2 Cor. 5:17).

The initiative in conversion is God's (John 6:44; Acts 11:18; 21:19; Phil. 1:6; 2 Tim. 2:25).

At the same time conversion is commanded by God: men and women are to be urged to repent and turn to God so that their sins may be wiped out (Acts 3:19).

Cornelius

Cornelius was a centurion in the Roman army, in what was known as the Italian Regiment, stationed at Caesarea. He was a God fearer, that is, a convert to the Jewish faith who had not gone so far as to be circumcised (Acts 10:1–2).

He was brought into contact with Peter by a remarkable vision of an angel of God (Acts 10:3–6).

His conversion—together with that of his family and household—marked the beginning of God's work among

Gentiles, and a gentile "Pentecost," in effect, took place (Acts 10:44–48).

Cornelius's conversion changed the direction of the whole missionary outreach of the early church (Acts 11:1–18; see also Acts 15).

Council. *See* Sanhedrin.

Covenant

A covenant is a compact or contract. When used with regard to God, it has the idea of a one-sided arrangement made by a superior party.

In the covenant with Adam, for example, God placed him on probation, promising life if he were obedient (Gen. 2:17).

The word is used particularly, however, of obligations God imposes on Himself for the reconciliation of sinful men and women to Himself (Gen. 17:7; Deut. 7:6–9; Ps. 89:3–4; Heb. 13:20).

Cross

The cross was an upright stake or beam used in punishing and executing criminals, particularly by the Romans.

The word describes the painful form of death Jesus endured, but it is more often used as a one-word summary of the good news of salvation, that Jesus died for our sins.

"The message of the cross" is "the preaching of the gospel" (1 Cor. 1:17–18).

Crucified, Crucifixion

Cicero described crucifixion as "the most cruel and revolting punishment."

Josephus called it "the most pitiable of deaths."

Originally inflicted by the Romans only on slaves, rebellious subjects in Roman provinces were later executed by this means.

The gruesome sight of the writhing and screaming victims was thought to be a powerful deterrent to crimes.

It was not a punishment permitted by Jewish law, but Judea under the Romans seems to have witnessed many crucifixions.

First, the hands were nailed to the main crossbar while the sufferer lay on the ground. Then the crossbar was drawn up by ropes and fixed to an upright stake. There was no footrest but a kind of seat that supported the weight of the body to prevent it tearing free the hands.

Death was usually drawn out, rarely occurring before thirty-six hours. The pain was intense, and after a while, the arteries of the hands and stomach were surcharged with blood, causing a throbbing headache. Eventually, traumatic fever and tetanus set in.

Curtain

The curtain referred to most often in the Bible is the one that separated the Most Holy Place from the Holy Place (Exod. 26:33; Heb. 9:3). It was made "of blue, purple, and scarlet thread, and fine woven linen. It shall be woven with an artistic design of cherubim" (Exod. 26:31).

It shielded the ark of the testimony from view (Exod. 35:12; 40:3).

A barrier symbolizing human separation from God because of sin, it was torn in two at the death of Jesus (Matt. 27:51; Mark 15:38; Luke 23:45), declaring that the way is now opened for sinners into God's presence (Heb. 10:20). *See* Most Holy Place.

Cyrene

Cyrene was the capital city of the North African district of Cyrenaica (modern Libya).

It was an old Greek colony, and many Jews settled there.

From 67 B.C., Cyrenaica was combined with Crete as a senatorial province and ruled by a Roman consul.

— D —

Daniel

When God delivered Jehoiakim, king of Judah, into the hands of Nebuchadnezzar, Daniel (whose name means "God is my judge"), a Jewish exile, was one of the young men from the royal family and nobility chosen to be trained for the king's service (Dan. 1:1–4; 5:13).

He was given a new Babylonian name—Belteshazzar—which he chose not to use because of its pagan connections (Dan. 1:7; cf. 4:8).

From the beginning Daniel held fast to his commitment to God and refused to defile himself with the royal wine and food (Dan. 1:8).

He came to public attention through his God-given ability to interpret King Nebuchadnezzar's dream (Dan. 2:16–49). Then as a result of his interpreting the significance of the writing on the wall during Belshazzar's feast, he was made the third highest ruler in the kingdom (Dan. 5:29).

Under Darius, Daniel continued as one of the three principal administrators of the kingdom, and he so distinguished himself that the king planned to set him over the whole kingdom (Dan. 6:1–4), an intention that provoked jealousy and intrigue, which ultimately turned out to Daniel's advantage (Dan. 6:5–28).

The prophetic parts of the book bearing his name relate the dreams and visions that he had and wrote down in the reigns of Belshazzar (7:1; 8:1), Darius (9:1), and Cyrus (10:1). What he foresaw disturbed and exhausted him (7:15; 8:27).

God gave Daniel remarkable insight (Dan. 9:22), as he set his mind to gain understanding and to humble himself before God (Dan. 10:12).

Daniel anticipated the coming of the Messiah, the Son of man (Dan. 7:13–14).

Daniel is spoken of elsewhere in the Old Testament because

of his righteousness—in common with Noah and Job (Ezek. 14:14, 20)—and his wisdom (Ezek. 28:3).

David

David was the youngest of the eight sons of Jesse (Ruth 4:17, 22; 1 Sam. 17:14) and from his youth was a shepherd (1 Sam. 16:19; 17:15).

Samuel anointed him as the second king of Israel—to replace Saul—and God's Spirit rested on him (1 Sam. 16:13).

David first came into the public eye with his defeat of Goliath (1 Sam. 17:12–51).

Throughout his life, he displayed great confidence in God (1 Sam. 17:37, 45–47; cf. Ps. 27:1).

David's successes in battle provoked Saul's jealousy and fear (1 Sam. 18:5–15), with the consequence that Saul hounded him (1 Sam. 26:2; 27:1–2).

Nevertheless, he had a special friendship with Jonathan, son of Saul (1 Sam. 18:1, 3; 20:1–42; 23:16).

God took David from looking after sheep to be ruler over His people Israel (1 Chron. 17:7). David was thirty when he became king, and he reigned for forty years (2 Sam. 5:4). He shepherded God's people with integrity and skill (Ps. 78:72).

He reigned over Judah in Hebron for seven and a half years (2 Sam. 5:5).

Having conquered Jerusalem, David made it his capital. He called it "the City of David," built his palace there (2 Sam. 5:6–7, 9, 11), and reigned in Jerusalem over all Israel and Judah for thirty-three years (2 Sam. 5:5).

Jerusalem continued to be known as the City of David (Luke 2:4, 11).

It was in David's heart to build a temple for God in Jerusalem, but that privilege was denied him because he had shed much blood and fought many wars (1 Chron. 22:8). The opportunity was promised to his son Solomon (1 Kings 5:5).

David was marked by integrity of heart, uprightness (1 Kings 9:4), and obedience to God (1 Kings 11:38; 15:5), apart from his tragic lapse with regard to Bathsheba (2 Sam. 11:1–27). He expresses his repentance in Psalm 51.

He was kind (2 Sam. 9:1–13), possessor of a tender conscience (1 Sam. 24:5; 26:9–11) and a keen sense of justice (1 Sam. 30:23–25).

David has the distinction of being called a man after God's own heart, willing to do all God wanted of him (Acts 13:22).

Seventy-three of the psalms are attributed to David (e.g., Pss. 23; 103; 110; see Ps. 72:20; 2 Sam. 23:1), and he had a musical gift (1 Sam. 16:23; 19:9).

David anticipated the coming of the Messiah (Ps. 110:1; Matt. 22:43–45; Luke 20:42–44; John 7:42; Acts 2:24–35).

Born into the family of Mary and Joseph (Matt. 1:20; Luke 1:27), Jesus was a descendant of David (Rom. 1:3; 2 Tim. 2:8; Rev. 22:16).

Jesus quoted from David's experiences (Matt. 12:3; 22:43; Mark 2:25; 12:36; Luke 6:3), and "Son of David" was a messianic title given to Him (Matt. 9:27; 12:23; 20:30–31; 21:9, 15; Mark 10:47–48; 11:10; Luke 18:38–39).

Dead Sea

The Dead Sea is the large salt lake between Jordan and Israel at the mouth of the river Jordan. Receiving the Jordan at its north end, it is 51 miles long and 11 miles wide at its greatest breadth. At 1,312 feet below sea level, it is the lowest point on the earth's surface. Its highest level is in early summer when the Jordan receives the melting snow of Mount Hermon.

Seawater contains about 3.5 percent salt, while the Dead Sea contains 24.5 percent, so that only the lowest form of animal life exists in its salt and acrid waters.

In the Old Testament the Dead Sea is called the Salt Sea (Gen. 14:3; Num. 34:3; Deut. 3:17; Josh. 3:16), the Sea of the Arabah (Deut. 3:17; 4:49; Josh. 3:16; 12:3), and the Eastern Sea (Ezek. 47:18; Joel 2:20).

The name Dead Sea was probably given to it after biblical times.

Dead Sea Scrolls

The Dead Sea Scrolls, found beginning in 1947, are the remains of a library of a community (probably a branch of the Essenes) that took refuge in the Qumran caves, located near the northwest corner of the Dead Sea, eight miles south of Jericho, during the persecution of Antiochus Epiphanes (175–163 B.C.).

Prior to their discovery, the oldest Hebrew texts in existence were no earlier than the ninth century A.D. They preserved a text edited into an established structure in the fifth century A.D.

The Scrolls constitute one of the greatest manuscript discoveries of all time. They contain the remains of copies of the Old Testament canonical Scriptures with the exception of Esther, plus books of the Apocrypha and other documents relating to the Essenes, the Qumran sect, which go back to the first and second (and possibly even third) century B.C.

Death

The sin of humankind brought the penalty of death (Gen. 2:17; 3:19), and death has spread to us all because we have all sinned (Rom. 5:12; 1 Cor. 15:21–22); death is a punishment for each individual's sin (Ezek. 18:4, 20; Rom. 6:23; James 1:15).

Death reigns (Rom. 5:14, 17). Its power enslaves us throughout life (Heb. 2:15), and we live in its shadow (Isa. 9:2; Matt. 4:16; Luke 1:79).

Guilty of trespasses and sins, we are already under the power of death (Eph. 2:1–2; Col. 2:13; 1 Tim. 5:6); in fact, we live in a state of spiritual death because we are cut off from God (Rom. 7:24; cf. Luke 15:24).

The Bible emphasizes death's finality (2 Sam. 14:14; Ps. 6:5) and our inability to escape it (Ps. 89:48). God alone can provide the answer (Ps. 68:20).

Jesus Christ shared in our humanity that by His death He might destroy him who holds the power of death—that is, the devil (Heb. 2:14).

Jesus Christ died the death we deserve (Phil. 2:7–8; Heb. 2:14), and He died for us (Mark 10:45; Rom. 5:6–8; 1 Thess. 5:10; Heb. 2:9–10).

To believe in Jesus Christ is to pass from death to life (John 5:24), to be ransomed from the power of the grave, and to be redeemed from death (Hos. 13:14; 1 Cor. 15:54–57).

The last enemy to be destroyed is death (1 Cor. 15:26): it has no place in the New Jerusalem, the life to come (Rev. 21:4).

Deity

Deity indicates divine character or nature, all that expresses God's nature as the Supreme Being (John 1:1; Rom. 11:36), who is Head over every power and authority (Col. 2:10).

Deity is the character that sets God apart as alone worthy of worship.

The wonder of Jesus Christ's incarnation is that God appeared in a body (Matt. 1:23; 1 Tim. 3:16) and that "in Him dwells all the fullness of the Godhead bodily" (Col. 2:9; cf. John 14:9).

The basic Christian confession is that Jesus Christ is Lord—that is to say, God (John 20:28; 1 Cor. 12:3; Phil. 2:11).

Demons

Demon possession seems to have been particularly rife at the time of Jesus' ministry, perhaps because of the imminent danger in which the kingdom of evil found itself.

Demons invariably recognized Jesus as the Son of God, and for that reason He forbade them to speak (Mark 1:34).

Distinction is made in the Gospels between ordinary illness, disease, insanity, and demon possession (Matt. 4:23–24; 9:32–35; 10:8).

Jesus regularly drove demons out of people (Mark 1:34, 39; 5:12, 15; Luke 8:30, 32, 35, 38; 13:11–12), and Mary Magdalene was one out of whom He had driven seven demons (Mark 16:9; Luke 8:2).

Beelzebub was regarded as the prince of demons (Mark 3:22). Jesus was accused by the teachers of the law of being possessed by him and driving out demons by his power (Mark 3:22).

The apostles were given authority to drive out demons (Matt. 10:8; Mark 3:15; 6:13; Luke 9:1; 10:17).

The driving out of demons was a sign that the kingdom of God was operative (Luke 11:20), and it was one of the many signs that accompanied the early believers (Mark 16:17).

Devil. *See* Satan.

Disciple, Discipleship

Disciple was something of a technical term used of anyone who attached himself to a teacher. A disciple is someone under instruction, and besides being used of Jesus' disciples, it was the term applied in the Gospels to people who followed the teaching of John the Baptist or the Pharisees.

Jesus chose the Twelve, to bring them under His instruction, so that later they would be able to convey His teaching to others (Matt. 28:19–20; cf. 2 Tim. 2:2).

But many more besides the Twelve were disciples (Luke 10:1–17), and the term is given generally to all professing Christians (Acts 11:26).

Jesus requires faithfulness and obedience to what He says as the major condition of discipleship (John 8:31).

Divorce

Divorce, according to the Hebrew words used in the Old Testament, means "a cutting off" (Deut. 24:1) or "a sending away" (Mal. 2:16).

Jesus taught that it is not our prerogative to break the marriage covenant in that the union it represents is an act of our Creator (Matt. 19:3–8).

The one ground Jesus gave for permissible divorce was unlawful sexual intercourse (i.e., adultery), which so damages the marriage covenant that it leaves the injured partner free to divorce and remarry if he or she so chooses (Matt. 19:9).

First Corinthians 7 seems to teach that if married people become Christians and their partners choose to leave them, divorce is then allowable. But the implication throughout is that, where possible, Christians should not want divorce, even if it is permissible.

— E —

Easter

Easter is not a Bible word, although it occurs once in the Authorized or King James Version (Acts 12:4) where the Greek is the word for "the Passover." It is a natural enough substitution, since Jesus' death and resurrection took place at the time of the Passover.

In common usage Easter describes the period when Christians celebrate the resurrection of Jesus Christ on a variable Sunday in March or April, that is, the first Sunday after the calendar moon.

Egypt

Egypt is in the northeastern part of Africa, and its borders have varied at different periods of history. It was renowned for its wisdom (1 Kings 4:30).

Egypt appears frequently in the biblical narrative because of its close proximity to Israel (1 Kings 4:21; 8:65), and trade links existed (1 Kings 10:28–29).

Egypt was a place of refuge in time of famine. Abraham went there (Gen. 12:10–20), as did Jacob and his family through the prominent position given Joseph, even though he had gone to Egypt originally as a slave (Gen. 37:28, 36; Acts 7:9; Gen. 46:8–27). Jacob's descendants lived in Egypt subsequently for 430 years (Exod. 12:40–41).

Moses, one of those descendants, was educated in Egypt and prepared for leadership by what he learned there (Acts 7:22; Heb. 11:24–26).

The first Passover took place in Egypt, when God passed over the Israelites' houses as blood of the Passover lambs was placed on the sides and tops of the doorframes of their houses, saving them from the destructive plague that fell upon the Egyptians (Exod. 12:13, 17, 27, 29).

The hard experiences the Israelites knew as aliens in Egypt were to be a constant reminder of their need to be sympathetic and kind to aliens in general (Exod. 22:21; 23:9; Lev. 19:34).

Egypt was also a place of refuge in time of danger (1 Kings 11:17–22, 40; 2 Kings 25:26). In Jeremiah's day some foolishly thought that they could escape God's judgment on Judah by fleeing to Egypt to settle there (Jer. 42:14–22; 44:12–14).

Throughout her history, Israel was subject to war and attacks from Egypt (1 Kings 14:25; 2 Kings 23:29; 2 Chron. 12:2–4).

In their folly the Israelites sometimes looked to Egypt's help against their enemies rather than to God's (Isa. 30:2, 7; 31:1; 36:6, 9).

Egypt had its place in the life of Jesus in that Joseph was warned in a dream to flee with Mary and the child Jesus to Egypt (Matt. 2:13–15, 19).

Jews from Egypt were present in Jerusalem on the day of Pentecost (Acts 2:10).

Elders

"Elder" is a time-honored title given to older men in a community.

Each town or city among the Jews had its elders in the Old Testament period (1 Sam. 16:4; Ezra 10:14).

After the return from Exile, the Sanhedrin, the governing council of the Jews, was made up of the elders.

In the New Testament, elders were the spiritual leaders of the early Christian churches and were appointed once churches were established (Acts 11:30).

Their precise functions are not clear, although pastoral care and rule fell to them as their particular responsibilities, and some had the additional task of teaching and preaching the Word of God (1 Tim. 5:17).

The qualifications for elders and overseers (or bishops) are more or less identical (Titus 1:6–9; 1 Tim. 3:1–7), and it is generally agreed that the two titles are interchangeable, referring to the same spiritual office.

Elect, Election

The elect are people God has chosen for Himself from humankind and drawn to Himself. In the Old Testament, the term is used of Israel (1 Chron. 16:13; Isa. 65:9, 15), and in the New Testament of Christians (Mark 13:22, 27; 2 Tim. 2:10).

Election is God's eternal, unconditional choice of guilty sinners to be redeemed and born again of His Spirit so that they may be brought finally to His everlasting glory (Rom. 8:30; Eph. 1:3–12; 1 Pet. 1:2).

Believers' experience of salvation, sanctification, and glory all flow from God's election (2 Thess. 2:13–14), which has no regard at all to any works or merit on their part (Rom. 11:6; 2 Tim. 1:9).

Elijah

Elijah was a Tishbite from Tishbe in Gilead, who exercised his principal prophetic ministry during the reign of Ahab and delivered God's judgments to Ahab as God's word came to him (1 Kings 17:1–2; 18:1–2, 15, 17–20; 21:17–29). His ministry continued during the reigns of Ahaziah (2 Kings 1:2–17) and Jehoram (2 Chron. 21:12–15), sons of Ahab.

His dress was distinctive: he wore a garment of hair, with a leather belt around his waist (2 Kings 1:8).

A number of amazing providences and miracles accompanied his ministry: he was fed by ravens at Cherith (1 Kings 17:4–6); the widow's jar of flour and jug of oil did not fail in a time of famine, and Elijah raised her son to life (1 Kings 17:8–24); he divided the waters of the Jordan with his cloak (2 Kings 2:8).

Elijah issued a dramatic challenge to Israel on Carmel, "How long will you falter between two opinions? If the LORD is God, follow Him; but if Baal, follow him" (1 Kings 18:21). God answered Elijah's prayer on Carmel by fire falling upon his water-soaked offering (1 Kings 18:24, 33, 36–38).

His sharing of our humanity (James 5:17) was seen in his fears, pessimism, and depression (1 Kings 19:3–18).

Nevertheless, he stood out as a powerful servant of God (1 Kings 18:15, 46), although accused by Ahab of being the "troubler of Israel" (1 Kings 18:17). He demonstrated the place God gives to earnest believing prayer (1 Kings 18:36–37, 42–45): he prayed earnestly that it would not rain, and it did not rain on the land for three and a half years (James 5:17).

At God's command, he called Elisha to succeed him as God's prophet (1 Kings 19:16, 19–21), and he was taken up into heaven in a whirlwind as a chariot of fire and horses of fire appeared (2 Kings 2:1, 11).

God's promise through Malachi was that before the Day of the Lord, the prophet Elijah would be sent (Mal. 4:5), whom Jesus identified as John the Baptist (Matt. 11:14; 17:11–12).

John the Baptist went before Jesus in the spirit and power of Elijah (Luke 1:17).

Elijah—with Moses—appeared at Jesus' transfiguration (Matt. 17:3).

Elizabeth

Elizabeth was the wife of Zacharias, a priest, and like her husband, she was a descendant of Aaron (Luke 1:5).

She was upright and obedient to God (Luke 1:6).

Barrenness was her condition throughout her years of potential motherhood (Luke 1:7), but according to God's promise given to her husband, she became pregnant, remaining in seclusion for the first five months (Luke 1:24).

She was related to Mary, the mother of Jesus (Luke 1:36). On being greeted by Mary, Elizabeth was filled with the Spirit, and she recognized the uniqueness of the One conceived in Mary's womb (Luke 1:39–45). Elizabeth's words to Mary occasioned Mary's song known as the Magnificat (Luke 1:46–55). Mary then stayed with Elizabeth for three months (Luke 1:56).

Elizabeth gave birth to a son, John—later known as John the Baptist (Luke 1:13).

Emmaus

Emmaus was a village about seven miles from Jerusalem (Luke 24:13).

It was the destination of Cleopas and his unnamed companion when they met Jesus on the day of His resurrection, without at first recognizing Him (Luke 24:13–32).

The site cannot be identified with certainty, and several have been suggested.

End

The end is the end of this world as we now know it (Dan. 8:17, 19), when all that can be shaken will be removed, and God's unshakable kingdom will remain (Heb. 12:26–28).

The end of the age and the Lord Jesus Christ's coming are one and the same (Matt. 24:3, 6; 1 Cor. 1:8).

The timing of the end is linked with the completed preaching of the gospel to the whole world (Matt. 24:13–14; Mark 13:10).

Although there will be signs of the end (Luke 21:5–36), it will be at God's appointed time (Dan. 8:19; 11:35; cf. Matt. 24:36).

The end will be like a time of harvest, with good consequences for Christian believers but tragic ones for those who have refused to believe (Matt. 13:39–40, 49; cf. 2 Thess. 1:8–10).

Christians' full and perfect salvation will be revealed at the end (1 Pet. 1:5).

Christians are to live remembering that the end is near—a constant New Testament emphasis (Rom. 13:12; 1 Cor. 7:29; Heb. 10:25; James 5:8–9; 1 Pet. 4:7; 1 John 2:18; Rev. 22:20).

Eternal

Eternal always conveys the idea of that without end (Luke 16:9; Acts 13:46 NIV) and, sometimes when God is spoken of, of that without beginning (Gen. 21:33; Isa. 26:4; Rom. 16:26; Heb. 9:14 NIV).

Eternal Life, Everlasting Life

Eternal life is never-ending life, the opposite of death and corruption (Rom. 6:22; Gal. 6:8 NIV).

It is the gift of God and the present possession of the Christian through believing in the Lord Jesus Christ (Rom. 6:23; John 3:16; 10:28 NIV).

Its essence is everlasting fellowship with God (John 17:3).

Evangelism, Evangelist

Evangelists are the ascended Lord Jesus Christ's gift to His church. They come before pastors and teachers in Ephesians 4:11 in that evangelists bring churches into being by the preaching of the gospel, and pastors and teachers then have the responsibility of nurturing them in the Christian faith.

Philip is the one person described as an evangelist in the New Testament (Acts 21:8), although Timothy is told to "do the work of an evangelist" (2 Tim. 4:5), and the apostles themselves evangelized (Acts 8:25; 14:7; 1 Cor. 1:17).

Evangelism is announcing the good news, that is to say, preaching the gospel to those who are without Christ (Acts 16:10; Rom. 1:15; 15:20).

It is the priority of the church in its responsibility to the world (Matt. 28:18–20; Mark 16:15; Acts 1:8; Phil. 2:15–16).

Evil Spirits. *See* Demons.

Exile

The Jewish people were taken into exile more than once (2 Kings 15:29; 17:3–6; 24:11–16; 25:11; Jer. 52:30; Dan. 1:1–6), and so we have to be careful about which exile we have in mind. The Assyrians twice conquered Israel (the northern kingdom); and Judah (the southern kingdom) was conquered once by Assyria and three times by the Babylonians. On each occasion Jews were carried off as captives.

When we refer to the Exile, we usually have in view the round figure of seventy years in which Judah was held captive by the Babylonians (605–536 B.C.).

Nebuchadnezzar, king of Assyria, invaded the entire land of Israel and deported into exile all Jerusalem, and in particular all the officers and fighting men, and all the craftsmen and artisans (2 Kings 17:5–6; 24:13–16).

A total of 4,600 people who had survived the sword were taken into exile (2 Chron. 36:20; Jer. 52:28–30).

Jeremiah exercised his ministry before and during the exile (Jer. 24; 29), and prophesied concerning it (Jer. 13:18–21; 20:4–6).

Through Jeremiah, God gave the people advice about how

to conduct themselves during their banishment (Jer. 29:4–7), and promised to bring the people back into their own land (Jer. 29:14; 30:10).

Jeremiah was not taken away (Jer. 40:5–6). He remained with the poor people who were left behind by the Assyrians under a governor's jurisdiction (2 Kings 24:14).

The Exile lasted seventy years until the kingdom of Persia came to power under Cyrus in fulfillment of God's promise to Jeremiah (2 Chron. 36:20–21; Ezra 1:1–4).

A remnant of the Israelites survived the Exile (Neh. 1:2–3) and returned under Nehemiah, who was appointed governor of Jerusalem (Neh. 2:5, 7–8, 11–18; 5:14–15).

Expiate, Expiation

Expiation is found in some Bible translations in place of *propitiation*. It is an action that has sin as its object in that the guilt of sin needs to be removed. It is the covering, or putting away, of the guilt of human sin so that it no longer constitutes a barrier to a right relationship with God.

Propitiation is the preferred New Testament word since it includes expiation but denotes the more profound concept of satisfying God's wrath by the death of our Lord Jesus Christ as the substitute for sinners.

Jesus Christ is the propitiation for our sins (Rom. 3:25; 1 John 2:2). *See* Propitiation.

— F —

Faith

In the New Testament, faith is both a decisive act and a sustained attitude, which is brought about not by the force of subtle human arguments but through the power of the Holy Spirit (1 Cor. 2:4–5).

It rests on certain facts that the apostles were careful to preach (1 Cor. 11:23–26; 15:1–5), truths concerning Jesus, the Son of God (John 20:31), and His death for our sins

(1 Pet. 2:24) and resurrection to life again (1 Pet. 1:3; Rom. 4:25), in accordance with what God promised beforehand in the Old Testament (1 Cor. 15:3–4).

These facts have to be received and a stand taken upon them (1 Cor. 15:1) so that faith moves beyond the facts to trusting a person—the Lord Jesus Christ (John 1:12; Acts 16:31)—and abandoning all reliance upon ourselves and our works to merit salvation.

After this, faith becomes the practice and habit of our lives (2 Cor. 5:7; Eph. 6:16; 1 Tim. 6:12; Heb. 11).

Fasting

Fasting is abstinence for a limited period from any form of food.

In the Old Testament, it was a preparation for meeting with God (Exod. 34:28; Deut. 9:9; Dan. 9:3).

It was especially associated with prayer (Ezra 8:21, 23; Neh. 1:4; Jer. 14:11–12).

It was usually for the period of a day (Judg. 20:26; 1 Sam. 14:24; 2 Sam. 1:12).

The Levitical law demanded fasting only on the Day of Atonement (Lev. 23:27–32; Num. 29:7).

Fasting became divorced from seeking after God and tended to be simply a religious act thought to give merit before God, and as such it offended Him (Isa. 58:3–7; Jer. 14:12).

Jesus fasted for forty days and forty nights before beginning His public ministry (Matt. 4:2).

He did not condemn fasting, but He did condemn the pride that could be behind it (Matt. 6:16–18).

The early church backed up prayer with fasting (Acts 13:3; 14:23) as an expression of earnestness.

Father, God the

The word *Father* is the distinguishing name of the first person of the Trinity in relation to the second person—the Son

(John 14:6; 20:17; Rom. 15:6; 2 Cor. 1:3). The relationship, which is unlike any other, is beyond our understanding. *See* Trinity.

The word is used, second, of the relationship God the Father has with those who believe in His Son (Rom. 1:7; 1 Cor. 1:3; 2 Thess. 2:16), a relationship of care and affection for us as His spiritual children. As such we are taught by the Holy Spirit to call Him Father (John 1:12; Rom. 8:15; 1 John 3:1)—our heavenly Father (Matt. 6:9, 14, 26, 32).

The relationship of God with men and women in general is seldom spoken of as fatherhood; indeed, the opposite is the case (John 8:44).

Fellowship

Fellowship is a favorite Christian word and is the name given to the common sharing of Christians in God's grace, the salvation Christ brings, and the indwelling Holy Spirit—the spiritual birthright of all Christians.

The fellowship that Christians have with one another, therefore, springs from the fellowship they first have with the Father, the Son, and the Holy Spirit (1 John 1:3).

Fellowship with God is a relationship in which Christians receive from, and respond to, all three persons of the Trinity in a relation of friendship (John 14:23; Rom. 5:5; 8:16; Eph. 4:30).

Such fellowship is the life of heaven begun on earth (John 17:3; 1 Pet. 1:8–9).

Firstfruits

Firstfruits are, as the name indicates, the first fruits both of crops and of animals, which were set apart for God before the rest could be put to ordinary use (Exod. 23:16, 19; 34:22, 26).

Giving firstfruits to God was part of people's honoring Him with their wealth (Prov. 3:9).

The term is applied to the early Christians in that they were the promise of a greater harvest to come (James 1:18; cf. Jer. 2:3; Rom. 16:5; 1 Cor. 16:15; Rev. 14:4).

It is also used of Jesus Christ who, through His resurrection, was the first to rise of those who have fallen asleep (1 Cor. 15:20, 23).

It is further employed to describe the "first installment" that the Holy Spirit's indwelling of Christians gives them of the eternal glory that is theirs in Christ (Rom. 8:23).

Forgiveness

Forgiveness is the canceling by God (Mic. 7:19; Eph. 1:7) of the sinner's debt and guilt on the basis of Christ's death for sinners (Matt. 26:28; Mark 14:24).

The conditions are repentance and faith in Christ (Acts 2:38; 5:31; 10:43; 1 John 1:9).

— G —

Gabbatha

Gabbatha (John 19:13) is the Aramaic word for the Stone Pavement in Jerusalem. *See* Pavement.

Gabriel

The name *Gabriel* suggests two meanings: "man of God" or "God is strong."

The angel Gabriel appeared to Daniel in the Old Testament as a heavenly messenger who revealed the future by interpreting his vision (Dan. 8:16), and who gave him insight and understanding (Dan. 9:21–22).

He described himself as one who stands in God's presence (Luke 1:19).

Gabriel appeared to Zacharias while he was burning incense in the temple, and he promised him and his wife, Elizabeth, a son—John the Baptist (Luke 1:11, 19).

Gabriel was also the angel sent to Nazareth to reveal to

Mary her impending conception by God the Holy Spirit of Jesus (Luke 1:26–38). *See* Angels.

Galilee, Sea of Galilee

Galilee is both a region and a lake in northern Israel.

As a region, it is for the most part a coastal plain, with the exception of its mountains such as Mount Carmel.

Galilee was the home area of Jesus—as of many of His disciples—and much of His ministry took place there.

In the Old Testament, the Sea of Galilee was called Chinnereth (Num. 34:11; Josh. 12:3).

The Sea of Galilee is where Jesus taught His first disciples (Matt. 4:18; Mark 1:16) and the Jewish people (Matt. 15:29–30).

It is also called in the New Testament the Sea of Tiberias (John 6:1) and the Lake of Gennesaret (Luke 5:1) because of the names of the towns on its shores.

It is thirteen miles long and up to seven and one-half miles wide at Magdala.

The Jordan flows through it from north to south.

Galilee's wealth was centered on the Sea of Galilee.

Violent and unexpected storms can suddenly erupt, as the Gospels indicate (Matt. 14:22–34; Mark 4:37; 6:45–53; John 6:16–21).

Gentiles

Gentiles was, to begin with, a name for the "nations."

The Jews knew themselves to be distinct from other peoples, and they used this term to describe all such.

In the New Testament, the word usually has Greeks in mind, and subsequently, it covers all who are not of the Jewish people.

Gethsemane

The word means "oil press." It was an olive orchard, across the Kidron (John 18:1) on the Mount of Olives (Luke 22:39).

Gethsemane was a favorite place of prayer for Jesus, and a frequent venue for meeting with His disciples (Luke 22:39–46; John 18:2).

Glorification, Glorified

Glorification is the term used to describe Christians' ultimate complete conformity to the image of Christ, a glorious work that will take place at Jesus Christ's coming (Col. 3:4; 1 John 3:2). It is the logical outcome of predestination, calling, and justification—a consequence so certain that it can be described as having already taken place (Rom. 8:30).

Christians are to share in the glory of our Lord Jesus Christ (Rom. 8:17–18; 2 Thess. 2:14). *See* Glory.

Glory

Glory is used of God Himself to sum up the perfection of all that He is and all that He does, and not least His grace, power, and righteousness—the latter revealing especially how far short men and women fall of God's standards (Rom. 1:23; 3:23; Eph. 1:17; Jude 24).

The word is also used to describe the eternal happiness that Christians are to enjoy in the life to come (Rom. 8:18, 21; 1 Pet. 5:1, 10).

Godliness

Godliness—closely linked with the fear of God (Heb. 5:7) —may be defined as doing what is right with an eye to God's approval alone. It describes the person who practices loyalty and faithfulness to God both in public and in private.

The knowledge of the truth—the truth of the gospel— leads to godliness (Titus 1:1).

Godliness is a quality of Christian life and character after which Christians are to strive (1 Tim. 4:7; 6:11; 2 Pet. 1:6–7).

Godliness is linked with virtues such as faithfulness (Ps. 12:1),

uprightness (Mic. 7:2), holiness (1 Tim. 2:2), and content-
ment (1 Tim. 6:6).

God's divine power has given us all we need for godliness
through our knowledge of Jesus Christ (2 Pet. 1:3).

Godliness holds promise for both the present life and the
life to come (1 Tim. 4:8).

Golgotha

From the Aramaic, translated "Place of a Skull," Golgotha
was the name of a hill or eminence near Jerusalem close to a
highway (Matt. 27:33), used as a place of execution, where
Jesus was crucified.

Luke describes it as "the place called the Skull" (Luke
23:33 NIV), or Calvary.

Two principal explanations have been given for its name:
first, the hill was skull shaped; second, skulls were found there,
as might have been expected since it was a place of execution.

Gospel

Gospel means "good news"—the good news concerning
God's Son Jesus Christ (Acts 10:34–43; 1 Cor. 15:1–8).

The good news is that Christ died and rose again for sinners, and that God has exalted Him to His right hand as Lord
and Savior that He might give repentance and forgiveness of
sins to all who repent and believe in Him (Acts 5:31). The gift
of forgiveness is accompanied by the gift of the Holy Spirit
(Acts 2:38–39) and eternal life (Acts 11:18)—in fact, all the
blessings of salvation (Eph. 1:3).

Gospels

The four Gospels—Matthew, Mark, Luke, and John—are
the New Testament books in which the story of Jesus Christ's
life and teaching is found.

They are not so much biographies of Jesus as written copies
of the apostles' teaching and preaching, with the emphasis on

His life and work through which God's salvation is made available to men and women—the good news after which the Gospels are named.

According to the four gospel writers, there is but one gospel—the gospel of Jesus Christ, the Son of God—delivered to, and preached by, the apostles (Acts 2:42; 1 Cor. 15:1–4).

Grace

Grace is God's undeserved love to men and women revealed in Jesus Christ, giving them through His saving work countless gifts and benefits they could never merit (Rom. 3:24; 5:15; 6:1; Eph. 1:6; 2:5, 7–8).

— H —

Heart

Heart covers the whole inward life of a person: thinking, feeling, and will (Matt. 13:15).

Sin has its roots in the heart (Matt. 15:19–20), and it is in the heart, therefore, that God's work of salvation begins (Matt. 13:19; Rom. 2:15; 2 Cor. 3:3; Heb. 8:10), so that we believe in our own hearts in the Lord Jesus Christ (Acts 15:9; Rom. 10:9–10).

Heaven

Heaven is the eternal dwelling place of God (Matt. 5:16; 12:50; Rev. 3:12; 11:13; 20:9) and of His angels (Matt. 18:10; 22:30; Rev. 3:5).

Our Lord Jesus Christ came from heaven (John 3:13, 31; 6:38, 42, 50; 1 Cor. 15:47) and at His ascension returned there (Mark 16:19; 1 Pet 3:22). It is from heaven that He will descend at His second coming (Matt. 24:30; Phil. 3:20; 1 Thess. 4:16; 2 Thess. 1:7).

Heaven is not part of this creation; it is quite different from it (Heb. 9:11). Heaven is marked by peace (Luke 19:38), holiness (Deut. 26:15; Ps. 20:6; Isa. 57:15), and indescribable happiness and satisfaction (Rev. 7:17).

It is described as paradise (2 Cor. 12:2, 4), a granary, with Christians being the wheat gathered in (Matt. 3:12), the Father's house (John 14:2), a city prepared by God for His people (Heb. 11:16; 12:22), a heavenly country (Heb. 11:16), a rest (Heb. 4:9), and Christians' inheritance (Matt. 25:34; 1 Pet. 1:4).

All who gain entry into heaven recognize that they do not deserve to do so by reason of their own merits (Matt. 25:37–39): they gain entry on the grounds of the mediation of Jesus Christ and the efficacy of His sacrifice (Heb. 12:22–24) for all who believe of every nation and language (Matt. 25:32; Rev. 5:9–10).

Christians' citizenship is already in heaven (Phil. 3:20), a truth that should influence the way they live (Col. 3:2) and not least how they regard their material possessions (Heb. 10:34).

Hell

Two words are translated "hell" in the New Testament: *Hades* and *Gehenna*.

Hades, corresponding to the Old Testament word *Sheol*, is the underworld as the place of departed spirits. It is sometimes translated "Hades" (Matt. 16:18; Rev. 1:18), "hell" (Luke 16:23 NIV), "the depths" (Matt. 11:23 NIV), and "the grave" (Acts 2:27, 31 NIV).

Gehenna comes from the Hebrew word for the Valley of the Son of Hinnom, a ravine south of Jerusalem, where refuse was dumped and burned. All the New Testament uses of the word, except one (James 3:6), are by Jesus Himself.

Gehenna is associated with punishment by fire (Matt. 5:22; 18:9; Mark 9:43, 47) and destruction of an eternal character (Matt. 10:28; 18:8; 25:41, 46; Mark 3:29; Heb. 6:2; Jude 6).

Hell is the place of eternal punishment and banishment from God's presence, the future dwelling place of all who have neglected God and disobeyed the gospel of Christ (2 Thess. 1:8–9).

Herod

Five Herods are mentioned in the New Testament, but three are prominent in the following historical order.

Herod the Great, not a Jew by birth, reigned from 37 to 4 B.C. He was given the title "king of the Jews" by the Romans (Matt. 2:1–19; Luke 1:5).

His dates remind us that our accepted practice of reckoning dates as so many years after Jesus' birth is inaccurate. Matthew 2:16 would make 6 B.C. a more accurate date for Jesus' birth.

He was greatly hated by the Jews, and at his death his kingdom was divided among three of his sons (Matt. 2:22; 14:1; Luke 3:1).

He was responsible for the rebuilding of the temple, which had been in progress for forty-six years when Jesus began His ministry (John 2:20).

Herod Antipas was the son of Herod the Great and Malthace, a Samaritan.

He was tetrarch of Galilee and Perea from his father's death until A.D. 39 (Matt. 14:1–12).

It was the people's custom to call him "king" (Mark 6:14), a title that he desired and that led to his ultimate downfall, according to Josephus, the Jewish historian.

He married the wife of his half brother Philip (Matt. 14:3), for which he was rebuked by John the Baptist, leading to the latter's beheading (Mark 6:14–29).

Herod Agrippa, a grandson of Herod the Great, received the title of "king" from Emperor Gaius in A.D. 37 with jurisdiction over territories northeast of Palestine. When his uncle Herod Antipas was banished in A.D. 39, Galilee and Perea were added to his kingdom, and later Judea and Samaria.

His persecution of the church seems to have been politically motivated (Acts 12:1–14), and his pride led to his dramatic downfall and death (Acts 12:20–23).

Herodians

The Herodians were influential supporters of the Herod family, and particularly in the New Testament period of Herod Antipas.

Preferring Herod's rule to the direct rule of the Roman administration, they wanted a united nation under Herod.

High Priest

The high priest was the head priest, the most senior of the chief priests (Num. 35:28; Matt. 26:3).

Always of the tribe of Levi, he represented the whole priesthood and the complete nation, whose twelve tribes' names he was to bear on his shoulders and over his heart (Exod. 28:12, 29). He alone could enter the Most Holy Place on the Day of Atonement (Lev. 16:17, 23; 1 Chron. 6:49).

The difference in his consecration to office compared with other priests seems to have been the wearing of additional symbolic garments (Num. 20:26–28).

The high priest's palace, with his retinue of servants, was in Jerusalem (Matt. 26:3, 51, 57).

Holiness, Holy

The idea behind the words *holy* and *holiness* is that of being cut off, separated, or set apart.

God sets His people apart from other peoples, and He calls them to separate themselves from all that displeases Him and is contrary to His will.

He calls them to be like Himself (1 Pet. 1:15–16).

Holy Spirit

The Holy Spirit is the third person of the Trinity, one with the Father and the Son (Matt. 28:19; 2 Cor. 13:14;

Eph. 4:4–6), and the qualities ascribed to Him are those attributed to God alone (Ps. 139:7–13; Luke 1:35; Rom. 8:11; 15:19; 1 Cor. 2:10; 12:13).

He was the Agent of God's first creation (Gen. 1:2; Job 26:13), and humankind was made by the Spirit of God (Job 33:4; cf. Gen. 2:7; Ps. 104:29–30).

He is the Author of the Scriptures (2 Tim. 3:16; 2 Pet. 1:21).

He was active with regard to the incarnation of our Lord Jesus Christ. By His power the virgin conception was accomplished (Matt. 1:18, 20; Luke 1:35), and He led and directed Christ throughout His ministry (Matt. 4:1; Mark 1:12), equipping Him with power (Matt. 12:28; Luke 4:1, 18; Acts 10:38), and finally raising Him from the dead (Acts 2:24; cf. 1 Pet. 3:18; Heb. 13:20; cf. Rom. 1:4).

He is the Agent of God's new creation in Christ, the church, since He is the Author of the new birth (John 3:5–6; 2 Cor. 5:17). He accompanies the preaching of the gospel with His power (1 Pet. 1:12), shows men and women their need of salvation by convicting them of sin (John 16:8–11), bears witness to Christ (John 15:26), and enables them to confess that "Jesus is Lord" (1 Cor. 12:3).

He binds Christians together in one body in spiritual unity (Eph. 4:3–4), allots varying gifts to them (Rom. 12:6–8; 1 Cor. 12:4–11), and equips them for work in Christ's service for the building up of the body of Christ (Eph. 4:11–13).

Hypocrisy

The New Testament word for hypocrite is that for an actor, and it conveys the meaning, therefore, of pretending to be what one is not.

A mark of hypocrisy is a person's parading spiritual activity (Matt. 6:2, 5, 16) and performing religious actions without inner devotion to God (Matt. 15:7–9; 23:28; Mark 7:6–7).

If not corrected, hypocrisy has a pervasive character like yeast, and it was a particular peril for some Pharisees (Luke 12:1).

— I —

Image of God (Christ)

Jesus Christ is the image of God (2 Cor. 4:4; Col. 1:15), the exact representation of God's nature (Heb. 1:3), the One at whom we may look and see what God is like (John 14:9).

Through Jesus Christ alone, God, who is otherwise invisible, is perfectly revealed. In Jesus Christ, we may see God as in a mirror, for whatever is in the person of the Father is in the person of the Son.

Immortality

Immortality is deathlessness. It belongs to God alone (1 Tim. 6:16; cf. 1:17).

Immortality describes the quality of life that is before Christian believers; it is the opposite of mortality (1 Cor. 15:50).

Christians receive immortality as a gift through the saving work of Jesus Christ (2 Tim. 1:10).

Immortality is not merely the survival of the soul after the death of the body, but the ultimate self-conscious existence of the whole person, body and soul together, in a state of eternal happiness (1 Cor. 15:53–55).

Incarnate, Incarnation

The word *incârnation* itself comes from Latin, meaning "becoming in flesh," and it describes the amazing fact of Jesus Christ, the Son of God, taking human flesh upon Him and living among men and women (John 1:14).

In both Old and New Testaments, Jesus Christ is declared to be both God and man, united in one person (Pss. 2; 22; 45; 72; 110; Isa. 9:6–7; John 1:1–3, 14; Col. 2:9).

His perfect deity and perfect humanity are essentials of the Christian faith (1 John 2:22–24; 4:1–6; 5:5–12; 2 John 7), although these glorious facts are beyond the understanding of the finite human mind (1 Tim. 3:16).

Inspiration

The word rendered in some Bible translations *inspired* means "God-breathed" (2 Tim. 3:16).

The Scriptures came about not by the impulse of people who wrote them, but by their being moved by the Holy Spirit to speak from God (2 Pet. 1:21; cf. Matt. 22:43; Mark 12:36).

Their responsibility was to transmit what they received (1 Pet. 1:10–12). The exercise of their natural faculties was not interfered with, yet spontaneously they produced what God planned—so perfectly so that what they said, God said (Dan. 9:10).

The Bible's authority springs from its divine inspiration (2 Tim. 3:16–17).

The conviction that the Scriptures are the Word of God is brought about in the heart of the Christian by the Holy Spirit (1 Cor. 2:4; 1 Thess. 1:5; 2:13).

Intercession

Intercession is an important aspect of prayer in which we pray for the needs of others rather than for our own (1 Sam. 7:5; 1 Kings 13:6; 1 Tim. 2:1).

Jesus Christ made intercession on the cross for those who put Him to death (Luke 23:34; cf. Isa. 53:12).

Intercession is the continuing work of Jesus Christ in heaven for His people. On the grounds of His sacrifice on their behalf, He unfailingly claims every spiritual benefit for them, secures forgiveness for all their sins, and makes their worship and service acceptable to God (Rom. 8:34; Heb. 7:25; 9:24; 13:15; 1 John 2:1).

A different kind of intercession is the Holy Spirit's work in Christians by which He disposes, teaches, and helps them to pray according to God's will. The Spirit gives both the inclination and the ability to pray (Rom. 8:26–27).

Isaiah

Isaiah (the Lord is salvation), son of Amoz (2 Kings 19:2), lived in Jerusalem. He was a contemporary of Micah (Isa. 1:1; Mic. 1:1) and exercised his ministry during the reigns of Uzziah, Jotham, Ahaz, and Hezekiah, kings of Judah (Isa. 1:1).

He was married and had two sons to whom he gave significant names (Isa. 7:3; 8:3).

He was called to be a prophet in the year King Uzziah died (Isa. 6:1)—that is, 740/739 B.C.

He protested against Ahaz's foreign policy prompted by unbelief (Isa. 7:3–25).

He was consulted by King Hezekiah (2 Kings 19:1–7) and was given messages from God for him (2 Kings 19:20–34; 20:1–11, 16–18; Isa. 37:6–7, 21–35; 38:4–8).

Isaiah looked forward to the coming of the Messiah (Matt. 3:3; 4:14; 8:17; 13:14; Mark 1:2; Luke 3:4; John 12:38–39; Rom. 15:12).

Isaiah saw Jesus' glory and spoke of Him (John 12:41; Isa. 6:1–8)—hence Philip's ability to preach Jesus to the Ethiopian from Isaiah 53 (Acts 8:28, 30).

Jesus quoted Isaiah (Matt. 15:7; Mark 7:6) and saw Himself fulfilling Isaiah's promises concerning the Messiah (Luke 4:17–21).

Israel

Israel (he who strives with God) was the name given to Jacob after his night of wrestling with God (Gen. 32:28; cf. 35:10; Hos. 12:3–4).

Israel then became the name given to the Hebrew nation, which traced its descent back to Israel (i.e., Jacob) through his twelve sons (Gen. 32:32; 34:7; 49:16, 28).

Israel was later the name appropriated by the ten northern tribes, which broke away from the southern kingdom of Judah after the death of Solomon (around 933 B.C.) and which were carried away to Assyria (around 721 B.C.).

But the name Israel, when not referring to that geographical division, includes all the Jewish people (Lev. 9:1; Num. 21:17; Deut. 4:1; Matt. 15:24; Luke 2:32; John 12:13; Rom. 11:26).

In 1948, a state once more arose with the ancient name of Israel.

Israel is the name the New Testament gives to the church—the new "Israel of God" (Gal. 6:16)—as it now inherits and shares the privileges of ancient Israel as God's covenant people (Eph. 3:6).

— J —

Jabbok

The Jabbok River, one of the main streams of Transjordan, was the river Jacob crossed the night he wrestled with God (Gen. 32:22–32).

The Jabbok River was the border of the Amorites (Num. 21:24–25) and Ammonites (Deut. 3:16; Josh. 12:2) when the Israelites came out of Egypt and took possession of the land from the Arnon River to the Jabbok River, all the way to the Jordan (Judg. 11:13).

Jairus

Jairus (meaning "God will enlighten") was a synagogue ruler whose daughter's illness drove him to seek Jesus' help (Mark 5:22–23; Luke 8:41–42).

Before Jesus arrived at Jairus's home, his daughter died, but Jesus brought her back to life again (Mark 5:41–42; Luke 8:54).

James, Brother of Jesus

James is mentioned with his brothers Joses, Simon, and Judas (Matt. 13:55; Mark 6:3).

Although he does not seem to have recognized Jesus' deity early on (Mark 3:21), he was later prominent among the early

Christians (Acts 12:17; 15:13; 21:18; 1 Cor. 15:7; Gal. 1:19; 2:9, 12).

It seems likely that he was the author of the New Testament letter of James.

James, Son of Alphaeus. *See* James the Younger.

James, Son of Zebedee

James, a son of Zebedee, is always mentioned after Peter and in association with his brother John (Matt. 4:21; 10:2; Mark 1:19).

He and John, his brother, were nicknamed "Boanerges, that is, 'Sons of Thunder'" (Mark 3:17).

Since his father employed men, James's background may have been affluent (Mark 1:20).

He was put to death by the sword of Herod Agrippa (Acts 12:2).

James the Younger

James, son of Alphaeus, is usually identified as James the younger, being younger than James, the son of Zebedee (Matt. 10:3; Mark 15:40).

Jehovah. *See* Yahweh.

Jerusalem

Probably the "Salem" of which Melchizedek was king at the time of Abraham (Gen. 14:18), and then later a Jebusite stronghold, it was captured by King David and made his capital (2 Sam. 5:6–9; 1 Chron. 11:4–8), from which he ruled for thirty-three years of his reign (1 Chron. 29:27).

Once Solomon built the temple in Jerusalem, it became the Jews' Holy City (1 Kings 6).

It is the city where God chose to put His name (1 Kings 11:36; 2 Chron. 6:6).

It is outstanding for its situation: high in the Judean hills (2,526 feet), with the ground dropping steeply away on three sides.

It suffered badly through many declines and wars. Under Herod the Great—made king by the Romans—the city was again repaired and a magnificent new temple built, the building that featured much in the life and ministry of Jesus.

Jews expected Jerusalem to become the focus of the whole world, and the place to which all nations would one day stream (Isa. 56:6–8).

Jerusalem, as God's city (Matt. 5:35), inevitably played a decisive role in Jesus' ministry, especially in the events leading to His death (Matt. 16:21; Luke 9:31).

Many of God's promises throughout the centuries focused on Jerusalem (Luke 2:38), and the Christian's focus is on the new and heavenly Jerusalem (Heb. 12:22; Rev. 3:12; 21:2).

Jesus

Jesus is a transliteration of the Hebrew *Joshua*, meaning "the Lord is salvation," that is to say, "the Lord is the Savior."

It was the name given to the Son of God at His incarnation as His personal name, at the command of the angel to Joseph, Mary's husband (Matt. 1:21).

It is the name by which the Son of God is usually known in the Gospels, although there are exceptions (Mark 16:19–20; Luke 7:13).

Jew

A Jew was originally a descendant of Judah (the fourth son of Jacob), but the word came to be used of all Abraham's descendants and then of all Israelites who adhered to the true worship of God in Jerusalem.

The word itself first occurs in the book of Esther—and then on eight occasions (2:5; 3:4; 5:13· 6:10; 8:7; 9:29, 31; 10:3)

—and thereafter once each in Jeremiah (34:9) and Zechariah (8:23) and twenty-two times in the New Testament.

A Jew is someone who is not a Gentile (Acts 14:1, 5; Gal. 2:14; 3:28), or a Samaritan (John 4:9), or a convert to Judaism (Acts 2:10).

The particular symbol of a Jew's belonging to God was circumcision, although that outward mark had no value to God apart from the inner reality of dedication to Him (Rom. 2:28–29).

John

Several men by the name of John are mentioned in the New Testament, but three are prominent—John the Baptist, the apostle John (son of Zebedee), and John Mark.

John the Baptist. The gospel record begins with John the Baptist's ministry (Acts 10:37)—"a man sent from God" (John 1:6).

He was the forerunner of the Messiah, promised in the Old Testament (John 1:23).

He was the only son of Zacharias and Elizabeth, Mary's cousin. His name was God-given (Luke 1:13), and he was filled with the Spirit from birth.

His ministry began during the priesthood of Annas and Caiaphas as God's Word came to him in the desert (or wilderness) of Judea (Matt. 3:1; Luke 3:2), and he preached a baptism of repentance for the forgiveness of sins (Mark 1:4; Acts 13:24), always with a forward look to the person and work of Jesus (Luke 3:16; John 1:15; Acts 13:25).

His dress and lifestyle were simple (Mark 1:6) and ascetic (Luke 7:33), and his message clear, honest, and blunt (Luke 3:7–14).

He gathered disciples around him, and he taught them to pray (Luke 11:1) and to be ready for Jesus' ministry (John 1:26).

His uncompromising preaching of repentance made his rebuke of Herod's adultery inevitable and caused Herodias to regard him as an enemy.

John was reluctant to baptize Jesus, but eventually, he acceded to His request (Matt. 3:13–15; Mark 1:9), and it prompted John's unique testimony to Jesus (John 1:29–34).

John thereafter pointed his disciples to Jesus as the One they should follow (John 1:35–36; 3:26–30; cf. Matt. 11:4–6; Luke 7:20–23).

John's imprisonment seems to have been the signal for Jesus to begin His public ministry (Matt. 4:12; Mark 1:14).

After John's death at the hands of Herod (Matt. 14:3–12; Mark 6:17–29), Jesus' miracles prompted Herod to think that Jesus was John raised from the dead (Matt. 14:2; Mark 6:16).

Jesus spoke highly of John's ministry (Matt. 11:11; John 5:35), a ministry that the Jewish people as a whole did not receive (Matt. 21:32).

John, Son of Zebedee. John, brother of James and likewise a fisherman (Matt. 4:21), was probably the younger of the two. He was an apostle and one of the Twelve (Matt. 10:2; Mark 3:17).

His family would seem to have been well-to-do since his father is said to have had "hired servants" working for him (Mark 1:20).

He was almost certainly a disciple of John the Baptist before Jesus called him.

With Peter and James, he was especially close to Jesus (Matt. 17:1–9; Mark 5:37; 14:33; John 19:26–27).

He was prominent in the early church (Acts 3—4; Gal. 2:9).

He was the writer of the fourth gospel, the three New Testament letters bearing his name, and the book of Revelation (Rev. 1:1, 4, 9).

John Mark. See Mark.

John. He was an unknown member of the Sanhedrin (Acts 4:6).

John, Father of Peter. Nothing is known of him (John 1:42; 21:15–17).

Jonah

Jonah, son of Amittai, from Gath Hepher (Jon. 1:1), was one of the "minor" prophets. He prophesied during the reign of Jeroboam II (790–750 B.C.), declaring the territorial expansion the latter would achieve at Syria's expense (2 Kings 14:25).

Jonah is most remembered as the runaway disobedient prophet who learned to be obedient (Jon. 1:1, 3; 3:3).

He experienced a remarkable deliverance when he was thrown overboard through God's provision of a great fish to swallow him and then to bring him to safety (Jon. 1:15, 17; 2:10).

Jonah proclaimed God's judgment on Nineveh (Jon. 3:3–4), a traditional enemy of Israel, and to his dismay, the whole city repented and God had mercy on it (3:10—4:11). Jonah learned the profound truth of God's compassion and love for His creatures.

It would seem that Jonah's remarkable deliverance (after three days and three nights in the great fish) was a sign to the Ninevites of which they took notice, and it prefigured the sign that Jesus' resurrection is to humankind (Matt. 12:39–41; 16:4; Luke 11:29–30, 32).

Jordan

The Jordan is the largest river in Israel.

The name aptly means "the descender" in that it begins in the foothills of Mount Hermon at a height of 249 feet above sea level and reaches the Dead Sea, via the Sea of Galilee, at 1,292 feet below sea level, having doubled the distance by its meanderings.

The Jordan is mentioned in connection with important incidents in the Old Testament (Gen. 13:10–11; 32:10; Deut. 3:23–25; Josh. 1:2; 3:1—4:24; 2 Kings 5:1–14; 6:1–7).

"The Jordan" is used to describe a whole region around the Jordan River and Valley (Matt. 3:5).

John the Baptist's ministry was at the Jordan, especially in the early days (Mark 1:5, 9; John 10:40), and it was there that he baptized Jesus.

Joseph, Husband of Mary

Joseph, a carpenter of Nazareth (Matt. 13:55; Luke 2:4), the husband of Mary (Matt. 1:16; Luke 3:23), the mother of Jesus, was of Davidic descent (Matt. 1:20; Luke 2:4).

He is described as a righteous, or just, man (Matt. 1:19), who was naturally concerned at the news of Mary's pregnancy prior to their coming together in marriage. An angel of the Lord explained the unique nature of the conception of Mary's child, and Joseph was obedient to God's instruction to marry Mary and to give the child the name "Jesus" (Matt. 1:20–25).

On two other occasions Joseph was addressed by an angel of the Lord in dreams: first, with instructions to escape to Egypt with Mary and the child (Matt. 2:13) and, second, later, to return (Matt. 2:19–20).

He was the father of Mary's four other sons—James, Joseph (or Joses), Judas, and Simon, and one or more daughters (Mark 6:3).

We do not know when Joseph died, but it would seem that his death occurred prior to Jesus' crucifixion (John 19:26–27).

Joseph of Arimathea

Joseph of Arimathea, a wealthy Jew who was waiting for the kingdom of God, was a prominent member of the Jewish council, the Sanhedrin (Matt. 27:57; Mark 15:43).

He was a secret disciple of Jesus until the time of Jesus' crucifixion when he sought permission from Pilate to bury the body of Jesus in a tomb he had prepared for himself (Matt. 27:57–60; Luke 23:50–53; John 19:38–42).

Joshua

Joshua, son of Nun, was Moses' young assistant (Exod. 24:13; 33:11; Num. 11:28), and he led the Israelites' attack against the Amalekites at Moses' direction (Exod. 17:8–13).

He was one of those Moses sent to explore the land of Canaan (Num. 13:16–20). He and Caleb expressed confidence about going forward (Num. 14:6–9) and therefore survived the wilderness experience and entered the Promised Land (Num. 14:38).

The Spirit of God was on Joshua, and Moses laid his hands on him to commission him as his successor (Num. 27:18–23; Deut. 34:9); that commission was confirmed by the Lord at Moses' death (Josh. 1:1–18).

Joshua led Israel to inherit the land of Canaan (Deut. 1:38; 3:28), and under his leadership, the Lord gave the Israelites rest from all their enemies (Josh. 23:1).

Joshua was faithful in giving the people all that Moses had delivered to Israel of God's will and words (Josh. 8:34–35; 11:15).

The secret of Joshua's success was God's presence with him (Josh. 6:27).

He died at the age of 110 (Josh. 24:29; Judg. 2:8).

Judas Iscariot

Judas always appears last in the list of the apostles, and usually with the description "who betrayed Jesus."

He was the treasurer of the disciples' common funds (John 13:29).

Some have suggested that his greed for money caused Judas to betray Jesus. Others maintain that, believing Jesus to be a political Savior and Messiah, he tried to force Jesus to take action to declare Himself as such by handing Him over to the authorities.

Luke's explanation is the true one: "Satan entered Judas, surnamed Iscariot, who was numbered among the twelve" (Luke 22:3).

Judea

Sometimes used as the name for all the land, including Galilee and Samaria, *Judea* is the Greek and Roman name for Judah.

Usually, it refers to the southern part of the country, with Jerusalem as its capital, in contrast to Galilee, Perea, and Idumea.

Judge, Judgment

Judgment is God's condemnation, which rightly falls on sinners (Rom. 2:2) and which will be executed at the Judgment when Christ will be the Judge and all will appear before Him (Matt. 25:31–46; John 5:22, 27).

The perfect justice of God and the undeniable guilt of all will be plain and beyond dispute (Gen. 18:25; Acts 17:31; Rom. 2:5–6).

Those justified through faith in Christ will be acquitted from the guilt of sin and will receive rewards according to their faithfulness (Rom. 5:1; 1 Cor. 3:9–15; 2 Tim. 4:8); the unbelieving will receive their final condemnation (Rom. 2:8; 2 Thess. 1:8–9; Jude 15; Rev. 20:15).

The Day of Judgment is the day when Christ returns (1 Cor. 3:13; 1 Thess. 5:4; Heb. 10:25) and all these things will take place.

Just

Just describes men and women who are upright or righteous in that they conform to the laws of God and humankind; the desire so to live is one of the motivations and evidences of new birth (1 John 2:29).

It is used of God Himself to describe the perfect fairness of His judgment of men and women and nations (Ps. 7:11; 2 Tim. 4:8).

It is used of Jesus, who is the perfect standard of obedience and uprightness (Matt. 27:19; Acts 7:52; 1 Pet. 3:18).

Justification, Justified

Justification has to do with God's justice and righteousness. He is the Lord and Judge of all the earth who always does what is right (Gen. 18:25), and His righteousness is seen in His judgment and condemnation of those who disobey His laws (Ps. 7:11; Isa. 5:16; Acts 17:31; Rom. 2:5).

Men and women are unrighteous before God (Ps. 143:2; Rom. 3:23). Although theoretically the law of God is a means of justification (Rom. 2:13; 10:5; James 2:10), none achieves it since all men and women everywhere have broken God's law (Rom 10:5; cf. 9:31).

God alone can deliver men and women from the condemnation that rightly awaits them, and His answer is the gospel— the revelation of His plan for imparting righteousness to sinners (Rom. 1:16–17).

God sets Jesus Christ before us as the One upon whom we are to believe because His sacrificial death has atoned for our guilt and removed the judgment that our rebellion against God brings on us (Rom. 3:22–25).

While God is the Judge, He is also the Justifier (Rom. 3:26, 30; 4:5; 8:33). On the basis of Jesus Christ's death, He reckons to believers His Son's righteousness (Rom. 3:23–26; Phil. 3:9), pronouncing them free from all guilt and just and righteous before Him (Rom. 3:26).

Justification is a free gift from God (Rom. 3:24; 5:17; Phil. 3:9), and the means of our entering into it is by faith (Rom. 1:17; 3:22, 26; 4:3–6, 13; 10:10).

— K —

Kingdom, Kingdom of God, Kingdom of Heaven

The kingdom of God, or the kingdom of heaven, is spoken of in at least three ways. First, it is God's reign or rule in human life, His acting as King (Matt. 6:33; Mark 10:15; cf. 1 Sam. 12:12; Isa. 41:21).

Second, it is the kingdom of which Christians are members because Christ, through the new birth (John 3:3, 5), actively rules as King in their hearts.

Third, it is the kingdom that Christians possess as an inheritance in the future (Matt. 25:34; Luke 22:16; 2 Tim. 4:18; Heb. 12:28).

Matthew alone uses the phrase "the kingdom of heaven"—thirty-one times. "Heaven" is used in place of "God" to avoid mentioning the divine name—a characteristic Jewish practice out of respect for God's name. Matthew probably did it out of regard for his intended Jewish readers.

— L —

Lamb of God

The Lamb is a prominent picture of Jesus Christ (used more than twenty times in the book of Revelation) to set Him forth as the One promised in the Old Testament (Isa. 53:7; cf. Acts 8:32) to obtain for others deliverance from God's judgment by the sacrifice of Himself (John 1:29; 1 Pet. 1:19)—God's purpose from the foundation of the world (Rev. 13:8).

In the Old Testament, the lamb was the principal sacrificial animal, and all such sacrifices looked forward to the one sacrifice that would deal with sin once and for all—the sacrifice of Jesus as the Lamb of God (Heb. 10:1–14).

Jesus Christ is our Passover Lamb, and as such, He has been sacrificed as an atonement for our sins (John 1:29, 36; 1 Cor. 5:7).

Although meekness characterized Jesus as the Lamb of God in His earthly ministry (Isa. 53:7; 1 Pet. 2:22–23), the symbol is used in the book of Revelation to express His position as the Conqueror and the Mighty One (Rev. 5:6; 7:14–17; 12:11).

Law

The word *law* is used to describe the whole of the Scriptures (Josh. 1:8; Ps. 119:97; Rom. 3:19), the first five books of the Bible, the Pentateuch (Rom. 3:21; Gal. 4:21), and more particularly the law of God, as summed up in the Ten Commandments (Exod. 20:1–17; Rom. 2:14, 17; 3:28; Gal. 5:3).

The law of God, which reflects God's nature and expresses His authority over us, can be summed up in the two great commandments (Matt. 22:34–40; cf. Gal. 5:14; James 2:8).

The law of God demands entire obedience (Gal. 3:2). No one, therefore, will be declared righteous in God's sight by observing the law (Rom. 3:20–21). Rather, it brings God's wrath on us because of our transgression of it (Rom. 4:15). The law was given so "that every mouth may be stopped, and all the world may become guilty before God" (Rom. 3:19).

Jesus came not to abolish the law but to fulfill it (Matt. 5:17); He set Himself to fulfill every demand of the law for a life of complete obedience to God, thus qualifying Himself to be a suitable and perfect substitute for sinners (1 Pet. 3:18).

Those under the law are in need of redemption, and God sent His Son, born of a woman, born under law, to redeem those under the law (Gal. 4:4–5).

In His death on the cross, Jesus Christ upheld the law's condemnation of all sinners: He became a curse for us, dying in the place of sinners (Gal. 3:13; cf. Deut. 21:23; Isa. 53:12; 2 Cor. 5:21).

The law of God makes us aware of our sin against God (Rom. 3:20) and thus drives us to realize our need of the salvation made possible by God through Jesus Christ (Gal. 2:15–16, 21; 3:24).

Christians desire to keep the law—not to gain salvation by works—but out of gratitude for salvation and in the liberty of those set free to love and obey God (Rom. 8:3–4; Gal. 5:1).

Lazarus

Lazarus is the name given to the beggar in the story Jesus told about the rich man in hell (Luke 16:19–31).

Lazarus is also the name of the brother of Mary and Martha, who lived with them in the village of Bethany (John 11:1; 12:1).

He died and was raised from the dead by Jesus when he had already been in the tomb four days (John 11:1–44), and as a result, many came to faith in Jesus (John 11:45; 12:10–11).

He was present at the dinner given in Jesus' honor when Mary, his sister, anointed Jesus' feet (John 12:1–2).

He became the subject of people's curiosity after his amazing resurrection, and the object of the chief priests' malice (John 12:9–11).

Levi

Levi, son of Alphaeus, was another name for Matthew, an apostle, one of the Twelve (Mark 2:14; Luke 5:27–29).

Levi may have changed his name to Matthew when he became a disciple of Jesus. *See* Matthew.

Lord

The word *lord* in the New Testament can be translated as "lord" or "master" when it relates to human beings.

But generally, *Lord* describes God, and it is the word used in the Greek translation of the Old Testament to render the name of God, Jehovah, or Yahweh.

It is used regularly of Christ, meaning that He is the divine Lord, having the highest place of all, worthy of our worship, service, and obedience (Acts 2:36; 1 Cor. 16:22; Phil. 2:9–11; Col. 3:24).

Since the Holy Spirit is Himself God, it is also used of Him (2 Cor. 3:18).

Lord's Supper

The Lord's Supper is a symbolic meal in that it proclaims Jesus Christ's death by words and symbols (1 Cor. 11:26).

It was foreshadowed by the Jewish Passover (1 Cor. 5:7–8; Exod. 12:21–30). As the Passover proclaimed God's mercy in redeeming His people under the old covenant, so the Lord's Supper proclaims God's redeeming mercy in the new covenant.

It took place at the time of the Passover and was established on the pattern of that feast (Matt. 26:17–19; Mark 14:1–2, 12–16; Luke 22:14–20; John 13:21–30; cf. Exod. 12:1–29).

Commanded by Christ for His disciples, it is appropriately called the Lord's Supper (1 Cor. 11:20; cf. 11:23).

By means of the Lord's Supper, Christians remember Christ's death, acknowledge their sharing in the benefits of His atoning sacrifice, make their thanksgiving to God, express their identity with other believers, and look forward to their Lord's return (1 Cor. 11:24–26).

Lost

Lost is used to describe the condition of people who live without Christ and therefore without the hope of eternal life. Men and women are either those being saved or those perishing (1 Cor. 1:18; 2 Cor. 4:3; 2 Thess. 2:10)—and to be lost is to be among the perishing.

Like lost sheep, unforgiven sinners are separated from the Shepherd they need (Matt. 10:6; Luke 15:4; 19:10).

The lost need to be found and saved through Jesus Christ, or else they will perish (Matt. 18:12–14; John 3:16).

Love

Love is unconquerable benevolence, and its source is God (1 John 4:7).

God is love (1 John 4:8, 16), and He is called "the God of love" (2 Cor. 13:11). There is nothing in Him that is incompatible with love, such as malice, coldness, or indifference.

Love characterizes every aspect of God's relationship with His people (Hos. 2:19).

God's love was demonstrated in His sending His Son into the world to be the atoning sacrifice for our sins (Rom. 8:32; Col. 1:13–14; 1 John 4:9–10).

When we respond to His love in Jesus Christ, we have the assurance that nothing can separate us from it (Rom. 8:38–39).

Born into God's family, we are to show to the world that we are God's children and Jesus Christ's disciples by the display and practice of love (John 13:35; 1 John 3:14; 4:7).

The love required of us is a totally unselfish love, a matter of will and action, expressed in service of the unworthy as much as the worthy (Matt. 5:44), based on the pattern of the love set forth in the cross of our Lord Jesus Christ (1 Cor. 13; Gal. 5:22; 1 John 3:16).

Luke

Luke was a Greek-speaking Gentile (Col. 4:14; cf. v. 11), and he had perhaps been a convert to Judaism before he became a Christian. He was probably a native of Antioch.

He is the anonymous author of the gospel bearing his name and of the Acts of the Apostles. He set himself to be a careful investigator and to provide an orderly account of the life and ministry of Jesus and of the birth of the early church.

He wrote evangelistically and with the purpose of defending the faith (Luke 1:3–4).

There are passages in the Acts where he uses the word *we*, telling his readers that he was present when the events recorded occurred (Acts 16:10–16; 20:5—21:18; 27:1—28:16).

He had access to reliable sources for his work—the apostle Paul (as in the *we* passages), Philip (Acts 21:8) who was one of the Seven (Acts 6:5), and John Mark (Col. 4:10–14).

He is outstanding for his historical accuracy (Luke 2:1–2; 3:1–3), and not least in his accurate naming of officials (Acts 13:7; 17:6).

He was a doctor, and in his two books there are at least twenty-three technical medical expressions that occur only in his writings (e.g., Luke 14:2; Acts 28:8).

He was a close friend (Col. 4:14; 2 Tim. 4:11) and fellow worker of Paul (Philem. 24).

Tradition has it that he was unmarried and that he died at the age of eighty-four in Boeotia in Greece.

— M —

Magi

The word *Magi* is Persian in background and describes wise men, priests, or experts in astrology, the interpretation of dreams, and other secret practices.

The Magi in the birth narrative of Christ came from the East, and they declared that they had read in the stars of the birth of the messianic king.

They were guided not only by a particular star they saw but by a dream (Matt. 2:12).

Malachi

Malachi's name (meaning "my messenger" or "angel") is mentioned only once in the Bible in the first words of the book bearing his name (Mal. 1:1).

He appears to have lived in or near Jersusalem since he had intimate knowledge of worship practices in the temple (Mal. 1:6—2:9).

Manoah

Manoah was the father of Samson and came from Zorah, of the clan of the Danites (Judg. 13:2).

His wife had been childless (Judg. 13:2) until the promise of Samson's birth to be the deliverer of Israel from the Philistines (Judg. 13:3–7).

Manoah's prayerful concern was to know how his son should be brought up (Judg. 13:8–23).

Mark

Mark was also called John (Acts 12:12, 25), John being his Hebrew name and Mark his Roman or Latin name. He was probably the young man mentioned in Mark 14:51–52 since Mark's gospel is the only gospel that refers to the incident.

His mother's home was a regular meeting place for members of the Jerusalem church (Acts 12:12).

He was the writer of the second gospel and gained much of his firsthand information from the apostle Peter.

Mark accompanied Barnabas and Paul on their first missionary journey (Acts 12:25) as their helper (Acts 13:5), but he left them at Perga to return home to Jerusalem (Acts 13:13). Paul clearly regarded it as an act of desertion, causing a division between Barnabas and himself and an end to their partnership (Acts 15:36–41).

Barnabas, perhaps because he was Mark's cousin (Col. 4:10), felt Mark should have a second chance, so he took Mark on his second missionary journey (Acts 15:39).

Mark subsequently proved himself and restored himself to Paul's confidence (Col. 4:10; Philem. 24). He was helpful to Paul in his ministry (2 Tim. 4:11).

He also served with Peter, probably in Rome (1 Pet. 5:13; "Bablylon" here almost certainly stands for Rome).

Martha

Martha, with her sister Mary and brother Lazarus, lived at Bethany near Jerusalem (John 11:1). The family had a special place in Jesus' affections (John 11:5).

Martha is remembered most for her distraction from listening to Jesus because of her preoccupation with preparing a meal for Him, and the lesson he taught through the contrasting attitudes and priorities of the two sisters (Luke 10:38–42).

Mary (Mother of Jesus)

Mary, a virgin, was pledged to be married to Joseph, a descendant of David. Before they came together, Mary was found to be with child through the Holy Spirit (Matt. 1:18; Luke 1:27), a miracle explained to Mary and to Joseph—but separately—by an angel (Matt. 1:20–21; Luke 1:26–38).

Mary was related to Elizabeth, the mother of John the Baptist, and they shared three months of their pregnancies together when Mary stayed with Elizabeth (Luke 1:56). When Elizabeth identified Mary's unborn son as the Son of God, Mary was inspired to express outstanding praise to God known as the Magnificat—"my soul magnifies the Lord" (Luke 1:46–55).

Mary gave birth to Jesus at Bethlehem while she and Joseph were there during a census (Luke 2:1–7).

Mary witnessed many astounding events surrounding her child, such as the shepherds' account of the appearance of the angel and the heavenly host (Luke 2:8–18), the wise men bowing down and worshiping Him (Matt. 2:11), and the recognition of the identity of her son as the promised Savior by both Simeon and Anna in the temple (Luke 2:25–38). Mary treasured up and pondered in her heart all these amazing events (Luke 2:19).

Mary gave birth to four other sons (Matt. 13:55), and one or more daughters (Mark 6:3).

Mary stood near the cross at the time of Jesus' death (John 19:25) and was entrusted to John's guardianship, as he was handed over to her care (John 19:26–27).

Mary was one of the women who joined constantly in prayer with the apostles and disciples after the Ascension, waiting for the coming of the Holy Spirit (Acts 1:14).

Jesus did not deny Mary's unique privilege, but He refused to put her above all who hear and obey God's Word (Luke 11:27–28).

Mary Magdalene

Mary's name derives from Magdala, a Galilean town, and her life was transformed after Jesus drove seven devils out of her (Mark 16:9).

She was one of the women who witnessed Jesus' crucifixion and who followed Joseph of Arimathea and Nicodemus as they laid Jesus' body in the tomb (Matt. 27:56, 61; Mark 15:40, 47; John 19:25).

She was first at the tomb with the other women on the day of Jesus' resurrection to anoint His body with spices (Matt. 28:1; Mark 16:1; John 20:1).

She reported to Peter and John that the stone had been removed from the tomb's entrance (John 20:1-2).

Jesus' initial resurrection appearance was to Mary (John 20:10-17), and she became the first messenger of the Resurrection (John 20:18).

Matthew

Matthew, also called Levi, was the son of Alphaeus (Mark 2:14; Luke 5:27).

His name is found in all the lists of the twelve apostles (Mark 3:18; Luke 6:15; Acts 1:13).

The gospel bearing his name identifies him as the tax collector who served the Romans as such (Matt. 10:3; cf. 9:9).

Upon his call to discipleship, he revealed an immediate concern for his former colleagues (Luke 5:27-32).

Mediate, Mediator, Mediation

A mediator, literally, is a go-between. He mediates between two parties to produce peace by removing disagreement.

Jesus Christ is the one Mediator between God and men and women (1 Tim. 2:5-6). He was uniquely qualified to mediate, being Himself both God and man.

He voluntarily took His stand between the offended God and the offending sinner, so as to deliver the sinner by taking upon Himself God's wrath, which the sinner deserves (Gal. 1:3–4; 2:20; 1 John 2:1–2).

By His unique sacrifice for sins on behalf of sinners, peace between God and sinners was made possible—Jesus Christ Himself is our peace (Rom. 5:1–2; Eph. 2:14).

Messiah, Messianic

Messiah means "Anointed," and it was the title given to the coming Deliverer promised in the Old Testament.

The word indicated that the Deliverer or Savior was to be specially consecrated for His tasks, in the same way as a king or a priest might be.

Among the Greeks the title "Messiah" was translated *Christos,* or *Christ* as we now know it.

Jesus' temptations at the beginning of His ministry (Matt. 4:1–11) indicated the kind of expectations Jews had of the Messiah: miraculous food, world dominion, and supernatural signs.

Micah

Micah (who is like the Lord?), an eighth-century B.C. prophet from Moresheth, a town in the lowlands of Judah, prophesied in the reigns of Jotham (ca. 742–735 B.C.), Ahaz (ca. 735–715 B.C.), and Hezekiah (ca. 715–687 B.C.), kings of Judah (Jer. 26:18; Mic. 1:1).

He was a younger contemporary of Isaiah, and in the days of Hezekiah, he foretold God's judgment on Jerusalem (Jer. 26:18).

The book bearing his name records the vision he saw concerning Samaria and Jerusalem (Mic. 1:1–16), the capital cities of the two kingdoms of Israel and Judah.

Miracle

A miracle is an act or a work of supernatural origin or character, which would not be possible by ordinary or natural means.

Jesus' deeds of power were miracles in this sense (Matt. 13:54, 58; Luke 19:37).

Behind the word translated "miracle" in some New Testament translations is the Greek word for "sign," which is something more than a deed of power. *See* Sign.

Moses

Moses is one of the most prominent figures in the Bible, and his name occurs eight hundred times.

Of the tribe of Levi, son of Amram and Jochebed, and brother of Aaron and Miriam (Exod. 6:16–20), Moses was cared for by his natural family for three months after his birth. Then having been placed in the reeds along the bank of the Nile, he was discovered by Pharaoh's daughter and brought up as her son (Acts 7:20–21). She gave him his name *Moses*, meaning "drawn out of the water" (Exod. 2:10). As a consequence he was educated in all the wisdom of Egypt (Acts 7:22).

Brought up in Egypt, he did not lose his sense of identity with his own people (Exod. 2:11). At the age of forty, through the discovery of his killing of an Egyptian who illtreated an Israelite, he fled to Midian (Exod. 2:11–15; Acts 7:23–29), where he lived for forty years and married Zipporah, daughter of Jethro, a priest of Midian (Exod. 2:16–22; 18:1; Acts 7:30). Zipporah gave birth to his two sons, Gershom and Eliezer (Exod. 18:3–4).

Moses' key contributions to Israel's history were the Exodus and the giving of the law (John 1:17).

He received God's commission to deliver God's people from Egypt (Exod. 3:1—4:17).

As the leader of God's people (Mic. 6:4), he led the Israelites throughout their journeys in the wilderness and recorded them (Num. 33:1–49), and many acts of power were associated with his leadership (Deut. 34:12; Isa. 63:12).

Moses was God's trusted spokesman (Exod. 19:9, 20; 24:1–3; Lev. 8:5). He gave the people God's law (Exod. 20:1–17; 31:18; 34:28; Deut. 33:4), and he was a prophet whom the Lord knew face-to-face (Exod. 33:11; Num. 12:8; Deut. 34:10).

When the tent (or tabernacle) of meeting was established, Moses heard God's voice speaking to him from between the two cherubim above the atonement cover on the ark of testimony (Num. 7:89).

He was responsible for writing down God's words and laws (Exod. 24:4) and the first five books of the Bible—called the Pentateuch—(Mark 12:26; Luke 16:29, 31; 20:28; 24:27). The law of God became known as the law of Moses because it was so uniquely given through him.

As a man of God (Deut. 33:1; Ps. 90) and a servant of God (Josh. 1:7, 13; 12:6), Moses was outstanding for his faithfulness (Num. 12:7; Heb. 3:5), his concern for the best interests of God's people (Num. 27:16–17), his intercession (Exod. 17:8–13; 32:7–14), and his humility (Num. 12:3).

He forfeited his own entry into the Promised Land by his failure to trust God enough to honor Him in the sight of the Israelites (Num. 20:7–13; 27:12–14).

Having been shown the Promised Land from Mount Nebo (Deut. 34:1), Moses died in Moab at the age of 120, still full of vigor (Deut. 34:5, 7), and Joshua succeeded him (Num. 27:16–23).

The secret of his perseverance was that he saw God, who is invisible (Heb. 11:27).

He anticipated the coming of the Messiah both in what he recorded (Gen. 3:15) and in what he prophesied (Deut. 18:15; John 1:45; Acts 3:22).

He appeared with Elijah at Jesus' transfiguration to talk with Him about His death and "exodus" (Luke 9:30–31).

Most Holy Place

The Most Holy Place was the innermost sanctuary of both the tabernacle and the temple (1 Kings 6:16), being only fifteen square feet.

It was separated from the rest of the building by a curtain (Exod. 26:31–33).

Within it was the ark of the testimony or covenant (Exod. 26:33), which contained the two stone tablets of the law, together with the gold jar of manna and Aaron's staff that had budded (Exod. 25:10–16; Heb. 9:4).

The cover over the ark was the atonement cover, or mercy seat, upon which blood was sprinkled on the Day of Atonement (Exod. 26:34; Lev. 16:2). On each end was a golden cherub (Exod. 25:17–22).

Only the high priest had access and then just once a year on the Day of Atonement with appropriate garments when he entered bearing sacrificial blood (Lev. 16:17, 23; 1 Chron. 6:49; Heb. 9:7).

This careful procedure symbolized that the way into God's presence for men and women had not yet been disclosed (Heb. 9:8), but Jesus' death, followed by His resurrection and ascension, declares that way now open by His blood (Heb. 9:12, 25; 10:19).

Through Jesus Christ, believers have access to God's immediate presence—the Most Holy Place—because by Jesus' offering of Himself the curtain, or the barrier, has been broken down (Heb. 10:19–22).

Mount of Olives

Sometimes called Olivet, the Mount of Olives, the highest range of hills east of Jerusalem, is a small ridge of four summits overlooking Jerusalem and the Temple Mount from the east.

In the early first century it was thickly wooded with olive trees, but following Titus's siege of Jerusalem in A.D. 70, he stripped it bare of trees.

The Garden of Gethsemane was probably at the foot of the Mount of Olives on the western slope.

Mystery

A mystery or secret is truth that we would not be able to understand apart from God's gift of spiritual illumination.

The gospel is a mystery since we could not have conceived it of ourselves, and we cannot understand it unless God graciously enlightens our minds.

The Lord Jesus Christ is the center of the mystery: His coming into the world in human flesh to be the Savior, a secret we can understand only as God Himself teaches us (Matt. 16:17; 1 Cor. 2:7; Col. 1:27; 2:2).

— N —

Nathanael

Nathanael (God has given), a model Israelite, a man of integrity and openness to God (John 1:47), came from Cana in Galilee (John 21:2).

He was brought to Jesus by Philip (John 1:45).

He was initially skeptical of the Messiah coming from Nazareth (John 1:46).

He is the first of Jesus' disciples to be recorded as making his confession of Jesus as the Son of God—a consequence of his discovery of Jesus' perfect knowledge of him (John 1:48–49).

Because of his not being mentioned in the lists of the Twelve in the first three Gospels, he has been popularly identified as Bartholomew.

Nazareth

Nazareth was the Galilean town in which Joseph and Mary lived. It was, therefore, the hometown of Jesus. But the people there rejected Him (Luke 2:39; 4:16, 28–30).

Though somewhat secluded, it was close to several main trade routes, which gave it contact with the world outside Israel.

New Birth

New birth deals with our dead spiritual state (Rom. 8:4–8), about which we can do nothing (Jer. 13:23; Eph. 2:1; Titus 3:5).

It is the supernatural work of God the Holy Spirit in which He acts according to the will of God the Father (John 1:13; 2 Cor. 5:18; James 1:18), on the grounds of Jesus Christ's saving work (Titus 3:6; 1 Pet. 1:2–3), to make us spiritually alive (Eph. 2:1) as He brings us to repentance and faith in Jesus Christ (John 1:12–13; 2 Thess. 2:13) through His Word (1 Pet. 1:23).

The Spirit's work in new birth is a work of tremendous power (2 Cor. 4:6; 5:17), as sovereign, mysterious, and irresistible as that of the wind (John 3:8; Acts 9:1–9; Gal. 1:15–16).

Without new birth—regeneration—we cannot enter the kingdom of God (John 3:3).

Three outstanding proofs of new birth are given by John in his first letter: those who are born again believe that Jesus is the Christ (1 John 5:1), strive to do what is right (1 John 2:29; 3:9; 5:18), and love fellow Christians (1 John 4:7).

New Testament

The word *testament* means "covenant." The term *New Testament* came into general use in the latter part of the second century to describe the twenty-seven writings that fall into four divisions: the Gospels; the Acts of the Apostles; twenty-one letters; and the book of Revelation.

The great message of the New Testament is that God's promises of redemption have been fulfilled in the life, death, and resurrection of Jesus Christ.

His blood has secured the provision of a new covenant, according to God's will, so that all who believe and obey become God's people and Christ's church.

Nicodemus

Nicodemus (conqueror of the people) was a Pharisee, a member of the Sanhredin, the Jewish ruling council, who came to Jesus by night seeking the truth about Jesus and the kingdom of God (John 3:1–21).

He spoke up in defense of Jesus when his fellow Jewish leaders criticized Him and were planning to kill Him (John 7:48–52).

He accompanied Joseph of Arimathea after the Crucifixion in asking for permission to bury Jesus' body in Joseph's new tomb (John 19:38–42), with the clear implication that by then he had become a disciple of Jesus (Matt. 27:57).

— O —

Old Testament

The word *testament* is used especially in the Bible with the concept of a "covenant" in view. (*See* Covenant.) The term *Old Testament* came into general use in the latter part of the second century to describe the writings we know by that title.

The thirty-nine books were arranged by the Jews into three divisions: the Law, the Prophets, and the Writings. They deal particularly with the promises, or covenant, that God made with Israel.

They are the record of the outworking of God's redemption of His people, and they always look forward to the spiritual redemption to take place with the Messiah's coming.

— P —

Palestine

The term *Palestine* originally referred to the land of Israel's enemies, the Philistines (Exod. 15:14; Joel 3:4), on the southwestern part of Canaan, but then later to the whole land—a phenomenon not unique in history.

The older term *Canaan* (Gen. 10:15–19) has the same kind of history (Exod. 6:4; Acts 13:19).

The Romans used the term *Palestina*.

Today we employ the name *Israel* to describe the whole land, although originally it belonged to the northern realm of Israel, after the division of the kingdom into Israel and Judah.

It is described in the Bible by a variety of names: the land of Israel (1 Sam. 13:19), the land of the Hebrews (Gen. 40:15), the Lord's land (Hos. 9:3), Immanuel's land (Isa. 8:8), the Promised Land (Heb. 11:9), and the Holy Land (Zech. 2:12)—the latter title was taken up in the Middle Ages and has survived.

Parable, Parables

A parable is a saying, comparison, or story by which a spiritual or moral truth is conveyed.

Jesus frequently used parables (Matt. 13:3; Mark 4:2), especially in speaking to the crowds (Matt. 13:10, 34).

His purpose in speaking of God's kingdom in parables was that only those with discernment would understand (Matt. 13:13).

Some parables were directed at those who opposed Jesus (Matt. 21:45; Mark 12:1–12).

The disciples were privileged to receive Jesus' private interpretation of the parables, especially those relating to the kingdom of God (Mark 4:10; Luke 8:10).

Paradise

Paradise is an Oriental word, first used by the Persians, of an enclosure or a walled garden.

Taken over by the Greeks, it expressed the idea of a place of supreme happiness above the earth.

It is a description of the heavenly home to which believers' spirits go at death, and Jesus promised a place in paradise to the penitent thief (Luke 23:43).

"The tree of life" is spoken of as being in the paradise of God (Rev. 2:7).

Paul identifies paradise with a place of supreme blessedness (2 Cor. 12:4).

Passover

Passover was the name given to the feast that God appointed to keep in the Jews' memory their deliverance from Egypt (Exod. 12:1–30).

It was so called because God "passed over" or "spared" the Israelites when He punished the Egyptians. God's people had to offer up a lamb or a kid so that the destroying angel might "pass over" them.

The Passover was celebrated on the fourteenth of the month Nisan (March–April) and continued into the early hours of the fifteenth.

It was followed immediately by the Feast of Unleavened Bread on the fifteenth to the twenty-first. In practice the two feasts were merged and treated as one (Mark 14:12; Luke 22:1).

The central event was the killing of the Passover lamb (Exod. 12:21; Deut. 16:2, 6; Mark 14:12; Luke 22:7) and the eating of the Passover meal (Mark 14:16; Luke 22:8, 13).

Christians came to understand the Passover lamb as a picture of Christ, and He is called "our Passover Lamb" (1 Cor. 5:7 NIV) because His death has saved us from the judgment of God's wrath, which we deserve.

Paul

Paul, the Greek form of his Hebrew name Saul by which he is first introduced in the Acts of the Apostles, was a Jew who came from Tarsus in Cilicia (Acts 21:39) and was educated under Rabbi Gamaliel in Jerusalem (Acts 22:3). He possessed Roman citizenship (Acts 16:37–39; 22:25–29).

He came from the most religious section of the Jewish nation (Phil. 3:4–6).

He was converted on the road to Damascus when he was intent on persecuting the Christians there (Acts 9:1–9; Phil. 3:6).

Called to be an apostle, and the last to receive such a call, he was like "one born out of due time" (1 Cor. 15:8; Rom. 1:1).

Having been befriended by Barnabas (Acts 9:27; 11:25–26), Paul was commissioned with him by the church at Antioch to go to the Gentiles with the gospel (Acts 13:1–4), and they worked in Cyprus, Antioch in Pisidia, Iconium, Lystra, and Derbe (Acts 12:25—15:35) until their disagreement about Mark (Acts 15:36–41). Then Paul took Silas as his companion (Acts 15:40) and soon afterward Timothy, also (Acts 16:1–4).

Beginning always with the Jewish people in any place, "Paul was compelled by the Spirit, and testified to the Jews that Jesus is the Christ," and he taught the Word of God (Acts 18:5, 11). When the Jews rejected his message, he turned to the Gentiles (Acts 18:6–8; 19:8–10).

He traveled from place to place strengthening disciples (Acts 18:23).

Paul's ministry provoked considerable opposition from his own Jewish people wherever he went, and as a result of their trying to kill him while he was in Jerusalem (Acts 21:30–32), he was arrested by the Roman authorities (Acts 21:33). As a result of a Jewish conspiracy to kill him (Acts 23:12–22), he was transferred to Caesarea and ultimately to Rome itself for trial (Acts 27—28), where we get our last glimpse of him maintaining his witness and testimony to Jesus Christ (Acts 28:30–31). It seems likely that he was released, and then rearrested, to die at the hands of Nero around A.D. 67.

Miracles (Acts 19:11; 20:9–10), amazing deliverances (Acts 14:19–20; 28:3–6), and special revelations from our Lord Jesus Christ (Acts 16:9–10; 18:9–10; 23:11; 2 Cor. 12:1–10) were associated with his ministry.

His New Testament letters were soon recognized to be written with God-given wisdom (2 Pet. 3:15).

Pavement

The Stone Pavement (which in Aramaic is *Gabbatha*) was the courtyard outside the military headquarters in Jerusalem, and the location of the judge's seat, where, for instance, Pilate, the Roman governor, passed sentence on Jesus (John 19:13).

Peace

Peace means well-being in general, not only the absence of strife but the presence of positive blessings. In the New Testament, it expresses all the blessings that flow to us from the grace of God.

Peace follows on our experience of God's grace (Rom. 1:7; Eph. 1:2; 1 Thess. 1:1; 2 Thess. 1:2).

Peace, therefore, is harmony with God restored, made possible by the reconciliation God has accomplished through the death of Jesus Christ (2 Cor. 5:20–21), into which we enter by faith.

This peace brings with it glorious access to God (Rom. 5:1–2).

At peace with God, we strive after peace with others (Matt. 5:9; Mark 9:50; Gal. 5:22; Eph. 4:3).

Pentecost

Pentecost—meaning literally "the fiftieth"—was the Jewish festival celebrated on the fiftieth day after the Passover.

It was called the Feast of Weeks because seven weeks (forty-nine days) had elapsed since the Passover, with the day after—the fiftieth—being Pentecost.

Pentecost was, to begin with, the festival of the firstfruits of the wheat harvest, when they were dedicated to God, and it finds its fullest description in Leviticus 23:15–22 (cf. Num. 28:26–31).

It was a day of rest, when no regular work was to be done (Lev. 23:21).

It was on the day of Pentecost that the Holy Spirit came on the disciples in Jerusalem (Acts 2:1–13).

Some have suggested that the firstfruits of the spiritual harvest—which the church represents—were symbolized on the day of Pentecost as thousands put their faith in Jesus Christ, but we cannot be dogmatic about this suggested symbolism.

Peter

Peter's original name was Simon, a later form of Simeon (Acts 15:14; 2 Pet. 1:1).

He came from the town of Bethsaida (John 1:44).

His name was changed by Jesus to *Cephas* or *Peter*, meaning "rock" (John 1:42).

His father's name was Jonah (Matt. 16:17) or John (John 1:42; 21:15–17), and his brother was Andrew (Matt. 4:18). Peter was married (Mark 1:30).

His name is linked particularly with James and John, for example, in some of the miracles (Mark 5:37; Luke 8:51), at the Transfiguration (Matt. 17:1, 4; Mark 9:2, 5; Luke 9:28, 32), and in the Garden of Gethsemane (Matt. 26:35; Mark 14:33, 37).

He spoke Aramaic with a strong north country accent (Mark 14:70).

He was a man of impulsive devotion (Matt. 14:28; Mark 14:29; Luke 5:8; John 21:7).

He was the regular spokesman for the disciples (Matt. 15:15; 18:21; Mark 1:36–37; 8:29; 9:5; 10:28; 11:21; 14:29; Luke 5:5; 12:41).

His denial of Jesus was his low point (Matt. 26:58–75; Mark 14:54–72; Luke 22:54–62; John 18:15–27).

Following his restoration after his act of denial, he was recommissioned to feed Christ's flock (John 21:15–17).

The nature of his death was foretold by Jesus (John 21:18–19).

In the early days of the church, he stood out as the leader (Acts 1:15; 2:14, 37–38; 3:12; 4:8; 8:14, 17, 25; 10; 12).

Although he had to be rebuked once by Paul for compromise (Gal. 2:11), he was rightly reckoned to be a pillar of the church (Gal. 2:9).

Two New Testament letters bear his name—1 and 2 Peter.

Pharisees

Pharisees means "separated ones." They originated as a group around 135 B.C. as they separated from other Jews who did not choose to keep the law.

As the religious teachers of the Jews (Matt. 16:12), they were primarily concerned with keeping God's law, so as to be God's faithful people preparing themselves for the Messiah's coming. Most teachers of the law belonged to the Pharisee party.

The tragedy was that instead of pleasing God, many ended up placing the emphasis on externals, like fasting (Matt. 9:14), public prayer (Luke 18:10–12), and tithing (Matt. 23:23). They fell into the snare of hypocrisy or playacting (Matt. 23:27, 29).

They generally rejected John the Baptist's ministry (Luke 7:30).

Linked sometimes with the Sadducees, they were Jesus' foremost opponents and critics, questioning His lifestyle and teaching (Matt. 9:11; Mark 10:2; Luke 15:2).

Besides being Jesus' main accusers and opponents (Matt. 9:34; 12:24), they were ultimately responsible for the plan to put Jesus to death (Matt. 12:14).

There were exceptions, like Nicodemus (John 3:1), and some, like Paul, came to faith in Jesus having initially opposed Him (Phil. 3:4–9).

Philip, One of the Seven

Philip, a Greek-speaking Jew, was one of the seven men chosen by the early church in Jerusalem to take charge of the daily distribution of food to needy people (Acts 6:1–6).

As a result of the persecution that broke out after Stephen's martyrdom, he proclaimed the gospel first in Samaria (Acts 8:4–13), and to Gentiles from then on from Azotus (Ashdod in the Old Testament) to Caesarea (Acts 8:40). He clearly had the gift of an evangelist (Acts 21:8) both in public preaching and in speaking to individuals (Acts 8:26–39).

He was married, and when Paul visited him in Caesarea, he had four unmarried daughters who prophesied (Acts 21:9).

Philip, One of the Twelve

Philip came from Bethsaida of Galilee (John 1:44; 12:21), the home of Andrew and Peter.

He was the disciple who told Nathanael about Jesus (John 1:43–46), and who became an apostle, one of the Twelve (Matt. 10:3; Mark 3:18; Luke 6:14; Acts 1:13).

He was the disciple who brought Gentiles to Jesus (John 12:20–22). He said to Jesus, "Lord, show us the Father, and it is sufficient for us" (John 14:8).

Phoenicia, Phoenicians

Phoenicia was the name given to the territory on the east Mediterranean coast between the rivers Litani and Arvad, the seacoast of central Syria, with Tyre and Sidon as the most important cities (Acts 11:19; 15:3; 21:2).

It was one of the places where Christians found refuge during the time of persecution that followed Stephen's death (Acts 11:19).

Matthew and Luke refer to it as "the region of Tyre and Sidon" (Matt. 15:21; Luke 6:17).

Pilate

Pontius Pilate was the Roman procurator, or governor (Luke 3:1), of Judea (A.D. 26–36).

Pilate took firm action against Galileans in an incident of which details are not given in the New Testament (Luke 13:1).

A stone slab was discovered in 1961 at Caesarea, bearing the name of Pontius Pilate.

There is evidence that he made mistakes in his administration, and he was sensitive to bad reports going back to his masters in Rome.

His role in Jesus' trial was decisive, and he gave the order for the Crucifixion (Matt. 27:2–26; Mark 15:1–15).

His wife also figures in the Gospels' narrative (Matt. 27:19).

Prayer

Prayer is the communion we may know with God as our Father through our Lord Jesus Christ, in which we express our dependence upon Him, offer up our desires (Ps. 62:8), and ask for the good things He desires us to request, both for ourselves and for others (Matt. 7:7; Luke 11:9–10; Col. 1:9).

Prayer is being with God, since it is not always asking but sometimes simply an expression of fellowship with God, with the desire on our part to be in His presence (Ps. 27:4; cf. Deut. 4:7).

Christians must always endeavor to pray in the way God has set forth: through Jesus Christ (Eph. 2:13) and in the Holy Spirit (Eph. 6:18; Jude 20). Through Jesus Christ, Christians have confidence to come before God (Heb. 10:19), and by the Holy Spirit, they are enabled to offer true prayer (Rom. 8:9, 26–27).

Preach, Preaching

We tend to use the word *preaching* in terms of teaching directed at believers, but in the New Testament, it is directed primarily to non-Christians.

Preaching constituted one of Jesus' principal activities (Isa. 61:1; Matt. 4:17; Mark 1:38; Luke 4:18, 43, 44), and He commanded His disciples and apostles to preach (Mark 3:14; 16:15; Luke 9:2; Acts 10:42).

Preaching is the authoritative proclamation of God's message by His appointed messengers (Titus 1:3).

Its context is the gospel or the good news about Jesus Christ (Luke 9:6; Acts 8:12; Rom. 1:15; 10:15).

Preaching is the proclamation of Jesus Christ (Rom. 16:25; 2 Tim. 4:17) and in particular His death (1 Cor. 1:23; 2:2).

His death for our sins, followed by His resurrection and exaltation, is the central content of Christian preaching (1 Cor. 15:12).

It is by preaching that God's Word is brought to light (Titus 1:3), His call goes out, and faith in Jesus Christ is brought to birth (Rom. 10:8–17).

Priesthood, Priests

The background of the Jewish priesthood is God's call to His people to be holy (Lev. 11:44–45).

Early in Israel's history the priesthood was given to the tribe of Levi, the smallest tribe, "to bear the ark of the covenant of the LORD, to stand before the LORD to minister to Him and to bless in His name" (Deut. 10:8). The priests also decided all cases of dispute and assault (Deut. 21:5).

Not having a property inheritance like other tribes, the Levites were supported by the people's tithe (Num. 18:21, 24), a tenth of which in turn was given to the priests (Num. 18:26–28).

All priests were Levites, but not all Levites were priests (Deut. 17:9; 24:8; Judg. 19:1). Levites who were not priests assisted the priests (Num. 1:50; 3:6, 8; 16:9; 1 Chron. 23:28).

The primary function of the priests was the offering of sacrifices on the altar (Lev. 1—7) in either the tabernacle or the temple.

They also sought God's guidance on behalf of the people through the Urim and Thummim (Exod. 28:30; Judg. 18:5; Ezra 2:63), the ephod (1 Sam. 23:9–12), or the drawing of lots (Lev. 16:8).

They distinguished between the holy and the common, and they taught the people the decrees God had given through Moses (Lev. 10:10).

They passed judgments on matters of ritual purity (Lev. 11—15).

By the time of Jesus' ministry, the priests were part of the Jewish aristocracy and possessed great influence in society, although they were divided into a number of parties and sects.

The chief priests claimed to be descendants of Zadok, the priests men of Aaronic descent, and the temple servants who remained were of Levitical parentage (1 Chron. 24). The chief among the chief priests, the high priest, was the only priest who was anointed for his task (Lev. 21:10).

The ordinary priests formed twenty-four divisions of service in four to nine family groups (1 Chron. 24; cf. Luke 1:5, 8), and the divisions performed their service in the temple in turn, a week on each occasion. For the rest of the time, they fulfilled their calling in the surrounding area. Priests often undertook the reading and exposition of the Law in the worship of the synagogue.

Levites who were not priests were divided into temple musicians and temple servants (1 Chron. 6:16–48), and were in twenty-four divisions of service like the priests. They had no access to the altar (Num. 18:3), and they lived in Levitical cities (Josh. 21).

Prophecy, Prophets

Prophecy in the Bible represents the speaking forth of the mind and counsel of God.

Although prophecies sometimes referred to future events, prophecy was not necessarily foretelling the future. Rather, it was the setting forth of truth that could not be known by natural means.

Prophets in the Old Testament were God's spokesmen: individuals supernaturally instructed in God's will, and inspired and commissioned to make known His will to men and women, as to both present and future events (Isa. 51:16; Jer. 1:9–10; 2 Pet. 1:20–21).

The Holy Spirit who inspired the prophets caused some of them to write their messages down for the benefit of future generations.

In the New Testament, prophets are mentioned after apostles in our Lord Jesus Christ's gifts to His church (1 Cor. 12:28; Eph. 2:20; 4:11).

Nowhere in the New Testament is the gift of prophecy explained, but it appears plain that the prophets were the spiritually inspired counselors who told the churches what to do in specific situations, a ministry that was especially relevant before the New Testament Scriptures were readily available. Their work is never put on a par with that of the Old Testament prophets.

Propitiation

To *propitiate* is "to placate or appease." The reaction of God's holiness to sin is wrath, displeasure, and vengeance.

The purpose of propitiation is the removal of God's wrath.

By His death upon the cross for our sins, Jesus Christ, God's Son, propitiated God's wrath and rendered God well disposed to His believing people—and this He did as the provision of God the Father's great love for sinners (1 John 4:8–10).

In the Bible, therefore, the initiative in propitiation is God's, and the wonder of it is that God offered Himself in propitiation for our sins.

Psalms

Psalms means "praises" and gives its name to the longest book in the Bible.

The 150 psalms came from different authors, although many—seventy-three—are said to have been written by David. They were like a hymnbook for Solomon's temple.

Reflecting many varieties of human experience, they offer strength and help to believers in their own experiences of life.

— Q —

Qumran

Qumran is an Arabic word for a wadi (a ravine or valley that in the rainy season becomes a watercourse and stream), and it describes the wadi that empties into the northwest end of the Dead Sea, where the Dead Sea Scrolls were found beginning in 1947 and thereafter.

The Qumran community was a Jewish sect. The members considered themselves a faithful Jewish remnant, living at the end of the age.

— R —

Ransom

Ransom is an Old Testament word, as much as a New, meaning a "redemption price." In the Old Testament, it usually indicates the transfer of ownership from one to another through the payment of a price or the provision of a substitute.

In the New Testament, the term is used by Jesus Himself (Matt. 20:28; Mark 10:45), Paul (1 Tim. 2:6), and the writer to the Hebrews (9:15 NIV) as the payment of a ransom price that is substitutionary in character in which Jesus offered His life for ours (Titus 2:14; 1 Pet. 1:18–19).

Reconcile, Reconciled, Reconciliation

The idea behind the word *reconciliation* is that of making peace after a quarrel, the bringing together of two parties who have been estranged. Its opposite, therefore, is alienation.

The harmony that humankind knew with God in the beginning has been completely spoiled by humankind's sin so that God's attitude of wrath is the only right one humankind can deserve.

Men and women constitute themselves God's enemies by their sins (Rom. 5:10; Col. 1:21) because God's just demand for righteousness means that He is always opposed to evil.

Reconciliation, in this situation, is achieved by God's dealing with the root cause of the quarrel—human sin.

By the death of His Son, God dealt with sin finally and effectively (Rom. 5:10–11). God caused Jesus Christ, who Himself had no sin, actually to be sin for sinners, so that in Jesus Christ, they might be made righteous and acceptable to Him (2 Cor. 5:21).

Men and women may now be reconciled to God as they respond to God's gracious offer in Jesus Christ (2 Cor. 5:20).

Redeem, Redemption

Redemption is a term by which Christ's work for sinners may be viewed. Redemption is deliverance from captivity, bondage, or death by purchase or ransom.

The biblical picture behind it is that of slavery. By nature, we are slaves to sin, deserving the punishment of death (John 8:34). The price paid to purchase sinners from the slavery of sin was the death of the Lord Jesus Christ (1 Cor. 6:20; Eph. 1:7).

Through Christ, believers become free from the power of sin and death, but they have a privileged obligation, as a consequence, to glorify God in their bodies (1 Cor. 6:20).

Regeneration, *See* New Birth.

Repentance

Repentance is turning from sin to God as a result of a change of mind and heart about sin.

God commands it on the part of all (Acts 17:30), and it is a condition of salvation (Matt. 4:17; Luke 24:47; Acts 26:18).

It yields fruits, which demonstrate its genuineness (Matt. 3:8; Luke 13:6–9).

Resurrection

Resurrection hope (Acts 23:6) was present in the Old Testament (Job 19:26–27; Ps. 16:9–11), although subsequently there were some, like the Sadducees, who denied the possibility of resurrection (Matt. 22:23; Luke 20:27; Acts 23:6, 8).

That resurrection hope was filled out immeasurably by the resurrection of Jesus Christ from the dead as His resurrection became and is the promise, guarantee, and prototype of the resurrection of those who believe in Him (John 11:24–26; 1 Cor. 15:13, 20, 35–57).

The resurrection of the dead will take place at the second coming of the Lord Jesus Christ (1 Cor. 15:23; 1 Thess. 4:14).

There will be a resurrection both of the righteous and of the wicked (John 5:28–29; Acts 24:15; Rev. 20:11–15), but addressed as it is to Christians, the New Testament concentrates on the resurrection of believers (John 6:40; 2 Cor. 4:14; 1 Pet. 1:3).

Life after the resurrection will be different in many respects from life as we now know it. For example, we shall neither marry nor be given in marriage, but we shall be like the angels in heaven (Matt. 22:30; Luke 20:35–36). Above all, in body and in character we shall be like our Lord Jesus Christ (Phil. 3:20–21; 1 John 3:2).

The resurrection of the dead is a fundamental Christian doctrine (2 Tim. 2:8–13; Heb. 6:2), so much so that Christian believers are called the "children of the resurrection" (Luke 20:36 NIV).

Righteous, Righteousness

Righteousness is a characteristic of God, expressing the rightness of all that He is and does (Rom. 3:5–6).

It is used to represent, too, whatever is pleasing to God (Matt. 3:15; 5:6, 10, 20).

The most important use is when it describes the right relationship into which men and women are brought with God when they believe in Christ (Rom. 1:17). They are made righteous in Him, that is to say, they become in Christ all that God requires men and women to be (1 Cor. 1:30; 2 Cor. 5:21).

Rome

First a city-state in Italy, Rome became an empire ruling much of the Western world by the first century A.D.

Rome's highway system began in 312 B.C., and by the second century B.C., first-class roads existed to every part of the empire—an important factor for the spread of the gospel in the first century A.D.

Rome was the largest city of the empire, with a population of almost a million by the end of the first century A.D.

It is not known when Jews first went to live in Rome, but it is reckoned that about twenty thousand lived there in the first half of the first century A.D. Certainly thirteen synagogues were established there, although not all were necessarily in existence at the same time.

Roman Jews were in Jerusalem on the day of Pentecost (Acts 2:10), and they may have been the founding members of the church in Rome.

— S —

Sabbath

The Hebrew word *shabbath* translated "Sabbath," the seventh day of the week, means "cessation, intermission, or rest."

The fourth commandment relates to the keeping of the Sabbath, and it is elaborated upon more than the others (Exod. 20:8–11).

The Sabbath is God's invitation to rejoice in His creation and in His lordship over our time (Gen. 2:2–3; Exod. 20:11).

It was a sign of God's covenant with Israel and a means of her declaring her loyalty to God (Exod. 31:13–17; Ezek. 20:12, 20).

The Jews were also taught to connect the Sabbath with their exodus from Egypt (Deut. 5:15), a fact that ties in well with the Christian church's decision to connect the Sabbath with Christ's resurrection.

The Sabbath guarantees employees a day of rest (Exod. 20:10; 23:12; Deut. 5:14), which they might otherwise not be at liberty to take.

Jesus' initial conflict with the Jewish religious leaders related to the Sabbath. They had surrounded it with so many laws of their own making that they had lost sight of its original purposes.

Sacrifice, Sacrifices

A sacrifice among the Jews in the Old Testament was an act of worship by which an offering was made to God of some object belonging to the worshiper—although never another human being (Deut. 18:10)—the purpose being to please God and to obtain His favor (Lev. 17:5).

High priests were selected from among men and appointed to represent men and women in matters related to God, to offer gifts and sacrifices for sins (Heb. 5:1; 8:3).

The animal sacrifices of the Old Testament were intended to teach the method of salvation (Exod. 12:25–27; 1 Cor. 5:7). They always had the idea of cleansing behind them, and the indispensable element was the shedding of blood (Heb. 9:22–23). But their repetition only pointed out their ineffectiveness (Heb. 10:2), and they were not able to clear the consciences of worshipers (Heb. 9:9).

Thus, the sacrifices reminded men and women of sin, revealed the need of atonement, and prepared the way for the coming of Jesus Christ (Heb. 10:1–4).

The term *sacrifice* is used of the sacrificial death of Jesus Christ, for He offered for all time a single sacrifice for sins (Heb. 10:12), doing what the Old Testament sacrifices could never do.

His sacrifice is effective for all time, cleansing our consciences (Heb. 9:14), and guaranteeing perfect forgiveness (Heb. 9:26).

Sadducees

The Sadducees were the other main party of the Jews with the Pharisees, although a considerably smaller group.

They denied the resurrection (Matt. 22:23; Luke 20:27), and the existence of angels and spirits (Acts 23:8).

Most of them were from the rich, landowning class, and many of the chief priests were from among their number.

They were generally opposed to the Pharisees, but they united with them in their opposition to Jesus (Matt. 22:34).

Salvation, Save

Salvation is deliverance from the guilt and penalties of sin to enjoy, instead, the unchanging favor of God forever through repentance and faith in the Lord Jesus Christ (Acts 4:12; Rom. 10:10).

It is known and felt in the present by the gift of the Holy Spirit (Acts 2:38) and the forgiveness of sins (1 John 1:9).

But it will be completely disclosed in the future in the full enjoyment of everlasting life and all its benefits (Acts 2:38–40; 16:30–31; 1 Thess. 5:8–10; 1 Pet. 1:5, 13).

Samaria

Samaria, the name of both an area and the northern Israelite capital, was associated in the Old Testament with many idolatrous shrines (1 Kings 13:32; Isa. 8:4; 9:9–10; Jer. 23:13; Ezek. 23:4; Hos. 7:1; Mic. 1:6).

The city received its name from the former owner of the hill, Shemer, when the hill was bought by King Omri (1 Kings 16:23–24). It became the burial place for many of the kings of Israel (1 Kings 16:28; 22:37; 2 Kings 10:35; 13:13).

Ahab continued his father Omri's building work (1 Kings 22:39) and reigned in Samaria (1 Kings 16:29; 20:43); it became the seat of government for the northern kingdom of Israel (2 Kings 10:36; 13:1, 10).

Ahab set up an altar for Baal in the temple of Baal that he built in Samaria (1 Kings 16:32).

God's judgment upon Samaria, because of the continuing heathen practices that had been introduced, was to allow her to be captured in 722 B.C. by the king of Assyria, and for the inhabitants to be deported to Assyria (2 Kings 17:6–23).

The king of Assyria brought people from Babylon, Cuthah, Ava, Hamath, and Sepharvaim to settle in the towns of Samaria as replacements for the Israelites (2 Kings 17:24), and Samaria stood out for its intermingling of religious practices and its population of people of mixed ancestry (2 Kings 17:24–41). As a consequence, the worship of God by the Samaritans was confused (John 4:22), and Jews did not associate with them (John 4:9).

The woman to whom Jesus spoke at the well, revealing Himself as the Messiah and the giver of the living waters of eternal life, was a Samaritan (John 4:4–26). Her testimony caused many Samaritans to believe in Him (John 4:39).

In the story Jesus told about kindness to a wounded traveler, a Samaritan showed love for his neighbor, in contrast to the Pharisee and the Levite (Luke 10:33).

The one man with leprosy—out of the ten—who returned to express his thanks to Jesus was from Samaria (Luke 17:16).

The apostles were commissioned to preach the gospel in Samaria (Acts 1:8; 8:14; 9:31).

After Stephen's death, Christians were scattered throughout Judea and Samaria (Acts 8:1).

Philip the evangelist exercised a significant ministry in Samaria (Acts 8:4–13).

Sanhedrin

The Sanhedrin was the highest governing body in Judea.

It was composed of high priests, elders, and teachers of the law, and it met under the presidency of the ruling high priest.

It was the ultimate authority in all religious matters and in all legal and government affairs where it did not encroach on the Roman governor's authority. The Roman governor, for example, had to confirm any death sentence passed by the Sanhedrin.

Sarah

Sarah, wife of Abraham (Gen. 11:29), set out from Ur of the Chaldeans to go to Canaan with her husband and father-in-law (Gen. 11:31).

The tragedy of her early married life was her barrenness (Gen. 11:30).

She was a woman of exceptional beauty and was persuaded twice by Abraham to pretend she was his sister on that account (Gen. 12:11–13; 20:1–18).

In view of her barrenness, Sarah suggested to Abraham that he should have a son by her Egyptian maidservant, Hagar, and thus Ishmael was born (Gen. 16:1–3). Sarah later put the blame for this action on Abraham after Hagar despised Sarah upon Ishmael's birth (Gen. 16:4–5).

Her name was changed from Sarai to Sarah (meaning "princess" or "royal lady") when Abram's name became Abraham (Gen. 17:5, 15).

God's plan was that Abraham should have a child through Sarah (Gen. 17:6; 18:10–12; 21:1–7; Heb. 11:11). She gave birth to Isaac at the age of ninety (Gen. 17:17) when she was past the age of childbearing, proving that nothing is too hard for God (Gen. 18:11–15; 21:1–3).

She lived to be 127 years old and died at Hebron where she was buried in the cave of Machpelah near Mamre (Gen. 23:1–2, 19), the place Abraham was also buried later (Gen. 25:8–10).

Sarah is presented in the New Testament as an example of wifely submission (1 Pet. 3:6; cf. Gen. 12:13; 18:6; 20:13).

Satan

Satan is the name of the prince of evil, commonly called the devil.

Satan is one of the fallen angels exalted in rank and power above all the rest (Jude 6; 2 Pet. 2:4), who fell from the truth in which he once stood (John 8:44), probably by reason of pride (1 Tim. 3:6). He is represented as a star fallen from heaven to earth (Rev. 9:1).

He is the great enemy of God and men and women, the opposer of all that is good, and the promoter of all that is evil (Acts 13:10; Rev. 12:9–11).

He has already been defeated by Christ's death and resurrection, and this defeat will be complete and clear to all at the end of this present age (Matt. 25:41; Col. 2:15; Heb. 2:14).

The multiplicity of names by which he is described—the "wicked one" (1 John 2:13–14), the "prince of the power of the air" (Eph. 2:2), the "ruler of demons" (Matt. 9:34), the "god of this age" (2 Cor. 4:4), Beelzebub (Matt. 12:24), the "tempter" (Matt. 4:3), "that serpent of old" and the "great dragon" (Rev. 12:9)—indicates the diverse nature of his evil activities.

Savior

A Savior is a deliverer or preserver, and as a title for Jesus Christ, it is especially appropriate because of His saving work on the cross on behalf of sinners, promised by God throughout the centuries (Luke 2:11; Acts 13:23; Phil. 3:20).

As the Savior, Jesus gives repentance and forgiveness of sins (Acts 5:31), and life and immortality (2 Tim. 1:10) to all who believe on Him (John 3:16).

Scribes

Scribes were the rabbis, ordained theologians, who were experts in the law. They proclaimed God's will by instruction, judgment, and preaching. Their reputation was high among the people (Mark 12:38–39; cf. Matt. 23:6–7).

Luke indicates that a distinction is to be made between Jesus' sayings against the scribes (Luke 11:45–52; 20:46) and those against the Pharisees (Luke 11:37–44).

Jesus criticized the scribes for their failure to practice what they preached (Luke 11:46), their misapplication of Scripture (Mark 7:9–13), their pride (Matt. 23:5–7), selfishness, and insincerity (Mark 12:40).

Some of their representatives, with the chief priests and elders, formed the Sanhedrin (Matt. 16:21; 27:41; Mark 8:31; 11:27; 14:43, 53; Luke 9:22).

Scriptures

The word *Scriptures* means "writings," and in the New Testament, it refers to the Old Testament (Luke 24:44–45; 1 Cor. 15:3–4).

The term is often used by Christians to describe both Old and New Testaments.

Septuagint

The Septuagint is the Greek version of the Old Testament, which derives its name from the unsubstantiated story that it was achieved by seventy or seventy-two Palestinian Jews at the request of Ptolemy Philadelphus (285–246 B.C.), and completed by them in seclusion on the island of Pharos in seventy-two days. The reference to seventy explains why it is commonly abbreviated LXX.

It was the Bible of the early Christians and of most of those involved in the writing of the New Testament.

When the New Testament writers quote from the Old Testament, it is usually from the Septuagint.

For Jews who settled in the gentile world, the Septuagint enabled them to hold on to their faith when Greek replaced Hebrew as their first language.

It also served as an introduction for Gentiles to Jewish history and religion.

Shepherd

God describes Himself as the Shepherd of His people (Ezek. 34:12, 16), and the title is frequent in the Old Testament (Gen. 49:24; Pss. 23:1; 80:1), indicating His love for, protection of, and rule over His people.

Those appointed by God for the care of His people, whether as kings (2 Sam. 5:2; 7:7; Ps. 78:71), prophets, pastors, or teachers (Jer. 17:16; John 21:15–17; Acts 20:28; 1 Pet. 5:2), are to see themselves as shepherds.

"Shepherd" was a messianic title (Mic. 5:4 NIV; Matt. 2:6).

Jesus delighted to speak of Himself as the Shepherd of His people (Matt. 26:31; John 10:11, 14, 16)—as the Shepherd who laid down His life for His sheep (John 10:15).

He is the Great and Chief Shepherd of the sheep (Heb. 13:20; 1 Pet. 5:4)—a relationship that will be just as meaningful in the life to come (Rev. 7:17).

Sign, Signs

A sign, like a miracle, is a work or an event that is contrary to the usual course of nature.

Jesus' miracles recorded in John's gospel are all described as "signs," for besides being supernatural in character, they provided evidence of His deity, sufficient to bring a person to living faith in Him (John 20:30–31).

Simeon, A Prophet and Teacher

Simeon, called Niger, is mentioned after Barnabas as one of the prophets and teachers in the church at Antioch (Acts 13:1).

Simeon of Jerusalem

Simeon was a righteous and devout Jew, who waited for the "Consolation of Israel" (Luke 2:25).

Prompted by the Holy Spirit, he went into the temple courts the very moment Mary and Joseph arrived to present Jesus to the Lord, as the custom of the law demanded (Luke 2:27).

The Holy Spirit had revealed to him that he would not die until he had seen the Lord's Christ (Luke 2:26). Simeon immediately recognized Jesus as the promised Messiah, took Him into his arms, and praised God in a song (Luke 2:28–32) we know as the *Nunc Dimittis* (now let me depart in peace).

He blessed Joseph and Mary and prophesied the wonderful destiny of Mary's son, and the sorrow that would be hers (Luke 2:34–35).

Simeon Peter

Simeon was a name of Simon Peter (Acts 15:14; 2 Pet. 1:1)—a variant of Simon. *See* Peter.

Simon the Zealot

We do not know whether Simon was a zealot in the religious or the political sense (Matt. 10:4; Mark 3:18; Acts 1:13). Political zealots led a revolt against Rome in A.D. 66.

Sin, Sins, Sinner

Sin is basically rebellion against God (Dan. 9:5; Rom. 3:23; 1 John 3:4).

Arising from the corruption of the human heart, it is the cause of our separation from God, and the reason for our deserving God's wrath (Rom. 1:18; 3:5; John 3:36).

Sin is our greatest problem (Isa. 53:6; Rom. 5:9; 1 Pet. 3:18).

Son, Son of God

"Son" or "Son of God" was a title Jesus rarely used, although He spoke of Himself sometimes as "the Son" (Matt. 11:27; Mark 13:32).

He is not the Son in the same sense as we may become sons and daughters of God through faith (Luke 2:49; John 20:17).

He is uniquely God's one Son, the One whom He loves (Mark 12:6), in a way no one else can be.

He and the Father are one, a fact that the disciples fully appreciated at the Resurrection (John 20:28; Rom. 1:3–4).

All the works, glory, and perfection of God may be attributed to Him (Mark 2:5, 7; John 1:3; Col. 1:16–17; Heb. 1:2).

Son of David

"Son of David" is a messianic title of great significance.

Matthew in particular records the crowds' use of the title (nine occasions compared with Mark's and Luke's three occasions each).

There was an understanding on the part of the Jewish people that the Messiah and "the Son of David" were one and the same (Matt. 22:42).

It was the crowds' recognition of Jesus as the Son of David that so angered the Jewish authorities at the time of His triumphal entry into Jerusalem (Matt. 21:9, 15).

Son of Man

"Son of man" was a description Jesus often used of Himself —it occurs eighty-two times in the Gospels.

It was a particularly useful title because it expressed both His humanity and His deity.

In Hebrew, "son of man" can simply mean a man as an individual (Num. 23:19; Dan. 8:17), but it was also a prophetic description of the Messiah (Dan. 7:13–14).

People could read into the title what they wanted. For the majority, it expressed Jesus' identity with humankind. For those with insight, it indicated His messiahship and deity (Mark 2:10, 28).

Sovereignty

Sovereignty is supreme authority and absolute dominion, and it belongs to God alone by right.

God works out everything in conformity with the purpose of His will (Eph. 1:11); He is over all things, and He does what He will (Rom. 9:15, 18; cf. 11:36).

Spirit

The word *spirit* is used in many different ways in the Bible.

It can refer to an individual's inner life, and it is sometimes used in place of the soul (Eccles. 12:7; Luke 1:46–47; 23:46; Acts 7:59; 1 Cor. 5:3, 5) and the heart (Ps. 78:8).

It is more important than the body, since it is the part of us that thinks, feels, and wills, and lives forever (Matt. 16:26; 2 Cor. 5:8; 2 Tim. 4:22).

The Bible speaks of the spirits of the dead (Job 26:5) with whom no communication is to be sought by means of mediums and spiritists (Lev. 20:6, 27; Deut. 18:11; 1 Sam. 28:7–20).

God is described as the "God of the spirits of all flesh" (Num. 16:22), and the Father of our spirits (Heb. 12:9).

Spirit can can also have reference to a person's disposition (Gal. 6:1).

Spirit can refer to an independent being who cannot be perceived by human senses, such as God Himself (John 4:24), and to good spirits (Heb. 1:14).

Spirit describes God's own nature. He is spirit, that is to say, there is nothing material in His nature (John 4:24), and He has no body.

Like the wind—the identical word in Greek—*spirit* is invisible, immaterial, and powerful, and these characteristics belong perfectly to God.

Spirit is the term especially employed to describe the third person of the Trinity (John 1:32; 3:34; Acts 2:17; Rom. 8:13). *See* Holy Spirit.

The word *spirit* is also used of a demon or evil spirit (Matt. 8:16; Luke 10:20). *See* Demons.

A gift of the Holy Spirit is the distinguishing of spirits (1 Cor. 12:10; cf. 1 John 4:1).

Stephen

Stephen was one of the seven men appointed to relieve the apostles from administrative tasks such as the daily distribution of food to widows (Acts 6:1–5).

He was a Greek-speaking Jew who sought to evangelize his own people (Acts 6:9).

He was full of the Holy Spirit and of faith, grace, and power, so that he did great wonders and miraculous signs among the people (Acts 6:5, 8; 7:55).

He was falsely accused of blasphemy and stoned to death (Acts 6:11–12; 7:57–60).

He was outstanding for following Jesus' example in the manner and spirit in which he submitted to his suffering (Acts 7:54–60).

There seems little doubt that his death had a profound effect upon Saul (Paul), who witnessed it (Acts 7:58).

A great persecution of Christians followed Stephen's martyrdom (Acts 11:19).

Synagogue

Synagogue (place of assembly), rather like the word *church*, described both the meeting place of the Jews in a community and the congregation itself.

Rulers of the synagogue (Mark 5:22, 35, 38) were responsible for the general oversight of worship and teaching (Luke 13:14; Acts 13:15).

Attendants (Luke 4:20) were paid officers whose particular duty was to care for the general fabric and the rolls of Scripture.

The sermon or "word of exhortation" (Acts. 13:15) came after the readings from the Pentateuch and the Prophets.

Any competent male worshiper might be invited to give the sermon (Luke 4:16–17; Acts 13:15), which explains why the synagogues were so important for the early spread of the gospel among the Jews (Acts 13:14, 42; 14:1; 17:1, 10, 17; 18:4, 7–8, 19, 26; 19:8).

— T —

Tax Collectors

The system of farming out sources of government revenue from taxes was common among the Greeks and Romans. Such concessions were sometimes auctioned annually.

The Roman authorities farmed out contracts for obtaining their taxes from the Jews, and the possessors of the contracts in turn employed subordinates—the tax collectors—usually from the Jewish population to collect the taxes from their own people.

It is not surprising that they became a hated and despised group.

Strict Jews were offended by the close contact tax collectors had with their gentile overlords, and such connections made them ceremonially unclean. Hence they were linked with the notorious sinners of the community (Matt. 9:10–11; Luke 15:1).

Temple

A temple is regarded as the dwelling place of a deity.

In heathen religions, it was, and is, the place where an idol might be found (2 Cor. 6:16).

The first temple was built by Solomon in Jerusalem on

Mount Moriah (2 Chron. 3:1), and it was destroyed when Jerusalem fell to the Babylonians in 587 B.C.

In 538 B.C., the Jews returned from exile in Babylon and began to rebuild the temple, completing it in 515 B.C.

In 63 B.C., the Romans captured Jerusalem and took the temple. It was not harmed, but it was later plundered of its gold.

The temple at the time of Jesus' ministry was in the process of being rebuilt (having been begun by Herod the Great). It was done in a piecemeal fashion so as to enable all the temple services to continue.

At the beginning of Jesus' ministry the rebuilding had been going on for forty-six years (John 2:20), and more than thirty further years were required to complete it. Made of white marble and plated with gold, it was a building of dazzling grandeur.

When Jerusalem fell to the Roman armies in August, A.D. 70, the temple was burned, and only the Wailing Wall of Herod's temple remains.

The word *temple* is also used to describe Christians collectively as God's dwelling (1 Cor. 3:16–17; 2 Cor. 6:16; Eph. 2:21).

Temple of the Body

Jesus used the word *temple* of His body, which was to be destroyed by death and then resurrected (John 2:19–22; Matt. 26:61; 27:40; Mark 15:29).

It is also used of the Christian's body as the temple of the Holy Spirit (1 Cor. 3:16–17; 6:19).

Temptation

Temptation is used in both a good and a bad sense, and it can have the meaning of test as much as to tempt.

In the good sense, God tests men and women so that they may prove themselves true (Heb. 11:17). In this sense, our Lord Jesus Christ was tested by God (Heb. 2:18; 4:15).

In the bad sense, it is seduction into disobedience to God, which is the devil's work (Matt. 4:1; 1 Cor. 7:5; Gal. 6:1; James 1:13). As such, it is to be viewed as a constant peril, and it is overcome only by daily watchfulness (Mark 14:38; 1 Cor. 10:12–13) and dependence on God (Eph. 6:10–18).

Thaddaeus

Thaddaeus's name appears only in the list of the apostles, and nothing more is known of him (Matt. 10:3; Mark 3:18).

Thomas

Thomas was one of the twelve apostles (Matt. 10:3; Mark 3:18; Luke 6:15).

Thomas's background is not known, except that he was a twin. *Didymus* (John 11:16; 20:24; 21:2 NIV) is the Greek equivalent of the Hebrew *Thomas*, both meaning "twin."

He was outstanding for his loyalty to Jesus (John 11:16) and for his honesty when he did not understand his Lord's teaching (John 14:5; 20:24–25).

On seeing the risen Jesus, he made the crucial confession, "My Lord and my God!" (John 20:28).

Tiberias

Tiberias is a city on the west shore of the Sea of Galilee.

It was founded by Herod Antipas around A.D. 20 as his capital, and it was named in honor of Emperor Tiberius.

The Sea of Tiberias is another name for the Sea of Galilee (John 6:1; 21:1).

Tiberius

Tiberius was the son of Augustus Caesar.

He was adopted as heir when it was clear there was no direct succession.

He was Caesar during the period of Jesus' ministry, and he is specifically mentioned by name in Luke 3:1.

He was Caesar for twenty-three years, from 14 to 37.

Timothy

Timothy's father was a Greek and his mother, Eunice, a Jew and a Christian believer (Acts 16:1). Eunice's mother, Lois, Timothy's grandmother, was also a Christian (2 Tim. 1:5).

Timothy's home was in Lystra, which is where Paul first met him, and Paul's reference to him as his "son" implies Timothy was converted through his ministry (1 Cor. 4:17; 1 Tim. 1:2, 18; 2 Tim. 1:2).

He became a well-proved helper of Paul in his work (Acts 19:22; 20:4; 2 Cor. 1:19; Phil. 1:1; 2:22; Col. 1:1; 1 Thess. 1:1; 3:2), visiting places like Thessalonica and Corinth on Paul's behalf (1 Thess. 3:1–6; 1 Cor. 4:17).

He was outstanding for his pastoral concern and devotion to Jesus Christ (Phil. 2:19–23).

He received Paul's two letters addressed to him while he was giving leadership to the church in Ephesus (1 Tim. 1:3).

Titus

Titus was a Greek (Gal. 2:3), and from Paul's description of him as his "true son" (Titus 1:4), we may deduce that he came to faith through Paul's preaching.

He accompanied Paul and Barnabas to Jerusalem at the time of the gentile controversy (Gal. 2:1), and he became one of Paul's regular partners and fellow workers (2 Cor. 8:23).

Paul sent him to Corinth (2 Cor. 8:17) where his special responsibility was the organization of the collection of funds for God's people in need elsewhere (2 Cor. 8:6). It would seem that he carried a letter from Paul to the Corinthians, which has been lost—the severe letter (2 Cor. 2:3; 7:8).

Titus made more than one visit to Corinth, and the

Corinthians proved the truth of Paul's testimony to his exemplary character (2 Cor. 7:13–15; 8:6, 16; 12:18).

After Paul's release from imprisonment in Rome, it seems that Titus accompanied Paul to Crete, and he was left there to "set in order the things that are lacking" (Titus 1:5).

Once his task was complete and others had replaced him, he was instructed to do his best to rejoin Paul at Nicopolis (Titus 3:12), and he subsequently went to Dalmatia (2 Tim. 4:10).

Titus, Emperor

Titus was the son of Vespasian. The latter was appointed by Emperor Nero to take charge of affairs in Palestine, and he quelled the Jewish rebellion in Galilee in A.D. 67.

When Vespasian was proclaimed emperor in 69, the command of the Palestinian forces was given to Titus, and by the end of 69, all Judea had submitted except Jerusalem and three strongholds overlooking the Dead Sea.

In the spring of 70, Titus besieged Jerusalem, and on August 8, the temple itself was destroyed by fire. The revolt as a whole was not brought to an end until April 15, 73, with the overcoming of Masada.

Titus followed his father Vespasian as emperor in 79, only to die in 81.

Transfiguration

Transfiguration is the term used in the Gospels to record what three of the apostles witnessed of Christ's glory.

For a brief time, the heavenly glory of Christ, which was usually hidden by the conditions of His human life, shone through His body and clothing (Matt. 17:2; Mark 9:2–3).

This revelation was accompanied by a statement of God's approval of His Son (Matt. 17:5; Mark 9:7).

There is a spiritual transfiguration Christians are to experience as their minds are renewed, enabling them to discover and do God's will (Rom. 12:2).

Transgression

Transgression is the violation of God's law, the overstepping of the bounds laid down by His law. "Where there is no law there is no transgression" (Rom. 4:15; cf. Gal. 3:19).

When we do what God's law forbids, we transgress; we step over the bounds of what God has set (Dan. 9:11).

Transgressions are synonymous with willful sins (Ps. 19:13).

Twelve

The Twelve was the regular corporate description given to the twelve apostles (thirty-two occasions in the New Testament).

All the Twelve were personally called and chosen by Jesus and given power and authority for their ministry (Mark 6:7; John 6:70).

They were the particular recipients of Jesus' teaching and fellowship (Matt. 11:1; 26:20; Mark 3:14; 4:10; 9:35; 10:32; 14:20; Luke 18:31).

— W —

Witness

The common word for "witness" in the New Testament is that from which we obtain our English word *martyr*. To bear witness is to give testimony or proof of truth.

The apostles gave their witness to Jesus and in particular to His resurrection (Matt. 10:18; Acts 1:8, 22; 2:32; 3:15; 5:32; 10:39; 13:31; 22:15–16; 1 Cor. 15:15).

All Christians are called upon to bear their witness to Jesus Christ (Matt. 10:32; Rom. 10:9; cf. Matt. 5:14; 1 Pet. 3:15), for it is the spontaneous and natural consequence of an experience of His power and grace (Mark 5:20; Luke 8:39; John 4:29).

Witnessing is God's ordained means of spreading the gospel to all (Matt. 28:19–20).

The central subject of Christian witness is what God has achieved through the work of His Son, Jesus Christ (1 Cor. 1:6; 15:15; 1 John 1:1–4).

Witness of life and witness of speech go together, but there is an undoubted implication that the witness of life must come first (Phil. 2:15–16; 1 Thess. 1:7–8; 1 Pet. 3:1–2).

Word of God

The expression "the Word of God" is used in three particular senses.

First, the Lord Jesus Christ is called the Word of God (John 1:1), in that God has spoken through Him, giving in Him His final and complete revelation (Heb. 1:1–3).

Second, the gospel is called the word of God (Mark 4:14; Luke 5:1; 8:11; 11:28) because it is God's message to sinful men and women (Rom. 1:16; 15:16).

Third, the Scriptures are the Word of God. Christ and the apostles spoke of the Old Testament and quoted it as God's Word (Mark 7:13; Acts 3:22–25; Rom. 1:2; 2 Tim. 3:16). The Word of God taught by the Lord Jesus Christ and afterward by His apostles, whom He inspired by His Spirit, is the content of the New Testament, thus constituting the whole Bible the Word of God.

World

The word *world* is used sometimes simply to describe the world in a geographical sense (John 1:10), or the men and women of the world (John 3:16–17).

Most frequently, it refers to the life of men and women as organized and dominated by the god of this world, Satan (2 Cor. 4:4; 1 John 2:15–17; 5:19), whose powers are dark (Eph. 6:12).

The world without God (Eph. 2:12) is a prisoner to sin (Gal. 3:22) and is marked by corruption because of evil desires (2 Pet. 1:4).

Jesus Christ gave Himself for our sins to rescue us from this present evil world (Gal. 1:3–4), and as a consequence, Christians are not to love the world (2 Tim. 4:10; James 4:4; 1 John 2:15–16). Rather, they are to live as aliens and strangers in the world (1 Pet. 2:11) because their true citizenship is in heaven (Phil. 3:20).

Wrath, Wrath of God

God's wrath is the inevitable expression of His holiness and righteousness against sin (Rom. 1:18–20).

By nature, we are the objects of God's wrath because of our sin (Eph. 2:3).

God's righteous wrath against sin demands that He, the righteous Judge, shall finally reckon with it. The Day of Judgment will be the day of God's wrath about which John the Baptist and Paul warned (Matt. 3:7; Luke 3:7; Rom. 2:5; Col. 3:6).

Propitiation—atoning sacrifice—is the removal of God's wrath from believing sinners. Jesus Christ, by His propitiatory sacrifice, saves us from God's wrath (Rom. 5:9; 1 Thess. 1:10; 5:9).

God's wrath remains on people who reject His Son, Jesus Christ (John 3:36).

— Y —

Yahweh

Yahweh is the only truly personal name of God. Other names are titles or descriptions.

The name consists of the four consonants *YHWH*, and for that reason we cannot be sure of its proper pronunciation. Jews considered it too holy to pronounce (Exod. 20:7; Lev. 24:11).

The consonants *YHWH* are linked with God's revelation of His name to Moses in Exodus 3:14: "I AM WHO I AM" or "I WILL BE WHAT I WILL BE."

The English form *Jehovah* arose from a Latinized combination of the four consonants *YHWH* with vowels from *Adonai* (my Lord).

Since the Septuagint (LXX) translated *Yahweh* or *Jehovah* as "Lord," most modern translations do the same.

The name Yahweh exalts God as the unique, sovereign, and almighty Controller of everything.

— Z —

Zacchaeus

Zacchaeus, a wealthy chief tax collector, lived in Jericho (Luke 19:1–2).

Wanting to see Jesus but being short in height, he ran ahead and climbed a sycamore tree to watch and hear Jesus as He entered and passed through Jericho (Luke 19:1–4).

His conversion prompted criticism of Jesus as He became Zacchaeus's guest (Luke 19:5–7).

Jesus used Zacchaeus's conversion to underline His mission to save the lost (Luke 19:10).

Zacharias

Zacharias, a priest belonging to the priestly division of Abijah, lived in the time of Herod, the king of Judea. Both he and his wife were descendants of Aaron (Luke 1:5).

While he was burning incense in the temple, he received a revelation from an angel of the Lord concerning the birth and destiny of a son to be born to him and his wife in their old age (Luke 1:8–17).

Because of his initial unbelief at the angel's message, he was unable to speak until the time for the naming of the child (Luke 1:18–20, 59–64).

Recovering his powers of speech, he prophesied concerning his son and the Messiah for whom his son—John the Baptist —was to prepare the way (Luke 1:67–79).

Zebedee

Zebedee was a fisherman on the Sea of Galilee (Mark 1:20).

He was the father of James and John (Matt. 4:21; Mark 1:19).

He was the husband of Salome (cf. Matt. 27:56 with Mark 15:40; 16:1).

He seems to have been affluent in that he employed others (Mark 1:20).